THE ECONOMICS AND POLITICS OF OIL IN THE CASPIAN BASIN

The Caspian Basin has been a booming region since the late 1990s due to new oil discoveries, new pipelines that diversify the countries' transport options, and world oil prices that rose from below $10 in 1998 to $70 in 2006. This book analyses the experience of the Caspian countries during the oil boom. It is founded on empirical studies, using either macroeconomic tools or an analysis of public budgets, or microeconometric analysis of household survey data or fieldwork in oil-producing regions. Moving from aggregated to disaggregated analysis and, in keeping with its emphasis on rigorous empirical analysis to the greatest extent possible, several chapters are written by specialists on the Caspian region. Whilst there is an emphasis on the economic consequences of the oil boom, the interdisciplinary aspects of the phenomenon are also recognized. Overall, the analysis is firmly rooted in the region, yet the empirical studies also provide a basis for drawing broader lessons about the effects of an oil boom.

Boris Najman is Associate Professor at the University of Paris XII, France and researcher at CES-ROSES, a joint research unit of University of Paris I and the French National Centre for Scientific Research, CNRS. He is an expert on labour and social policies in transition economies.

Richard Pomfret has been Professor of Economics at the University of Adelaide since 1992. In 2006–7 he was the AGIP Professor of International Economics at the Johns Hopkins University Bologna Center. He is the author of *The Central Asian Economies since Independence* (2006). His research interests have centred on economic development and international economics.

Gaël Raballand received his PhD in economics from the University of Paris I (Sorbonne). Currently, he works as a Young Professional and Economist at the World Bank in Washington DC. Prior to this, he was a consultant for the French Institute of International Relations (IFRI), Paris.

CENTRAL ASIA RESEARCH FORUM
Series Editor: Shirin Akiner
School of Oriental and African Studies, University of London

Other titles in the series:

SUSTAINABLE DEVELOPMENT IN CENTRAL ASIA
Edited by Shirin Akiner, Sander Tideman and John Hay

QAIDU AND THE RISE OF THE INDEPENDENT MONGOL
STATE IN CENTRAL ASIA
Michal Biran

TAJIKISTAN
Edited by Mohammad-Reza Djalili, Frederic Gare and Shirin Akiner

UZBEKISTAN ON THE THRESHOLD OF THE
TWENTY-FIRST CENTURY
Tradition and survival
Islam Karimov

TRADITION AND SOCIETY IN TURKMENISTAN
Gender, oral culture and song
Carole Blackwell

LIFE OF ALIMQUL
A native chronicle of nineteenth century Central Asia
Edited and translated by Timur Beisembiev

CENTRAL ASIA
Aspects of transition
Edited by Tom Everrett-Heath

THE HEART OF ASIA
A history of Russian Turkestan and the Central Asian Khanates from
the earliest times
Frances Henry Skrine and Edward Denison Ross

THE ECONOMICS AND POLITICS OF OIL IN THE CASPIAN BASIN

The redistribution of oil revenues in Azerbaijan and Central Asia

Edited by Boris Najman, Richard Pomfret and Gaël Raballand

Routledge
Taylor & Francis Group

LONDON AND NEW YORK

First published 2008
by Routledge
2 Park Square, Milton Park, Abingdon, Oxfordshire OX14 4RN

Simultaneously published in the USA and Canada
by Routledge
711 Third Avenue, New York, NY 10017

*Routledge is an imprint of the Taylor & Francis Group,
an informa business*

© 2008 Editorial selection and matter, Boris Najman, Richard Pomfret and
Gaël Raballand; individual chapters, the contributors

Typeset in Times New Roman by
HWA Text and Data Management, Tunbridge Wells

First issued in paperback 2011

British Library Cataloguing in Publication Data
A catalogue record for this book is available from the British Library

Library of Congress Cataloging-in-Publication Data
The economics and politics of oil in the Caspian Basin: the redistribution
of oil revenues in Azerbaijan and Central Asia / edited by Boris Najman,
Richard Pomfret and Gaël Raballand.
p. cm. – (Central Asia research forum series)
Includes bibliographical references and index.
1. Petroleum industry and trade–Economic aspects–Caspian Sea Region.
2. Petroleum industry and trade–Political aspects–Caspian Sea Region.
I. Najman, Boris, 1969– II. Pomfret, Richard W.T. III. Raballand, Gaël.
HD9576.C372E27 2007
338.2´72809475–dc22
2007007141

ISBN13: 978-0-415-43410-2 (hbk)
ISBN13: 978-0-415-53317-1 (pbk)
ISBN13: 978-0-203-94054-9 (ebk)

CONTENTS

vii

ILLUSTRATIONS

LIST OF ILLUSTRATIONS

TABLES

CONTRIBUTORS

Richard Auty is Professor Emeritus in Economic Geography at Lancaster University. He has recently been a consultant for the DFID, EBRD, IUCN, National Bureau of Asian Research, UNU/WIDER and the World Bank. He has published nine books including: *Energy Wealth and Governance in the Caucasus and Central Asia* (2006, Routledge); *Resource Abundance and Economic Development* (2001) and *Sustainable Development in Mineral Economies* (1998, with Ray Mikesell).

Balázs Égert is at the Austrian National Bank, EconomiX at the University of Paris X (Nanterre), and William Davidson Institute, University of Michigan.

Régis Genté is a French freelance journalist based in Almaty, Kazakhstan, since November 2005. He covers Central Asia for several French media such as Radio France Internationale, Le Point, *Le Bulletin de l'Industrie Pétrolière* and Russia Intelligence. He also writes about the Caucasus, where he was based from January 2002 to November 2005.

Carol S. Leonard is a university lecturer in regional studies of the post-Communist states at the University of Oxford and has been a Fellow of St Antony's since January 1997. Before that she spent two years as resident adviser for the US Treasury to the Ministry of Finance of the Russian Federation.

Natalie Leschenko is a researcher at the Institute for Economic Research and Policy Consulting in Kiev/Ukraine. Her main research field is fiscal policy.

Michael Lewin was a senior economist at the World Bank at the time of writing his chapter. Among other things, he has worked and written extensively on macroeconomic issues of oil producing countries for all regions of the Bank. He is currently teaching economics at Gettysburg College. Before joining the Bank he was Assistant Professor of Economics at Johns Hopkins School of International Studies

Peter Lohmus is a senior economist at the International Monetary Fund and a former Deputy Governor of the Bank of Estonia.

Matthias Luecke is a research economist, specializing in economic development and international trade, at the Kiel Institute for the World Economy. He was a senior economist at the International Monetary Fund from 2000 until 2003, working with the IMF country teams for Azerbaijan, Kazakhstan, and Turkmenistan.

Mathilde Maurel is a researcher at the Centre d'Economie de la Sorbonne, CNRS – University of Paris I (Pantheon-Sorbonne), ROSES.

Boris Najman is Associate Professor of Economics at University of Paris XII, and a researcher at Centre d'Economie de la Sorbonne, CNRS – University of Paris I (Pantheon-Sorbonne), ROSES.

Richard Pomfret is Professor of Economics at the University of Adelaide, and in 2006–7 was the AGIP Visiting Professor in International Economics at the Johns Hopkins University Bologna Center. He is an Honorary Fellow at ROSES.

Gaël Raballand is an economist at the World Bank, Washington, and Observatoire des Etats Post-Soviétiques, Paris. He was the first OSCE Economic and Environmental Expert in Kyrgyzstan. He has published extensively articles on Central Asian economies, especially on water, energy, trade and transport issues. His PhD on the economics of landlocked countries was published in 2005: *L'Asie Centrale ou la Fatalité de l'Enclavement?* (Paris: L'Harmattan).

Patricia Sourdin lectures at the University of Adelaide and is a Professorial Lecturer at the Johns Hopkins University Bologna Center.

Anna Ter-Martirosyan is an economist in the Middle East and Central Asian Department of the International Monetary Fund in Washington, DC.

Natalia Trofimenko is a research economist, specializing in international trade and public finance, at the Kiel Institute for the World Economy. She has an MS in statistics from Miami University (Ohio) and is finishing her PhD in economics at Syracuse University (New York). In 1998–9 she worked with the UNDP and the IMF country teams for Kyrgyzstan.

Manuela Troschke is senior researcher in the Department of Economics at the Institute for Eastern European Studies (Osteuropa-Institut) in Munich. She works on transition economics and Central Asia in several national and international research projects.

Saulesh Yessenova is a postdoctoral research fellow at the Max Planck Institute for Social Anthropology in Halle/Saale, Germany.

PREFACE

The 'resource curse' occurs when a country provided with a resource rent does not manage it well, and its growth is deprived by this resource. Whatever the channels through which growth is impeded, and even if, in principle, oil revenue can educate and provide jobs for the people, it does not. Rarely have developing countries used oil money to improve the lives of the majority of citizens or to bring about steady economic growth. More often, oil revenue causes crippling economic distortions and is spent on showy projects. As emphasised by Jean Bodin,[1] 'Men of a fat and fertile soil, are most commonly effeminate and cowards; whereas contrariwise a barren country makes men temperate by necessity, and by consequence careful, vigilant, and industrious'. The fact that the majority of developing countries owning a resource rent do not perform well is well-known. Six channels of transmission from abundant natural resources to sluggish economic growth have been identified in recent literature, as indicated in Chapter 1.

- The first explanation is the overvaluation of the national currency. A natural resource boom and the associated surge in raw-material exports drive up the real exchange rate and hurt other exports (Corden 1984). Exchange rate volatility increases (Gylfason *et al.* 1999; Herbertsson *et al.* 1999), which can be bad for both the volume of export and its composition, away from high-tech and other manufacturing correlated with economic growth, as emphasised by Frankel and Romer (1999). Balázs Égert and Carol S. Leonard (in Chapter 4) examine the exchange rate explanation and conclude that the real exchange rate is not affected in Kazakhstan by the oil price development and oil revenue.
- The second explanation lies in the observation by Jean Bodin that economies rich in natural resources, inhabited by effeminate and cowardly men, seem prone to damaging rent-seeking behaviour, as opposed to countries less richly endowed, but inhabited by careful, vigilant and industrious people. The rent-seeking behaviour is used to explain why the resource-rich states of Latin America fell behind resource-poor East Asia in the 1970s and 1980s, the latter moving away from import-substituting industrialization (ISI) and adopting vigorous export-promotion strategies while the former persisted with ISI policies even long after they proved to be counterproductive. Within this class

of arguments which emphasise the consequences of the resource abundance on the quality of governance, Boris Najman, Richard Pomfret, Gaël Raballand and Patricia Sourdin (in Chapter 7) argue that the increase in the demand for a redistribution policy from poor regions to suddenly rich regions suffered from the low quality of the redistribution system, worsened by the resource abundance. According to Ross (2001), oil revenue is used to 'reduce social pressures that would otherwise result in demands for greater accountability'. Thanks to oil revenue, governments are less likely to tax their populations and the latter are less likely to demand accountability; governments are more prone to spend on patronage, on preventing the formation of social groups that could be inclined to demand more accountability.

- Third, natural resource abundance may provide individuals with a false sense of security and lead governments away from good economic management, including free trade, bureaucratic efficiency and institutional quality (Sachs and Warner 1995). A striking analogy is given by Thorvaldur Gylfason (2001) 'Rich parents sometimes spoil their kids. Mother Nature is no exception'. Gylfason reviews how political diversification, as opposed to political power in the hands of an authoritarian elite, and economic diversification, as opposed to a narrow specialisation in oil extraction, correlate in developing economies. A very appealing conclusion is that natural resource is a curse if it is not accompanied by sound political institutions, including freedom and democracy.

- The fourth explanation lies in the inadequate attention to the development of the human resources and their education. As emphasised by Gylfason *et al.* (1999), the Organization of the Petroleum Exporting Countries (OPEC) send 57 per cent of their children to secondary school compared with 64 per cent for the world as a whole and they spend less than 4 per cent of their gross national product on education on average compared with almost 5 per cent for the world as a whole (the figures refer to 1997). According to the graph below (Figure 0.1), reporting the spending on education in percentage terms of the gross domestic product (GDP) for Azerbaijan, Kazakhstan, the Kyrgyz Republic and Tajikistan, the latter is clearly below the highest line representing spending in OECD countries. This line of educational argument (also reflected in Table 0.1) is close to the claim that there is a need to strengthen social capital at both the local level and the national level, and of fighting against a sort of widespread rent-seeking behaviour described by Auty (in Chapter 9) as follows: 'Both firms and individuals look to the government to provide benefits and locals harbour deep cynicism over the likelihood of success, a scepticism that the domestic populace extends to the MNCs. There is an urgent need to strengthen civic voice and to build self-help civic associations so that local governments, firms and society can cohere to identify and achieve legitimate community interests within mining regions.'

- Moreover, it is likely that state ownership of resource industries softens the budget constraints of resource-exporting governments, producing fiscal laxity and a tendency to overborrow. This fifth explanation may be particularly

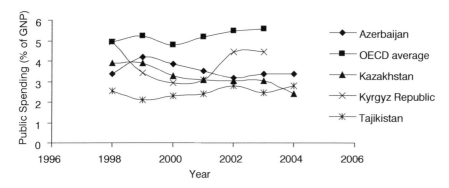

Figure 0.1 Public spending on education, percentage of GDP: Azerbaijan, Kazakhstan, the Kyrgyz Republic, Tajikistan and the OECD average, 1998–2004

Source: World Bank indicators, based on data from the United Nations Educational, Scientific, and Cultural Organization (UNESCO) Institute for Statistics. Recent data are provisional.

Table 0.1 Inadequate attention to economic growth and to the development of the human resources and their education

	Kazakhstan	Norway	Uzbekistan
Are development and economic growth a priority for the political power, above simple declarations (statements)?	3	3	2
Are development and economic growth a priority for the local public elites (hauts fonctionnaires, universitaires...) ?	2	4	2
Do parents devote high attention to the education of their children?	3	4	4

Source: French Ministry of Economy and Finance, 2006.

Note: The scale ranges from 1 = low effort to 4 = high effort.

relevant for formerly planned economies where the soft budget constraint (Kornai 1986) was, until recently, generalized to the whole economy.

*   Sixth and lastly, the failure of states to enforce property rights makes it difficult for manufacturing firms to conduct normal business, i.e. normal business, in which anticipated profits outweigh the risk of investing. By contrast, resource extraction can still proceed, since firms in the rentier sector are sufficiently rich to pay criminal organisations for the private enforcement of their property rights (Lane 1958; Klein *et al.* 1978). The result is that the correlation between slow growth and resource exports is spurious: both are the result of poorly enforced property rights. As soon as corruption is taken into account, the significance of large resource exports for explaining poor economic performance disappears.[2] According to data retrieved from the website of the Economic Freedom Network (www.freetheworld.com), the quality of the legal system and property rights is twice as high in Norway as

Table 0.2 Property rights enforcement

		Kazakhstan	Norway	Uzbekistan
If informal systems of property rights exist (as opposed to formal or modern system of property rights), do they provide with the security of property rights?	0 = do not exist 1 = very low security 4 = very high security	0	4	2
Security of formal property rights		3	4	2
Efficiency of judiciary means for defending property rights amongst private individuals	1 = weak efficiency 4 = high efficiency	2	4	3
Arbitrary actions from the state (for example from the administration) against private owners	1 = very often 4 = very rare	2	4	2
Security of commercial contracts (between private agents)	1 = weak 4 = high	2	4	2
Judiciary independence with respect to the state when a commercial disagreement occurs		2	4	1
Judiciary efficiency (speed in particular) when a commercial disagreement occurs		2	3	3
Application of the bankruptcy law	1 = slow and non-efficient 4 = quick and efficient	2	4	1
Are non profitable enterprises bailed in (1 or 2) or bailed out (3 or 4)?		2	3	3

Source: French Ministry of Economy and Finance, 2006.

compared with Azerbaijan. The same qualitative conclusion but more detailed is reported by the MINEFI,3 which systematically reports lower scores for Caucasian rentier countries than for Norway (see Table 0.2).

A striking feature of this literature is that it focuses on macroeconomics, and often neglects the potential redistribution of the rent and its welfare implications for the local mining communities. By contrast, a very important contribution of

PREFACE

this book, beyond the contributions already mentioned, is to focus on the welfare consequences and challenges of the extraction activities, from two different perspectives: first, the question of spatial redistribution from rich oil-producing areas to poor regions, by three different actors – the government, the mining companies, and the redistribution through small business generated by the oil activities; second, the question of intergenerational redistribution, i.e. investing for generating future revenue and for sterilizing oil revenue when it exceeds the absorbing capacity of the state.

Boris Najman, Richard Pomfret, Gaël Raballand and Patricia Sourdin (in Chapter 7) focus on unofficial redistribution taking place in Kazakhstan, which occurs when the additional activity generated by oil extraction is accompanied by the expansion of self-employment and small unregistered business. Their research strategy is based upon the LSMS (Living Standards Measurement Study) household surveys, and they consider that unofficial redistribution is dominant when expenditures are higher than twice the total income (which includes social transfers and wages). The main result is that the strongest mechanism of redistribution is informal.

This result is corroborated by the fact that company redistribution, which is the second redistribution mechanism, is not at work in oil-producing economies. Macroeconomic statistics indicate that the changes in employment do not echo the extraordinary surge of GDP: in Kazakhstan, 'direct employment in the oil sector is estimated to be less than 50,000 people [...], which is equivalent to less than 1% of Kazakhstan's active population' (see Chapter 7). The fact that mining activities generate inflated expectations that are not fulfilled is well-known, and Richard Auty (in Chapter 9) provides the reader with several explanations, such as the fact that a large share of the revenue leaks abroad to service capital. Moreover, according to Di Boscio (2004), the share of purchased inputs in the gross value of mining is 40 per cent or lower compared with 70 per cent for manufacturing. Although mining companies in Central Asia increasingly understand that benefits from the extraction activity must benefit the largest share of the population and satisfy requirements in terms of environmental safety, their efforts to boost local benefits fall well short of the expectations. Again, weak public governance and market failures magnify the problem. The level of corruption and the lack of transparency in public spending are particularly high in oil-producing countries. Auty (1999) adds that illicit costs and market imperfections may reduce the efficiency of capital to one quarter of the efficiency that could be achieved. Inadequate financial markets depress investment. For example, banks are often unable to recover their capital, given the failures in the judicial system. The picture is quite pessimistic, nevertheless three ways to push local welfare are proposed: establish *ex ante* a set of feasible targets, promote sustainable local business, and strengthen social capital. This has to be done through Production Sharing Agreements (PSAs), backed by sanctions imposed by the international financial institutions, and extended to embrace businesses linked to the mineral project. Mining companies and non-governmental organizations (NGOs) can work together towards strengthening local governance against rent-seeking and corruption. The contrast between what should be done

xxi

and the reality is particularly striking when one reads the fascinating chapter written by Saulesh Yessenova (Chapter 10), who opposes the petroleum projects and the official statement of promoting sustainable development and what she calls 'the real economy'. What emerges from this colourful analysis is that the reality is very different from the dream.

Official public redistribution is the third and last identified way of sharing the benefit of the rent. By focusing on Azerbaijan, Matthias Luecke and Natalia Trofimenko look at the redistribution of the benefits from the oil-producing regions to the rest of the country, from the groups directly involved in the extracting sector or transferred to the rest of the population and to its poorest members in particular. These issues are tackled with the help of household surveys and regional budget data from before (1995) and after (2004) the start of the most recent oil boom. The result is that while in 1995 a large part of the revenue was retained in the producing regions and urban areas, in 2002, after the oil boom and thanks to a public strategy targeted towards reducing the highest poverty, the level of state support was lowest for the residents of Baku and increased significantly in the resource-poor areas of the country.

Natalie Leschenko and Manuela Troschke (in Chapter 6) argue that decentralization is more efficient if a sufficient level of political and administrative decentralisation is achieved and if governance is strong enough. They show that

Table 0.3 Qualitative indicators of fiscal (de)centralization, transparency and quality of economic policy

		China	*Kazakhstan*	*Norway*	*Uzbekistan*
Level of centralization/ decentralization: fiscal autonomy	1 = low autonomy; 4 = 100% of local resources are taken locally	3	2	3	1
Transparency of public action in the economic field	1 = low level of transparency; 4 = high level of transparency	2	2	4	1
Transparency of economic policy (fiscal, monetary and exchange rate regime policy)		2	3	3	2
Corruption	1 = high level of corruption; 4 = low level of corruption	2	2	4	1
Efficiency of fiscal policy	1 = high level of informal economy, high tax evasion 4 = low level of informal economy, low tax evasion	2	2	3	2

Source: French Ministry of Economy and Finance, 2006.

the conditions are not fulfilled in Central Asia. The qualitative figures in Table 0.3 demonstrate, indeed, that fiscal autonomy is low, despite the similarity of local budgets as a percentage of GDP in Turkmenistan, Kazakhstan and Uzbekistan (respectively 10 per cent, 12 per cent and 15 per cent of GDP), as compared to the figure for Organisation for Economic Co-operation and Development (OECD) countries, which is 14.9 per cent. The system lacks transparency and is corrupted, reflecting the difficulty during the transition period of giving up more autonomy to local authorities, because the latter lack the capability of defining clear assignments and positive incentives. As a consequence, the scope for public redistribution is quite limited, a result which echoes the findings of Chapter 7. If the capacity to administrate oil revenue in a transparent and efficient way is limited, then the benefit from the option of saving oil revenue to meet long-term expenditure commitments and to provide a capital stock for future generations after reserves are exhausted, increases.

The question of intergenerational redistribution is examined in Chapter 2 by Gaël Raballand and Régis Genté, in two countries, Azerbaijan and Kazakhstan. While the former achieved its oil production record in 1941, the latter was specialized until recently in 'agriculture, livestock farming (over two-fifths of GDP in 1990) and coalmining and metal smelting'. Amongst the usual risks associated with investing in oil countries, one specific to the Caspian countries is the inherited political dependence *vis-à-vis* Russia's pipeline. This risk has reduced since 2001, with the creation of the first private transport consortium, the Caspian Pipeline Consortium (CPC). Oil discoveries in Kazakhstan pushed it into the top 10 world producers of energy. Needless to say, this unexpected and extraordinary increase in national wealth created extraordinary expectations, and the difficult task of choosing the appropriate level of spending/saving, compatible with the absorbing capacity of the economy. A danger to be avoided is the corruption of the functioning of the administration by softening the budgetary constraint.

Authorities in the Caspian Basin face the trade-off between, on the one hand, spending the minimum amount for alleviating the social pressures created by the conflict with Armenia in Azerbaijan and by the rate of poverty in both countries, which are among the highest amongst the former Soviet countries, and, on the other hand, investing in infrastructure and more generally for future generations. The governments in both countries advocate limiting current spending while their Parliaments ask for higher spending today – spending which may be far from superfluous, for example, subsidizing fuel for rural citizens, providing rural citizens with potable water, ensuring major repairs of roads and building public health buildings, etc. The attempts to put in place efficient institutions (Centralized Oil Funds, whose actions must be rationalized and transparent, and strong governance from the political centres to the local governors, who have to justify their actions and can be dismissed in case of failure) and to optimize the management of the oil wealth is described in great detail in Chapter 2.

Chapter 5 examines the level of inter-temporal optimal consumption, if the objective is to share, on an equal basis, oil revenue between current generations and future generations. The idea is that if consumption is higher than its optimal

PREFACE

level, then oil wealth will decline faster and the current generation will benefit from a higher share of wealth than future generations. Peter Lohmus and Anna Ter-Martirosyan show that in Kazakhstan, this optimal share is set at 6 per cent of GDP. Beside the task of centralizing the use of oil revenue and saving it efficiently but leaving some room for today's spending in a context of extreme poverty, as emphasised in Chapter 2, the National Fund of Kazakhstan (NFRK) has to implement a medium-term budget strategy, which takes into account the level of optimal consumption, while guaranteeing a sustainable budgetary position, and which is provided with a sufficient level of flexibility to adapt to unexpected changes in the value of future oil earnings.

To conclude, this book shows in a very convincing way that the question of 'blessing or curse' is a complex question, and that the focus on the macroeconomic performance of resource abundant economies does not provide unambiguous conclusions. It shows that the best way of understanding the phenomena is to look, at the micro level, at the concrete consequences of an oil boom: sudden increase in budgetary revenue, huge increases in individual and regional inequalities, inflated expectations of compensation by the state and by foreign companies, which are not met by actual redistributions, whatever the form they take. The main ingredients of the resource curse, namely 'volatility and exhaustibility', in the words of Michael Lewin (conclusion to Chapter 3), suggest that smoothing the rent is the crux of a strategy aimed at managing efficiently the consequences of the oil boom. Whatever the objective of the spending, be it redistributing the rent towards the poorest regions and populations or finding the appropriate way of sharing the rent across generations, the main difficulty is to avoid governance failures, which are more likely to occur in developing countries. 'In short, the government can do best by doing what seems to work best in any development context, with or without resource abundance.'

Mathilde Maurel

Notes

1 Jean Bodin (1967) *Six Books of a Commonwealth* (ed. and trans. M.J. Tooley), New York, NY: Barnes and Noble, 5, 1: 565 – originally published in 1576 as *Les six livres de la République*.
2 For the evidence of a link between resource extraction and extralegal violence see Reno's history of the diamond industry in Sierra Leone's Kono District (Reno 1995), and Jonathan C. Brown's analysis of oil firms during the Mexican revolution (Brown 1992).
3 The French Ministry of Economy and Finance published in 2001 and 2006 a set of qualitative institutional indicators covering a wide range of countries.

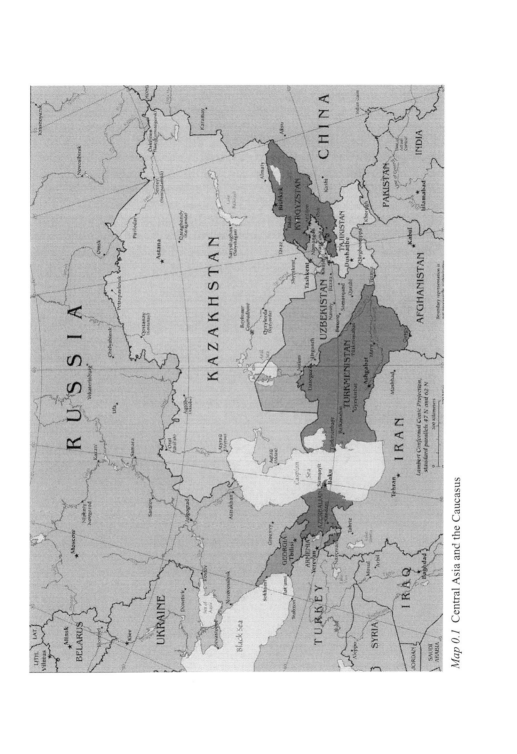

Map 0.1 Central Asia and the Caucasus

ACKNOWLEDGEMENTS

This book is based on a conference hosted by ROSES and held in Paris in June 2006. The editors acknowledge the contribution of all discussants and participants to the conference. The bibliography was prepared by Rachel Dunsmoor, and we thank the Johns Hopkins University Bologna Center for funding Rachel's time as part of her work-study program during her postgraduate studies.

Gaël Raballand and Régis Genté would like to thank Ferhat Esen for providing data on Azerbaijan. Balázs Égert and Carol Leonard are indebted to Karlygash Kuralbayeva for help in collecting some of the data used in their chapter. Natalie Leschenko and Manuela Troschke acknowledge financial assistance from the Volkswagen Foundation. Matthias Luecke and Natalia Trofimenko thank Yashar Pasha (Household Budget Survey and LSMS Department of the State Statistical Committee of the Azerbaijan Republic) and Ingilab Akhmedov (Public Finance Monitoring Center) for the data and Mary Gardashxanova (State Statistical Committee) for prompt response to all questions. Some material in Chapter 10 by Richard Auty is drawn from work undertaken for the EBRD, whose help is gratefully acknowledged, as is the assistance of the many companies and individuals within the Caspian region who kindly provided information.

Legal disclaimer

The views expressed in this book are personal and should not be attributed to any of the institutions with which the authors are affiliated.

ABBREVIATIONS

ACG	Azeri, Chirag and Gunashi (oilfields)
ADB	Asian Development Bank
AHBS	Azerbaijan household budget survey
AIOC	Azerbaijan International Operating Company
BTC	Baku-Tbilisi-Ceyhan pipeline
CIS	Commonwealth of Independent States
CPC	Caspian Pipeline Consortium
EBRD	European Bank for Reconstruction and Development
EITI	Extractive Industries Transparency Initiative
ENPT	enterprise profit tax
EPT	excess profit tax
ERZ	early reform zone
FDI	foreign direct investment
GDP	gross domestic product
HBS	Household Budget Survey (as inherited from the USSR)
IMF	International Monetary Fund
ISI	import-substituting industrialization
KEGOC	Kazakhstan Electricity Grid Operating Company
KMG	KazMunayGaz
LSMS	Living Standards Measurement Study
MNC	multinational corporation
MoU	Memorandum of Understanding
NFRK	National Fund of the Republic of Kazakhstan (oil fund)
NGO	non-governmental organization
NOEM	New Open Economy Macroeconomics
OECD	Organisation for Economic Co-operation and Development
OPEC	Organization of the Petroleum Exporting Countries
PIT	personal income tax
PFD	Parsons E&C and Fluor Daniel Corporation
PIH	permanent income hypothesis
PPP	purchasing power parity
PPS	Purchasing Power Standards
PSA	Production Sharing Agreements

LIST OF ABBREVIATIONS

SGP	Second Generation Project
SMEs	small and medium-sized enterprises
SOCAR	State Oil Company of Azerbaijan
SOFAZ	State Oil Fund of Azerbaijan
TCO	TengizChevroil
TNG	Trans Neft i Gaz
UNDP	United Nations Development Programme
VAT	value-added tax
WTO	World Trade Organization
$	all references to dollars are to US dollars, except where stated otherwise

1

INTRODUCTION

Boris Najman, Richard Pomfret and Gaël Raballand

As oil prices rose from less than $10 per barrel in 1998 to $60 and higher in 2005, and events in Iraq underlined the instability of the Middle East, the Caspian Basin emerged as an important new source of oil. The region around Baku in Azerbaijan was the oldest oil-producing area in the Russian Empire and had been crucial to the Soviet 1941–5 war economy. However, after 1945 the Caspian region was neglected relative to new oil regions in Siberia and the Russian Far East until the 1990 negotiations with Chevron to develop the Tengiz oilfield in north-western Kazakhstan, the largest foreign investment deal in Soviet history, appeared as a harbinger of future oil development in the Caspian Basin. Thus, although Caspian oil production had stagnated in the late Soviet era, expectations were high that after becoming independent at the end of 1991 energy-rich states such as Azerbaijan, Kazakhstan and Turkmenistan would flourish.[1]

The Caspian oil sector, however, was confronted with several handicaps in the 1990s. First of all, offshore prospecting was delayed for several years by disagreements over delimitation of national territories and by domestic wrangles over selling exploration rights to foreign firms possessing the technology needed to explore the offshore fields. Second, the existing pipelines were controlled by a Russian enterprise, Transneft, which overtly discriminated against non-Russian oil.[2] After the dissolution of the USSR, the government of Kazakhstan took over the state's share in the TengizChevroil joint venture, but Russia claimed rights to part of the oil and also controlled the pipeline about whose access no commitment had been made in the original agreement.[3] In Azerbaijan, development was hindered by war with Armenia in 1992, but after a ceasefire had been agreed the government moved swiftly to complete the 'deal of the century' by which foreign companies would develop the country's oil.

The situation turned around as oil prices started to rise at the end of the 1990s (see Figure 1.1). Major discoveries in the North Caspian mean that by 2010 Kazakhstan will have joined the club of the 10 largest oil exporters in the world. The International Monetary Fund (IMF) is forecasting oil revenue of $99 billion over the next 45 years for this country of 15 million people; compared to the current level, gross domestic product (GDP) per capita could be multiplied by four. Meanwhile, the pipeline situation finally started to improve. The opening in autumn 2001 of the first privately owned and commercially operated pipeline, the

1

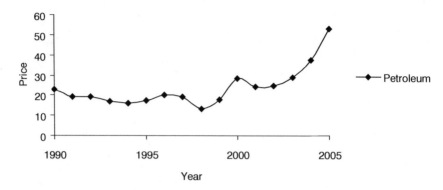

Figure 1.1 World price of oil, 1990–2005

Source: IMF International Financial Statistics.

Caspian Pipeline Consortium (CPC), provided an alternative route through Russia, which cut transport costs from Tengiz in half.[4] In early 2003 a 450 km pipeline was completed to link Kazakhstan's Uzen oilfield, which is operated by the Chinese National Petroleum Company, to the CPC. In December 2005 a 985 km pipeline was completed from Atasu, in central Kazakhstan, to the Chinese border, and this will eventually be part of a link between the major oilfields of Kazakhstan and the Chinese network. A pipeline to Turkey's Mediterranean coast was also opened in 2005. The Baku–Tbilisi–Ceyhan pipeline is more immediately important for Azerbaijan, but it also provides a valuable option for Kazakhstan as Azerbaijan's oil production is projected to plateau rather rapidly while Kazakhstan's production should continue to expand after 2015. The strategic importance of Caspian oil and its links to Turkey and western Europe and to China and, potentially, India is clear.[5]

This book focuses on the domestic impact and sustainability of the oil boom. Both Azerbaijan and Kazakhstan see their oil wealth as the basis for economic development. The cross-country evidence, however, suggests that oil can be a curse. The idea that mineral wealth can promote characteristics inimical to economic growth with equity is an old one, but the modern debate was sparked when Sachs and Warner (1995) found a negative relationship between resource abundance and economic growth in cross-country regressions. Subsequent contributions have refined the debate of oil as a curse, establishing that the relationship is conditional on variables proxying for institutions or on democracy; oil may be a blessing when corruption is absent and the economy is open and the workforce well educated. This fits with the observation that successful resource-rich countries like Norway, Australia or Malaysia have open economies and low levels of corruption, but does not address the issue of whether resource-abundance has fuelled corruption in countries like Nigeria or Venezuela.

The Sachs–Warner results are interesting, but beg the questions:

• What transmission mechanisms make a resource boom a curse?

- How is oil revenue redistributed in an oil economy?
- How should redistribution mechanisms be designed to benefit the population?

A fundamental issue is that, due to the capital-intensive nature of oil production, the direct impact on the local economy is likely to be small, and thus attention must also be paid to indirect effects or to taxation and redistribution of oil rents through the state budget. In economics the most rigorously argued connection between resource abundance and poor economic performance is the Dutch Disease effect, by which the resource boom makes production of other traded goods uncompetitive (Corden 1984). Another transmission mechanism (emphasised in the case studies in the World Bank project by Gelb *et al.* 1988) is that the volatility of resource earnings leads to poor investment decisions at the margin during the boom, which accentuate the subsequent recession. The nature of redistribution of oil rents through national or regional budgets is important; as oil exports grow, discontent in oil-producing regions and in the poorest regions of the oil country simultaneously grow, because oil-producing regions wish to keep a higher share of oil revenue while the poorest regions request a higher redistribution share.[6]

The main added value of this book is the empirical approach we use to assess the impact of the oil boom. Empirical tools are relatively well developed for examining macroeconomic linkages, such as Dutch disease effects which work through the exchange rate, and relatively straightforward when it comes to analysing the extent to which state budgets allow decentralized revenue-raising and expenditure decisions, but empirical work is more challenging in identifying microeconomic linkages. On the other hand, both Azerbaijan and Kazakhstan have high quality household survey data, reflected in a Living Standards Measurement Study (LSMS) survey in the mid-1990s and high quality annual data since the turn of the century.[7] One issue not addressed in this book because of its empirical intractability is the extent to which oil wealth has fuelled corruption, undermined the rule of law and created attitudes inimical to sustainable economic development.

The first part of the book provides background information on the hydrocarbon sector in the Caspian Basin and on the debate about whether resources are a curse or a blessing. The second part addresses the macroeconomic links via Dutch disease effects or through the state budget, both of which are shown to be weak in Kazakhstan (as well as in other Central Asian countries). The third part uses household survey data to analyse how oil boom effects can be picked up in reported income and expenditure; important differences between Azerbaijan and Kazakhstan are that in the former oil production is close to the capital city, whereas in the latter there are huge regional gaps between the oil-producing regions and the two large cities, where most of the benefits from the oil boom appear to accrue. The microeconometric analysis confirms the weak transmission through wages or state budgets, and that the main transmission mechanism to household income is through unofficial earnings. The fourth part takes us to the most disaggregated level based on fieldwork at the local level in Baku and Tengiz to examine how oil companies can promote local development and the extent to which they impose costs on the local inhabitants. The final chapter draws conclusions about the impact of the Caspian oil boom.

Notes

1 This book focuses on Kazakhstan and Azerbaijan as the main oil producers in the region. Turkmenistan's natural resource wealth is based on natural gas. Exploration for oil under Turkmenistan's part of the Caspian Sea has been hampered by the unwillingness of foreign firms to operate under the idiosyncratic regime imposed by the personalized autocracy of President Niyazov (Turkmenbashi the Great) and by jurisdictional disputes with Azerbaijan; this may change in the wake of Turkmenbashi's death in December 2006. Uzbekistan also has gas and oil but has yet to discover reserves which would make it an important net exporter.

2 The Russian state-owned pipeline company engaged in monopsonistic practices such as artificially high assessments of technical losses, arbitrary long route allocations and other discriminatory pricing, including absence of a quality bank which would recognize the higher quality of Tengiz oil. The net effect was that transit tariffs for Kazakhstan's crude were typically double those for Russian crude (estimates from IMF, *Cross-Border Issues in Energy Trade in the CIS Countries*, IMF Policy Discussion Paper PDP/02/13, December 2002). High transportation costs have been a severe obstacle to developing oilfields, especially in central Kazakhstan; expansion of the Kumkol field in the Kyzylorda region, for example, was constrained by transport costs of around $12 per barrel (Raballand and Esen 2006).

3 In the second half of the 1990s Kazakhstan's government was involved in selling off half of its share to Mobil, in a corrupt manner that led to a Mobil senior executive being imprisoned in the USA (Pomfret 2005), and then selling a fifth of its remaining quarter share to LUKoil in return for Russian cooperation. The current TengizChevroil ownership structure is as follows: Chevron (operator) 50%, ExxonMobil (25%), Republic of Kazakhstan/Kazmunaygaz (20%), LukArco (5%). For more details of the Tengiz project, see Chapter 10.

4 The CPC is half-owned by Russia (24%), Kazakhstan (19%) and Oman (7%), and the other half is divided among ChevronTexaco (15%), LUKoil (12.5%), ExxonMobil (7.5%), Rosneft/Shell (7.5%), Agip (2%), British Gas (2%), Kazakhstan Pipeline Ventures (1.75%) and Oryx Caspian Pipeline (1.75%). After the dissolution of the USSR, the CPC (then consisting of Transneft, Kazakhstan and Oman) was awarded the rights to transport oil from Tengiz to the Black Sea, but negotiations dragged on the question of how much Chevron should pay towards construction. After Mobil bought 25% of Tengiz and LUKoil/Arco purchased 5%, the Tengiz partners together with other investors took a half-share in the CPC.

5 Plans to construct a gas pipeline from Turkmenistan through Afghanistan to Pakistan and India, first raised in the mid-1990s but abandoned in 1997, depend upon the security situation in Afghanistan. The attractiveness of oil or gas pipelines to South Asia remains great as the Indian economy and its energy needs boom. The geostrategic advantage for the EU of not having to rely on Russian transit routes was underlined by the Russia–Ukraine energy conflict at the start of 2006 and by Russia's use later in 2006 of gas exports to Georgia and to Belarus as a policy tool.

6 Nigeria has experienced this conjunction of discontents for decades (Ikein and Briggs-Anigboh 1998). In Russia, approximately three-quarters of oil revenue flows to Moscow, creating a struggle between the politicians in regions of oil extraction and the central authorities (Dienes 2002: 451).

7 The Soviet household budget surveys (HBS) had become notorious for their biased samples. The World Bank sponsored new surveys within the aegis of the LSMS with superior sampling, and these practices have been carried forward by the national statistical authorities in their reforms of the HBS.

Part I

BACKGROUND

2

OIL IN THE CASPIAN BASIN

Facts and figures

Gaël Raballand and Régis Genté

Introduction

The Caspian Basin has been one of the world's major oil producing regions for over a century. In 1900, Azerbaijan accounted for half of the world's production of crude oil. However, in the last decade, the centre of gravity of the production in the Basin has moved from Azerbaijan to the Central Asian part of the Basin, primarily Kazakhstan.

Prior to the collapse of the Soviet Union, Western countries had known the producing potential of the Caspian Basin. In the early 1990s, the Caspian Basin became the focus of attention for the world oil industry for several reasons (Ebel 2001):

- the Caspian producing potential was judged to be world-class;
- this potential could not be realized within an acceptable time-frame without outside foreign participation;
- the oil and gas would not be developed to meet domestic requirements and most of the oil and gas to be produced would be for the export market.

In the early 1990s, the Caspian Basin was characterized as a new *El Dorado*. Several exploration campaigns later, statements on the potential of the Basin became more realistic. As Ebel states: 'Caspian oil will play an important role at the margin. […], it will add to diversity of supply for importers but its role will not be pivotal'.

Only two countries, Azerbaijan and Kazakhstan, will become major oil exporters from the Caspian Basin. Kazakhstan is going to become the most important oil producer from the Basin, Azerbaijan is going to combine oil and gas exports, whereas Turkmenistan should remain mainly a gas exporter. If output projections are confirmed, Kazakhstan and Azerbaijan will dominate the regional production with, respectively, 3 million barrels per day (mb/d) and 1 mb/d in 2015–20.[1]

With an expected revenue of billions of dollars in the next decade, local populations hope to see a dramatic improvement in their living conditions. In 2010, it is likely that Kazakhstan will join the club of the 10 largest oil exporters in the world. The IMF forecasts $99 billion in oil revenue over the next 45 years for this country where the current GDP per capita is less than $2,000 (IMF 2004).

The main challenge for national leaders is to satisfy these heightened expectations, although, unfortunately, the economic and social development outcome of many oil-producing countries is not encouraging. Will the Caspian Basin countries avoid the oil curse?

The next part of this chapter describes the extent of the expected new oil boom. In the third section 'Common strategies and differences of early oil revenue management', we assess the management of early oil revenue in Kazakhstan and Azerbaijan, which are the two main oil exporters of the Caspian Basin. The emphasis will be on oil funds, the governance of national oil companies and transparency of revenue management.

Reality of the new Caspian oil boom

During the Soviet period, the oil production of the Caspian Basin had been limited. When the USSR collapsed, the Caspian Basin successor states were presented as new *El Dorados*. Another reality, however, has appeared as exploration campaigns have been carried out. Caspian oil production will remain 'important at the margin' with two major exporters: Kazakhstan and, to a lesser extent, Azerbaijan.

Limited oil production during the Soviet times

After the Second World War, the Caspian Basin never accounted for more than 8 per cent of Soviet oil production – Azerbaijan, which has always been an oil economy, was the most important oil-producing Republic in the Caspian region (accounting for 3 per cent to 4 per cent of Soviet oil production). However, Azerbaijan set its production record in 1941.

During the Soviet era, Kazakhstan's two main economic pillars were agriculture and livestock farming (over two-fifths of GDP in 1990) and coalmining and metal smelting (Pomfret 1995: 80–5). Despite the fact that oil production dates back to the early twentieth century in Kazakhstan, oil production only started to grow significantly in the 1970s but then stagnated in the 1980s (see Figure 2.1). In the 1990s, the oil sector rapidly became the most important economic sector in Kazakhstan. Kazakhstan is becoming an oil economy for the first time in its economic history. During this period, due to the privatization process, Kazakhstan transformed its ownership structure from that of a Communist economy to an oil booming economy (Peck 2003; Pomfret 2005).

From the excessive expectations in the early nineties to reality

Oil reserves in the Caspian Basin are certainly significant, but oil reserves located in the Caspian Sea subsoil will never be able to compete with oil reserves from the Middle East. Caspian oil will remain 'important at the margin'.

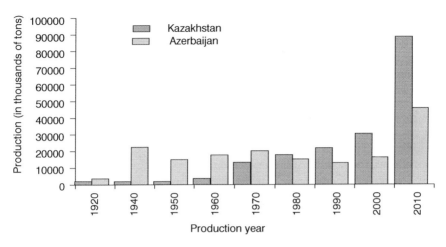

Figure 2.1 Azerbaijan and Kazakhstan oil production (1920–2010)

Source: Kazakhstan Statistical Committee, Radvanyi (1985) and Azerbaijan Statistical Committee.

When Azerbaijan and Kazakhstan became independent, the oil sector was confronted with major handicaps. When oil companies search for crude oil and natural gas, oil companies are confronted with three risks (Ebel 2001):

- Geological risk. Are the underground rock formations such that they would trap and hold crude oil or natural gas?
- Technical risk. If oil or gas is discovered, is available technology up to the task of bringing these resources to the surface at a cost which supports project viability?
- Political risk. The higher the political risk, the higher the return must be. Can the project yield a financial return commensurate with the perceived political risk?

Foreign oil companies could relatively easily overcome geological and technological risks. The geological risk was limited because oil had already been discovered in similar rock formations in the region. Moreover, offshore Western technology was more than adequate to develop oil production in the Caspian Basin.

For a decade, political risk in the Basin was crystallized on two major issues: the difficulties in reaching an agreement on the Caspian legal regime and the delay to reduce transport constraints by building new pipelines. Prospecting for new oil reserves under potentially oil-rich segments of the Caspian Sea has been delayed for several years because of the disagreements over Caspian Sea delimitation.[2] Exploration campaigns of Araz, Alov and Sharg oilfields have been suspended since 2001 because of a pending resolution of Caspian Sea borders between Azerbaijan and Iran. However, these fields have the same oil production potential as the current largest Azeri oilfield.

Concerning transport constraints, Kazakh authorities denied Russia's claims to share oil produced in the largest oilfield in Kazakhstan, Tengiz. The Russian authorities have consequently used the Russian state-owned pipeline company, Transneft, which has a monopoly on oil pipelines on the Russian territory to overtly discriminate against Kazakh oil.[3] In 1995, Russia allowed Kazakhstan to only export 70,000 b/d through the Transneft system, which seriously constrained Chevron's exports. Consequently, the US company arranged alternative means to export its oil, mainly by rail, or by swap arrangements. Transit tariffs for crude oil produced in Kazakhstan have been double those for crude oil produced in Russia.

It is worth noting that, during the Tsarist period, transport was already the main constraint for independent oil producers in Azerbaijan; owners of refineries were complaining in the 1880s against the directors of the railroad agencies, whom they charged with favouritism towards certain companies (McKay 1984: 610).

Between 1999 and 2003, Kazakhstan's oil production grew year-by-year by approximately 14 per cent, roughly doubling production since independence. In 2005, the Caspian region produced 1.9 mb/d or 2 per cent of the world's total output (see Table 2.1).[4] By 2010, oil exports could almost double in comparison with the 2005 figure. Kazakhstan is already among the 15 largest world oil exporters (see Table 2.2) and should enter the club of the 10 largest exporters by 2010.

Oil is produced from over 50 oilfields (see Map 2.1), the largest of which are: Tengiz (6 to 9 billion barrels of proven oil reserves) and Karashaganak (oil and gas condensate, 2.3 to 6 billion barrels of oil).[5] In the future, Kashagan (9 to 13 billion barrels of proven oil reserves)[6] and, to a lesser extent, Kurmangazy (more than 2.2 billion barrels of oil reserves) will contribute considerably to Kazakhstan's oil production. In Azerbaijan, the main oilfields are Azeri, Chirag and Deepwater Guneshli (6.5 billion barrels of proven oil reserves), Shah Deniz

Table 2.1 Oil and gas production, consumption in the Caspian Basin, 2004

		Oil production/ exports (mb/d)	Natural gas (m³ billion)
Kazakhstan	Production	1.22	20.51
	Consumption	0.22	15.75
	Net exports	1.00	4.76
Azerbaijan	Production	0.32	4.99
	Consumption	0.09	8.20
	Net exports	0.23	-3.21
Turkmenistan	Production	0.21	58.58
	Consumption	0.10	16.57
	Net exports	0.11	42.01

Source: US Department of Energy and Azerbaijan Statistical Committee.

Main Oilfields in Kazakhstan

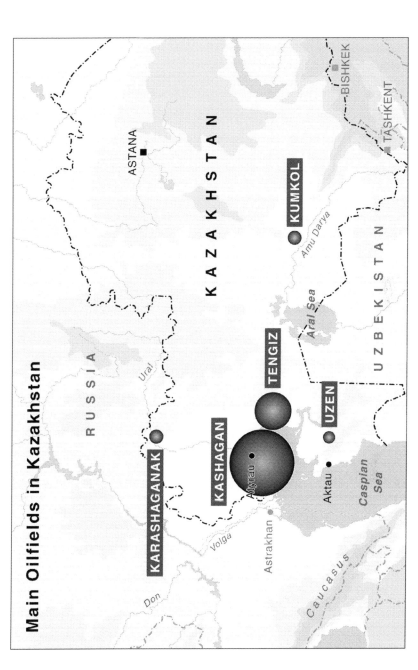

Map 2.1 Location of Kazakhstan production fields

Table 2.2 World oil exporters, 2005

Country	Net oil exports (mb/d)
1 Saudi Arabia	9.1
2 Russia	6.7
3 Norway	2.7
4 Iran	2.6
5 United Arab Emirates	2.4
6 Nigeria	2.3
7 Kuwait	2.3
8 Venezuela	2.2
9 Algeria	1.8
10 Mexico	1.7
11 Libya	1.5
12 Iraq	1.3
13 Angola	1.2
14 Kazakhstan	1.1
15 Qatar	1

Source: Information Agency of US Department of Energy.

(2.5 billion barrels of proven oil reserves) and, in the future, Inam (2.2 billion barrels of oil reserves) or Araz, Alov and Sharg.

In terms of proven oil reserves, although exploration campaigns are still going on, Kazakhstan holds 75 per cent of proven oil reserves of the Basin, Azerbaijan 17 per cent, Turkmenistan 6 per cent and Russia 2 per cent (Djalili and Kellner 2003). Although Kazakhstan only reached agreement with Russia in 2002 over delimitation of the Caspian Sea bed, oilfields explored in the late 1990s led to identification of major oilfields (such as Kashagan[7] in 2000), which will boost Kazakhstan's production in the next decade. The position is more favourable for gas reserves. If Uzbekistan's reserves are added to those of Kazakhstan, Turkmenistan and Azerbaijan, this region constitutes the fourth most important country/region in the world (behind Russia, Iran and Qatar).[8]

This oil boom has been made possible because large investments in oil exploration, production and transport have been carried out in the last decade. Kazakhstan has attracted the largest amount of foreign direct investment (FDI) per capita in the former Soviet Union. From 1996 to 2000, FDI inflows exceeded $1 billion per year and, since 2001, annual FDI to Kazakhstan has amounted to at least $2 billion, of which over 85 per cent has been invested in sectors intensive in natural resources. In 2003, investment flows into the oil sector reached $4 billion.

The pipeline issue has also taken time to resolve, but, since 2001, the situation is becoming more favourable to Kazakhstan. The opening ceremony in November 2001 of the first privately owned and commercially operated pipeline, the CPC, provided an alternative route through Russia, which has provided additional export capacity (see Map 2.2 and Figure 2.2).[9] In early 2003, a 450 km pipeline,

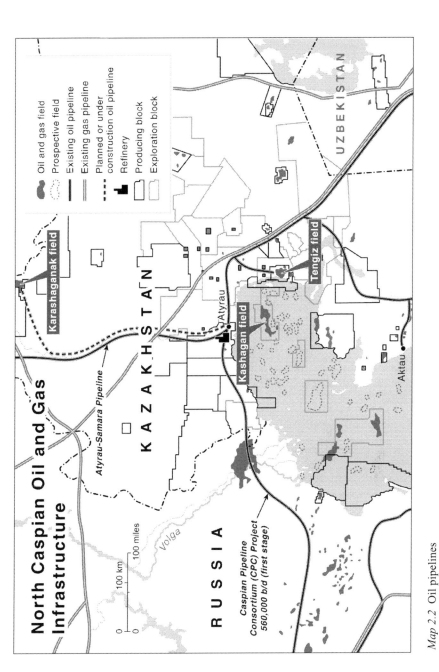

North Caspian Oil and Gas Infrastructure

Legend:
- Oil and gas field
- Prospective field
- Existing oil pipeline
- Existing gas pipeline
- Planned or under construction oil pipeline
- Refinery
- Producing block
- Exploration block

Karashaganak field

Atyrau-Samara Pipeline

KAZAKHSTAN

Atyrau

Tengiz field

Kashagan field

Aktau

Volga

RUSSIA

Caspian Pipeline Consortium (CPC) Project 560,000 b/d (first stage)

100 km

100 miles

UZBEKISTAN

Map 2.2 Oil pipelines

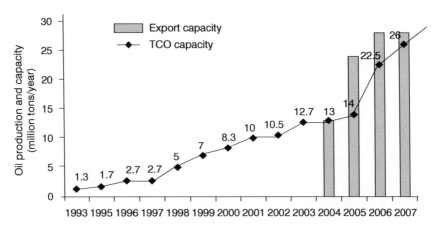

Figure 2.2 TengizChevroil oil production and CPC export capacity

Source: Chevron website, CPC website, Alexander's Gas and Oil Connections. Projected data for 2007.

operated by the Chinese National Petroleum Company, was completed to link the Uzen (Aktöbe region) oilfield to the CPC. A 985 km pipeline (second section of the Kazakhstan–China pipeline) linking Atasu, in central Kazakhstan, to Alatau pass (Xinjiang) was completed in December 2005.

In 2005, the Baku-Tbilisi-Ceyhan pipeline (BTC) was completed, which is of less immediate benefit to Kazakhstan but is likely to become an important outlet as Azerbaijan's oil production is projected to plateau rather rapidly while Kazakhstan's production should continue to expand after 2015. Azerbaijan and Kazakhstan have signed an agreement that 400,000 b/d to 500,000 b/d should be exported by tankers from Aktau to Baku and then through the BTC.

Although the least expensive option to export oil from Tengiz to the Black Sea has remained more or less constant, expanding capacity and rising oil prices have contributed to significantly reducing the transport constraint (see Figure 2.3). Today, land transport costs account for less than 7 per cent of international prices. However, in 1998, this ratio reached 26 per cent and, consequently, investment in oil transport was critical in order to expand capacity and reduce transport tariffs by expanding alternative routes and combining various modes of transportation.

Higher oil prices not only made Caspian oil worth more, but also encouraged foreign investors to change their minds about the economic value of pipelines and other investments. The size of the investments and the subsequent extent of the boom have also been magnified by the huge increase in oil prices which began in 1999 (see Figure 2.4).

The Caspian Basin will never compete with proven oil reserves located in the Middle East. According to BP's figures, proven oil reserves in the Caspian amount to 48 billion barrels (Cohen 2006), whereas the Middle East countries hold approximately 650 billion barrels (or 65 per cent of the proven oil reserves in the world).[10] The Caspian Basin should be able to produce approximately

16

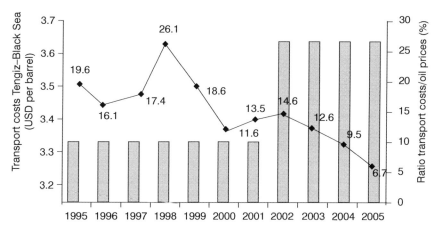

Figure 2.3 Transport costs from Tengiz to the Black Sea and oil prices

Note: Transport costs data for Atyrau–Samara–Novorossiisk from 1995 to 2002, CPC data thereafter. Although transport tariffs are adjusted regularly, we assumed constant transport costs because adjustments are marginal compared to current oil prices and remain below $4 per barrel.

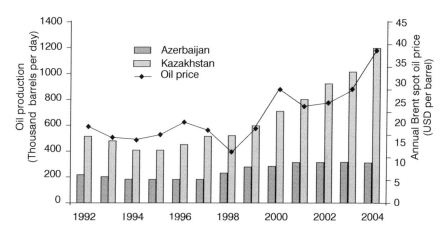

Figure 2.4 Azerbaijan and Kazakhstan oil production (1992–2004) and oil prices

Source: Data from Information Agency of US Department of Energy.

3.8 mb/d, i.e. less than 50 per cent of current Saudi Arabian or Russian production. In 2015, Caspian oil exports should reach 4 per cent of oil consumption in the world. The Caspian Basin will then be one of the two or three key oil-exporting regions apart from the Middle East, which will strengthen opportunities for oil-importing economies to diversify their sources of oil imports.

Common strategies and differences of early oil revenue management

For any large oil-producing country deciding how to use its oil windfall, the crux of the problem is to find an appropriate balance between spending now and spending in the future.[11] As the World Bank (2005) stated for Kazakhstan:

> On the one hand, the windfall could be used to support an expansionary fiscal stance that will aim at addressing bottlenecks, redistributing the oil wealth, or addressing social imbalances, but this could lead to overheating and reduced efficiency of public spending. It could lead to substantial waste if spending systems and the policy framework are inadequate. On the other hand, spending can be contained to help the economy cool down (like in China), but then Kazakhstan will, to a certain extent, be postponing the need to address important needs.

Pressure for redistribution of oil revenue is high in Caspian Basin countries because of the high poverty rate. In the meantime, Caspian Basin countries are becoming increasingly oil economies. In 2003, the oil sector in Kazakhstan represented approximately 35 per cent of export revenue and 20 per cent of budget revenue (or approximately 6.5 per cent of GDP).[12] This trend will be strengthened in the coming years. Oil production generates major revenue for Kazakhstan, especially since the tax code was amended in 2004 and Kazakh pressure on foreign oil companies increased.[13] The introduction of the rent tax on export of crude oil has raised the government's share of oil income to between 65 per cent and 85 per cent (US Department of Energy 2005).[14] The fuel sector is also growing in Azerbaijan: this sector represented 27 per cent of Azerbaijan's GDP in 2000 and it grew to 41 per cent in 2005 (Cohen 2006).

Authorities face a major trade-off between spending and saving for future generations, and a consensus has not been found even among Kazakh experts. In November 2006, Kanat Berentayev, head of the Department of Economics in Transition in Almaty, stated: 'measures targeting a reduction in the aggregated demand, in particular, freezing assets in the National Fund, may result in the stagnation of the real sector of the economy'. However, Anton Artemyev, head of the Kazakhstan Revenue Watch in Almaty (a program of the Soros foundation, Kazakhstan), stated that if oil revenue may be 'used to buy voters before elections by social spending only designed to seduce the people, disregarding economical rationality and the sustainability of projects', then 'money from the oil fund is used for long-term investments, mainly in infrastructure'.[15]

The pressure for redistribution and the trade-off between spending and saving

Expectations are extremely high in Azerbaijan and in Kazakhstan. In Azerbaijan, 45 per cent of the population still lives below the poverty line and due to the conflict with Armenia, more than 10 per cent of the population are refugees or internally displaced persons (Cohen 2006). In Kazakhstan, according to the United Nations Development Programme (UNDP), over 40 per cent of the population lives with a low income and over 20 per cent lives below the poverty line.

Parliament usually pushes for higher redistribution whereas the Ministry of Finance, backed by international financial institutions, laud restraint in spending. Such a debate took place in the fall of 2006 in Kazakhstan. During the discussion of the National Budget, the government advocated limited spending and transfers from the National Fund in order to control inflation and over-spending. On the other hand, the parliamentarians stated their preference for increased public spending, especially aimed at 'subsidizing fuel for rural citizens; providing rural citizens with potable water; ensuring major repairs of roads and building public health buildings …'.

Since the beginning of major oil flows to Kazakhstan, recurrent negotiations have taken place between those who wish to save for future generations and those who wish to spend part of the oil windfall.

Because the non-spending policy is impossible for any government to implement in a context of endemic poverty, the Kazakh government strives to rationalize the use of early oil revenue. In March 2006, a Sustainable Development Fund, named Kazyna, was created. Its overarching goal is 'to improve Kazakhstan capacity in industry and innovation and to create favorable conditions for economic growth'. Kazyna should rationalize the use of various Funds[16] aimed at providing financial assistance to improve economic diversification, financing breakthrough projects and technical innovation, financing infrastructure and supporting medium and small businesses. Kazyna is expected to facilitate investments both inside and outside Kazakhstan. Kazyna management is expected to build synergies, develop cluster projects and contribute to the implementation of the Strategy of Industrial and Innovative Development of Kazakhstan for 2003–15. During the next three years, authorities expect to channel over $10 billion into the non-mineral sector through Kazyna.[17]

Use of oil revenue is at the core of the bargaining process between central and regional authorities (akims or governors). As in Russia, the richest regions of the country (i.e. oil-producing regions) manage to keep a share of oil revenue. Central authorities usually give a certain financial leeway to the governors in exchange for transfers from oil-producing regions to the central budget. Thus, the onus is on the akims to pressure foreign investors. As pointed out by Luong (2003), it is possible for the president to revoke the akims. Nevertheless, the regime needs their financial and political support and cannot go completely against the interests of these 'new red barons', who were former directors of state enterprises and are powerful local businessmen or local powerful figures (see Figure 2.5).

In oil-producing regions, governors come from the oil and gas industry or from the local administration (such as tax administration). Liazzat Kiinov worked in the oil industry before becoming governor of Mangistau region and finally chairman of KazMunayGaz. Bolat Palymbetov, who was a vice-chairman of Trans Neft i Gaz, replaced L. Kiinov as governor of Mangistau.

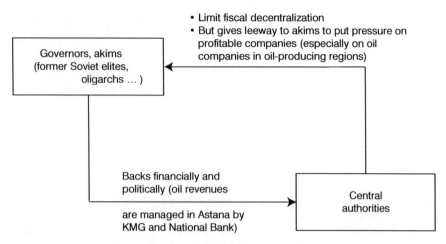

Figure 2.5 Centre–periphery relations in Kazakhstan

As in many oil-producing economies, Azerbaijan subsidizes industries by charging electricity and gas at below cost recovery. In Azerbaijan, although the situation is improving, tariffs remain below cost recovery and the collection of payments remains ineffective. The cost–recovery ratio of natural gas reportedly rose to 85 per cent by the end of 2004 from 50 per cent in 2002 but bill collection remains at around 50 per cent (Saavalainen and ten Berge 2006). Regarding electricity, the State Oil Company of Azerbaijan (SOCAR) continues to provide underpriced fuel and gas inputs for power generation. This scheme enables many large enterprises to postpone overdue reforms.

Oil funds, the Azerbaijan and Kazakhstan cases

Local authorities usually presented the establishment of oil funds as a panacea. The main advantage of such a stabilization mechanism is to avoid the excessive appreciation of the real exchange rate and make possible the saving of part of the oil windfall for future generations. However, this fund does not necessarily guarantee a sound and transparent use. Stevens (2003) points out that 'in many cases, the rules dictating the oil fund use are dependent on political circumstances'. According to Tsalik (2003), oil funds in Kazakhstan and Azerbaijan, when they were designed, had several apparent shortcomings, of which the two most important were: first, Parliament's role is more limited than it should be and, second, transparency *vis-à-vis* local populations remains inadequate.

The experience of the Azerbaijan Oil Fund[18] is instructive, and Kazakhstan seems to be going in the direction followed by Azerbaijan, with an increased role for Parliament to approve the use of oil revenue. In order to ensure that Azerbaijan has a single state budget rather than multiple parallel budgets, Parliament approves the consolidated budget, which includes the transfers from the State Oil Fund of the Republic of Azerbaijan (SOFAZ)[19] to the state budget. Annual transfers from the SOFAZ to the state budget are capped and decided by the President. By 2005, four presidential decrees had called for spending from the SOFAZ: three were aimed at improving the living conditions of refugees and displaced persons, and one requested funds for financing SOCAR's share of the BTC. From 2004 to 2024, direct contributions to the budget are projected to approach $20 billion. The government is expected to establish a sound comprehensive medium-term expenditure framework that takes account of the absorptive capacity of the economy and is designed to promote non-oil sector growth.

The National Fund of the Republic of Kazakhstan (NFRK) was established in January 2001.[20] As in Azerbaijan, the main objective of the Fund is to reduce the impact of volatile market prices and to smooth the distribution of oil wealth over generations. Initially, the authorities identified 12 major companies in the natural resources sector whose fiscal payments were to be transferred to the NFRK. However, this figure was reduced to six in 2004 and the list limited to petroleum companies. Flows consist of a *savings* component equal to 10 per cent of the budgeted baseline revenue, invariant to oil price changes, and a *stabilization* component that includes all revenue above the baseline price, fixed at $19 per barrel. The Fund's capital is supplied by shares of government income from the oil sector, royalties, bonuses and revenue from production sharing agreements (PSAs). The NFRK's funds are invested in foreign equities (Kalyuzhnova and Kaser 2005; IMF 2004: 19) and assets are managed by the National Bank, which reports on the Fund's management. Thus, a large share of oil revenue is allocated to the NFRK, which had accumulated $10 billion by July 2006.

In July 2006, a major change occurred in Kazakhstan, and the Parliament must now approve transfers from the National Fund to the state budget for a three-year period. For the first time since the establishment of the National Fund, the Parliament has the power to decide how much and how to use part of the oil windfall. Before that, Kazakhstan's president had full competency on the use of the NFRK because it was his mandate to determine 'the volume and use of the Fund'.

Non-governmental organizations (NGOs) involved in scrutinizing the use of oil revenue in Kazakhstan mainly complain about two major problems of transparency with the National Fund. First, oil and gas companies (including KazMunayGas) directly transfer their payment to the National Fund, bypassing the state budget. According to Mr Artemyev, 'the problem is that information of companies' payments is aggregated and we can't find out how much each company pays to the Fund'. Second, the legal and regulatory framework about the use of the National Fund remains too vague, although there is a section on the NFRK in the Budget Code. However, with the new rules in effect from July 2006, this criticism may be outdated. Kazakh NGOs usually recommend that a law should stipulate priorities for the Fund's expenditures and also provide a framework for greater transparency, and they would also like to become members of its Advisory Council. Many experts also recommend turning the NFRK into an independent legal entity, as in Azerbaijan and Norway.

Governance of national oil companies

Governance of national oil companies becomes increasingly critical because they own a growing share in local oil and gas production. Azeri and Kazakh oil companies own close to 30 per cent of proven oil reserves of the Caspian Basin or almost 15 billion barrels (see Figure 2.6).

That is why, in the first 15 years after independence, authorities have strived to achieve two main results:

1 ending the splitting up of the oil and gas sector, which was a result of the Soviet heritage;[21]
2 increasing the competency and efficiency of national oil and gas companies.

Fifteen years after independence, the splitting up of the oil and gas sector ended (with the potential problems of over-concentration of power in the hands of few key people). In one decade, the vertical integration of the oil and gas sector has been completed in Kazakhstan and in Azerbaijan. As far as the efficiency of these companies is concerned, initiatives have been recently taken in Kazakhstan;

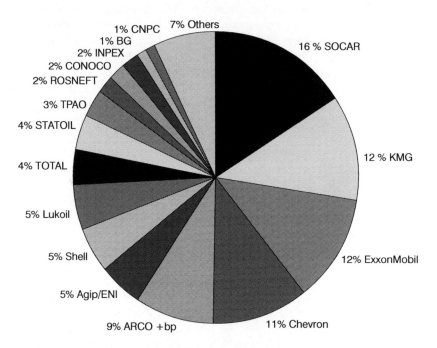

Figure 2.6 Share of Caspian oil reserves of the main oilfields in 2006

Source: Authors' calculations based on data on Azeri and Kazakh PSAs available at www.eia.doe.gov/emeu/cabs/Azerbaijan/azerproj.html and www.eia.doe.gov/emeu/cabs/Kazakhstan/kazaproj.html.

Notes: Calculations based on the lowest estimate of PSAs proven reserves. Oilfields below 500 million barrels have been excluded. Several PSAs are currently in negotiations in Kazakhstan.

although it is premature to assess the outcome of this restructuring, authorities seem aware of the importance of the management of oil companies.

In Azerbaijan, SOCAR is a major state-owned asset. As the equity owner of SOCAR, the government faces a number of specific challenges:

1   to effect a clear separation of the regulatory functions currently performed by SOCAR as the de facto 'competent authority' dealing with the upstream oil sector and the commercial functions SOCAR performs as an operator in the sector;
2   to ensure the state receives the full benefit associated with SOCAR's equity interest in PSAs and joint ventures;
3   to facilitate the transition of SOCAR from a Soviet-style state-owned enterprise to a commercially focused organization operating in accordance with best international practice; and
4   to ensure SOCAR's ongoing financial viability.

In order to address these challenges, the government has made a commitment to restructure the company. There are, however, certain decisions that the government should make with regard to the restructuring.

As in Azerbaijan, Kazakhstan's authorities have strived to put an end to the institutional splitting up of the sector and have achieved this objective in a decade. Several successive reorganizations took place, finally leading to the constitution of a single vertically integrated state company in the oil and gas sector, in which men related to President Nazarbayev's family have the power to take strategic decisions.

After 1991, the national company, Kazakhstanmunaigaz, managed Kazakhstan's oil sector, but it remained under the authority of the Oil and Gas Ministry. However, this aspect of the Soviet heritage rapidly disappeared as the mandate of the Minsitry was considerably reduced, especially after the creation of Kazakhoil in 1997. Nevertheless, oil exploration/production and oil transport remained in two distinct companies.

In December 1998, Nazarbayev announced that the oil and gas sector would not be privatised and the reorganization of the sector continued. In May 2001, a single transport company, Trans Neft i Gaz (TNG) was created by merging KazTransGas and KazTransOil. At that time, Timur Kulibayev, second son-in-law of Nazarbayev, was chairman of KazTransOil and then became chairman of the new entity, TNG.

The last stage took place in February 2002 with the dismissal of Balgimbaev at the head of Kazakhoil and the constitution of KazMunayGaz (KMG), which was the result of a merger between Kazakhoil and TNG. As Olcott (2002) put it, Balgimbaev, as a professional of oil, had succeeded in making of Kazakhoil a state within the state 'threatening the interests of Nazarbayev's family'. In the new entity, Liazat Kiinov, former governor of the oil province of Mangystau, was appointed chairman of the new company but Timur Kulibayev was appointed the first vice-chairman of KMG.[22]

Kazakhstan is striving to develop a model that combines leaders' self-interest and general interest through increased economic effectiveness. In that respect, 2006 was a particularly enlightening year: in February, President Nazarbayev signed a decree creating the 'Samruk' State Holding Company, a state holding designed to improve management of, initially, five large state-owned companies: KMG, Kaztelekom, Kazpost, Kazakhstan Temir Zholy (railways) and KEGOC (Kazakhstan Electricity Grid Operating Company).[23]

Inspired by the Singapore Temasek state holding, the main objective of this holding company is to improve the efficiency of government's asset management, corporate governance and financial management of these state-owned companies.[24] This strategy is the result of a political will to modernize the national economy and strengthen Kazakhstan integration into the world economy. A Council has been set up to develop strategies for these companies and define guidelines for dividends payment and use of profits.[25] The link between these state-owned companies and Ministries in charge of these sectors should be gradually reduced.

In the oil sector, KMG subsidiaries are assigned the task of securing the maximum profit for the Republic of Kazakhstan to take part in the development of all sector-related activities, and are even encouraged to take participations abroad. Earlier, the Samruk board of directors decided to restructure KMG's board of directors by replacing most of the government representatives with recognized experts in the field. 'This strategy gives a more professional and rational approach', explains an executive of a foreign oil sub-contractor company in Kazakhstan. 'For example, the new offshore KMG subsidiary, with which we are permanently in touch, call us regularly to learn about the new exploration technologies. That shows, in my opinion, a will to learn and better understand all phases of the oil and gas production'.[26] A new generation of managers is emerging in Kazakhstan. Often educated abroad, they are taking over the national oil company, bringing with them new management rules, more in accordance with those of Western Europe and the USA.

Although KMG seems increasingly managed in accordance with the law, suspicions about transparency problems remain strong among oil experts. Many of them involved in the country complain that state interests are in competition with the personal interests of some top managers of large Kazakh companies, including KMG. Indeed, these top managers usually use their own officially registered private enterprises, formally run by relatives but actually run by them, to benefit from oil-related contracts. These private enterprises are said to win tenders more easily than other sub-contractors.

In Nazarbayev's entourage, Timur Kulibayev is increasingly playing a key role in the management of Kazakhstan's oil and gas sector. Timur Kulibayev is Vice-Chairman of the Board of Directors of Samruk and, in July 2006, the Head of State announced that his son-in-law would also chair KMG's board of directors. Timur Kulibayev seems to be the President's man to combine the ruling elite's self-interests and Kazakhstan's interest. A major investor in Kazakhstan pointed out that 'he knows how to set up oil nationalism and taking care of the foreign investors'.[27] Most observers of the Kazakhstan oil and gas sector think that Timur

Kulibayev is the right man to enforce financial and economic discipline on state companies. He is said to have been behind the decision to list Kazmunaigaz Exploration and Production, a KMG subsidiary, on the London Stock Exchange in October 2006.

Transparency of early oil revenue management

Kazakhstan was late to endorse the Extractive Industries Transparency Initiative (EITI) mainly because of strong reluctance from the powerful Kazakh mining industry. The Transparency Initiative had been announced by British Prime Minister Tony Blair at the world summit on sustainable development in September 2002. Its goal is to increase the transparency of payments that oil, gas and mining companies made to the government and state revenue from extractive industries.

On the contrary, 'Azerbaijan is the leader for the activities carried out as part of the EITI' according to the US Ambassador in Baku, Reno Harnish. This process began in June 2003 for Azerbaijan. Twenty-two out of the 24 companies operating in the country's oil and gas sector have joined the EITI.

In recent years, there have been several corruption scandals in Kazakhstan. In April 2002, several high officials, including the Prime Minister, I. Tasmagambetov, they acknowledged the existence of such accounts. It was then indicated that these funds had made possible the financing of several investments in the new capital, Astana. Moreover, in April 2003, a New York judge charged J. Bryan Williams and James Giffen for a violation of the Foreign Corrupt Practices Act. The first acted on behalf of Exxon to negotiate swap agreements between Iran and Kazakhstan. The second was the chairman of merchant bank and had been an adviser to the Kazakh president for oil issues.

Contrary to what has happened in Azerbaijan, regulatory quality and control of corruption seems to be more and more problematic in Kazakhstan in the context of the oil windfall. This may explain why the redistribution of oil revenue may still be limited in Kazakhstan (see Figure 2.7 and additional analysis in Chapter 7).

The effect of 'Kazakhgate' made Kazakh oil management suspicious. As a result, the country recently launched a transparency policy to fight against this deep-rooted suspicion and also to be more integrated into the world economy because Kazakhstan's entry to the World Trade Organization (WTO) is one of the key priorities of the Kazakh government.[28]

In February 2005, President Nazarbayev announced that improving governance and transparency was a priority for the country. In June 2005, Kazakhstan endorsed the EITI. Four months later, the Kazakh government, 24 companies and representatives of Parliament signed a Memorandum of Understanding (MoU). Despite political will, the mining companies have not taken part actively in the discussions and have not joined the EITI, mostly because of disclosure concerns:[29] the fear of divulging confidential information and commercial secrets, which would undermine their competitiveness.

NGOs had called upon the government and companies to make the so-called 'social payments' (social projects of extractive companies aimed at local

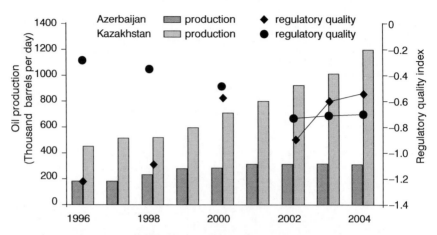

Figure 2.7 Oil production trends and regulatory quality

Source: Information Agency of US Department of Energy and World Bank.

development) part of the reporting mechanism under the umbrella of EITI. This proposal was not adopted. However, the NGOs agreed to co-sign the Memorandum only after a special body – the National Council of EITI Implementation – was established.

Conclusion

The Caspian Basin is expected to become a major oil exporting region in the next decade. However, to turn the oil windfall into economic and social development is a tremendous challenge. The management and redistribution of oil revenue will turn oil revenue into a curse or a success for local populations. The onus is on the leadership of these countries to turn the oil windfall into prosperity for local populations. As the World Bank states: 'economic theory provides no guidance for finding such balance [between saving and spending]'.

In September 2006, President Nazarbayev criticized the management of the state companies, especially the high salaries of several managers. In Kazakhstan, many observers understood that this surprising anger marked a decisive step to push state companies to become more competitive and be managed more efficiently. But was it just a 'public relations' statement or true anger signaling to everyone that nothing will be like it was yesterday?

Notes

1 Azerbaijan's production will peak around 2015 and that of Kazakhstan around 2020 because Kashagan's production will not start until 2009 at the earliest and will yield more production than expected.
2 An initial bilateral agreement was signed between Russia and Kazakhstan in 1998.
3 For more details on Transneft's policy, see Raballand and Esen (2006).
4 Kazakhstan accounted for 67% of Caspian production and Azerbaijan 22%.

5 The Tengiz field is the largest active field in Kazakhstan. Approximately 1 mmt corresponds to 20,000 b/d.
6 Kashagan's reserves were increased from 9 billion barrels to 13 billion barrels in November 2006.
7 Kashagan's development costs are estimated to be $29 billion (official data), implying that a large amount of FDI will flow into Kazakhstan.
8 Kazakhstan holds approximately 45% of gas reserves of the Caspian Basin, 44% for Turkmenistan, 10% for Azerbaijan, 2% for Russia. Gas reserves in the Caspian Basin cannot be compared with those of the Federation of Russia (32% of proven gas reserves in the world), nor with Iran (15% of the proven gas reserves).
9 The CPC is half-owned by Russia (24%), Kazakhstan (19%) and Oman (7%), and the other half is divided among ChevronTexaco (15%), LUKoil (12.5%), ExxonMobil (7.5%), Rosneft/Shell (7.5%), Agip (2%), British Gas (2%), Kazakhstan Pipeline Ventures (1.75%) and Oryx Caspian Pipeline (1.75%). After the dissolution of the USSR, the CPC (then consisting of Transneft, Kazakhstan and Oman) was awarded the rights to transport oil from Tengiz to the Black Sea, but negotiations dragged on the question of how much Chevron should pay towards construction. After Mobil bought 25% of Tengiz and LUKoil/Arco purchased 5%, the Tengiz partners together with other investors took a half-share in the CPC.
10 American officials recognized that, in 2020, the Persian Gulf should produce between 54% and 67% of world oil exports (Djalili and Kellner 2003).
11 Some experts argue that because of the risks related to governance of oil-related revenue, developing countries should leave the oil in their soil.
12 These figures are equivalent to Russian figures: the Russian oil sector represents 20% of GDP, 40% of total export revenue and 20% of fiscal revenue of the state budget (Cukrowski 2004: 295).
13 However, since the early 2000s, Kazakh authorities have strived to renegotiate contracts signed in the 1990s. A serious crisis took place in November 2002 between Chevron and Kazakh authorities about Tengiz. Chevron had announced that it had indefinitely postponed the implementation of the second phase of the project, aiming to nearly double output from 12.7 million tons to 22 million tons. Chevron and Kazakh authorities disagreed on the means to finance the required investments. Astana did not want TengizChevroil to reinvest their profits and consequently avoid paying taxes on profits for the next three years. KazMunayGaz argued that the consortium should borrow on international markets. An agreement was finally reached, which was different to the 1993 contract: for exploration and production activities, TengizChevroil would not reinvest profits from early oil sales and would finance new investments through international bonds or from profits generated by the second phase of oil production.
14 In Kazakhstan (but in any oil-producing country, revenue stems from exports and taxation). Kazakhstan's state benefit from the following revenue related to oil production:

- export sales of crude oil based on Kazakhstan's share in consortia (after deduction of cost recovery expenses under a PSA regime). Export of petroleum products remains a minor item; Kazakhstan still imports most of the petroleum products consumed in the country;
- tax applicable to subsurface users. They depend on the type of tax regime of the contract: excess profit tax (EPT) or PSA. In an EPT tax regime, the company is liable to pay bonuses, royalty, excess profits tax and a rent tax on export of crude oil, whereas in a PSA the company is subject to bonuses and gives up a share of production, rent on export of crude oil (except in fixed price PSA) and 'top up tax';
- taxation of business profit, such as corporate income tax and branch profits tax;
- indirect taxation such as VAT, excise and customs duties;

- other taxes such as environmental fees, property tax, land tax, vehicle tax and other fees and licenses.

15 Interview with Anton Artemyev in October 2006.

16 Kazyna includes Funds from the following institutions and projects: the Bank for Kazakhstan Development, the Investment Fund of Kazakhstan, the National Innovation Fund, the Export Credits and Investments Insurance Corporation, the Fund for Small and Medium Support and the Centre for Marketing and Analytical Surveys.

17 In Kazakhstan, Kazyna is partly financing the development of the Information Technologies park in Alatau, inaugurated in September 2006. Outside Kazakhstan, Kazyna should acquire equities in transport assets. As, according to Kairat Kelimbetov, Chairman of Kazyna Fund, Kazakhstan should finance the construction of a grain terminal in Lithuania, as well as the takeover of grain terminals in Poti and Baku.

18 For more details on SOFAZ and redistribution issues, see Chapter 8.

19 The State Oil Fund of the Republic of Azerbaijan was established in December 1999. At the end of 2006, assets of the fund reached $1.3 billion to $1.4 billion. For the period 2004 through 2024 contributions to SOFAZ (excluding investment earnings) are projected to exceed $50 billion. SOFAZ is required to invest its funds outside Azerbaijan in high quality securities. For more details, see Chapter 8, Appendix, 'The State Oil Fund of the Republic of Azerbaijan'.

20 For additional details, see www.nationalfund.kz/ and the analysis of the NFRK in Chapter 5 'The National Fund of the Republic of Kazakhstan'.

21 In his study of the oil and gas of the time of the USSR, Gustafson (1989) shows the institutional splitting up of the sector with a decision-making process divided between several Ministries and directorates. Vertical integration was non-existent with no less than four Ministries in charge of energy.

22 From 2002 to October 2005, Timur Kulibayev was the KMG's first Vice-President. He surprisingly resigned from this position few weeks before the December 2005 presidential elections.

23 In the future, Samruk Holding will also include another 17 companies that are entirely or partly owned by the state: KazKuat (100%) Ekibastuz Power Plant (100%), Chokin Kazakh Energy Studies Institute (50%), Bukhtarma Hydropower Station (90%), Kazakhstan Operator of Market of Electrical Power (100%), Shulba Hydropower Station (92.13%), Ust-Kamenogorsk Hydropower Station (89.99%), Astanaenergoservice (61.72%), Air Astana Airlines (51%), Mangistau Electric Power Distribution Company (94.25%), Kazmortransflot (50%), Kazakhstan Engineering (100%), Maikainzoloto (25%), Pavlodar Airport (100%), International Airport Aktobe (100%), International Airport Astana (100%), and Akbakai mining-and-metallurgical integrated works (33%).

24 Temasek Holdings, incorporated in 1974, is the main Singaporian holding company in charge of managing a diversified $80 billion (S$129 billion) portfolio, spanning various industries. Prior to the incorporation of Temasek Holdings in 1974, these stakes were held at first by the Ministry of Finance. 'Temasek was founded on the philosophy of managing for long-term value and the principles of integrity and excellence' (www.temasekholdings.com.sg). As of 2004, it owned stakes in many of Singapore's largest companies, such as SingTel, DBS Bank, Singapore Airlines, PSA International, Singapore Power and Neptune Orient Lines.

25 Since October 2006, Sir Richard Evans, former chairman of BAE Systems (which is a shareholder of Air Astana), has been the chairman of Samruk. Sixty people work for Samruk.

26 Interviews carried out by the authors in October 2006.

27 Interviews carried out by the authors in October 2006.

28 Negotiations appeared to be reaching their final stages in 2006.

29 A small number of mining companies signed the MoU in June 2006: Aluminii Kazakhstana, Sokolovsko-Sarbaiskoe Mining and Concentrating Enterprise, KazChrome, Eurasian Energy Corporation, as well as the Zhairemskii and Vasilkovskii mining and concentrating plants.

3

THE IMPACT OF OIL REVENUE ON ECONOMIC PERFORMANCE

Analytical issues

Michael Lewin

Introduction

This much is certain: large oil revenue (relative to the size of the economy) *will* have an impact. New oil revenue flows, or significant increases in existing ones, will transform an economy for better or worse. Usually, expectations are high. Governments and private citizens consider the oil to be a bonanza and the increased income a windfall. Disappointment often follows. Certainly, oil revenue has the potential to make an economy unambiguously better-off but it also produces large risks that the potential benefits will not be fully realized or indeed, that may make an economy worse-off than before.

This chapter will discuss in general terms the likely impact of oil revenue and the associated risks of negative outcomes. In the first section, we discuss the so-called 'resource curse' question: is an oil endowment beneficial, a blessing or a curse? Indeed, any analysis without some reference to this question would be incomplete. Nevertheless, it is a question that probably cannot be answered even if the welfare criteria are precisely defined. In practical terms, there is very little likelihood that any government is going to knowingly forego oil production. It is therefore probably more productive to try to determine the likely economic impact of oil revenue, the risks to realizing its benefits and to develop policies to maximize those benefits and minimize the risks.[1] Therefore, in the second section we turn to an analysis of the macroeconomic impact of oil, its potential benefits and its possible costs. The final section looks at policies to help avoid the dangers that the oil windfall poses.

The focus here will be on the macro-economy as much of the literature and policy discussion concerns the effects of oil revenue on aggregate economic growth, consumption, investment, fiscal deficits/surpluses and the balance of payments. These are also the indicators typically used in evaluating overall economic performance and stability.

Preliminaries: on blessings and curses

Some doubts about the question. The idea that resource abundance is a 'curse' has taken hold in the literature on the subject[2] and the question of whether resource endowment is a blessing or curse is all but ubiquitous. If it could be shown than an economy was worse off after the windfall than before it; or, if it could be demonstrated that an economy is worse off with oil (or some other resource) than it would have been without it, then the resource could reasonably be called a curse. And if this was shown to be a likely outcome, then it might be best to leave the oil in the ground (as implied, for example, by the Oxfam report (Ross 2001)). But how would one demonstrate such an outcome? To answer the question one must clearly define the criteria. Thus, much of the empirical work on the subject focuses on long run aggregative growth performance. For example, Sachs and Warner argue that oil abundance is a key negative determinant of economic growth. These empirical results are themselves controversial (discussed briefly below) but the point here is to argue that the criterion itself is not sufficient.

Lower growth in the long run does not *necessarily* mean that the oil is curse. A country can experience a windfall, which raises income and consumption in all periods but does not produce faster growth, and indeed it may even slow growth. Even if growth slows after the windfall, consumption, the usual aggregative measure of welfare, may still remain higher in all periods because disposable income is higher than if the economy had not had a windfall but had grown faster. Thus, the empirical observation referred to above, that resource abundant economies tend to have lower aggregative growth, is not in itself sufficient to demonstrate that oil is a curse.

Much macroeconomics assumes that the marginal propensity to save is positive. This means, other things being equal, that oil windfalls (and other transfers such as aid) by raising income will raise capital accumulation and growth. However, if 'permanent income' or wealth is the key determinant of saving, then it cannot be ruled out that a windfall discovery of oil could have a negative effect on saving. Assume, for argument sake, that the oil wealth accrued to private households. In calculating their permanent income or wealth, taking into account the future expected income from oil, consumers may save less: with increased expected income they may feel less of a need to save. In other words, the wealth effect on saving is negative. Consumers believing they have 'inherited' an asset may feel less need to accumulate as much as they did before or at least may not be inclined to increase accumulation. For the economy as a whole, saving and growth may still be positive and so future generations can still enjoy higher income, even after the oil is exhausted, than generations before it came on stream enjoyed.[3] Thus, long-run growth performance is not a sufficient indicator of increased welfare. The usual aggregative indicator of welfare is consumption and that may be at least as high as it would have been even if oil caused the economy to grow at a slower rate.[4]

The policy implications of the above are not trivial. If the oil is a curse, that is if economies are likely to be worse off producing it than not, then it is best to leave it in the ground (e.g. Ross 2001). Oil may, indeed, be a curse but reaching this conclusion from empirical evidence that oil economies tend to grow at a slower rate would be misleading. Slower growth does not necessarily imply a relative welfare loss.

Similarly, the decline of the non-oil sector is not necessarily a curse. Most economic change comes at a cost and, as argued above, there is no *a priori* reason to assume that this cost outweighs the benefits from the oil. However, there are plausible arguments that the decline of the non-oil tradable sector has an overall negative effect on the economy. This will be discussed in the section below on the 'Dutch disease'. The point here is to note that booming and declining sectors are a feature of all change and not necessarily evidence of a curse.

This is not to deny that the windfall may turn out to be a curse. In the following sections we will show how the combination of volatility, exhaustibility of the resource, and the harmful effect that oil revenue often has on governance, may indeed contribute to setting an economy on an inferior trajectory in terms of consumption and poverty reduction. The purpose of the analysis is to use the understanding of the risks to help minimize them. We turn to this in the section on 'Dutch disease'.

Empirical evidence

The above argument shows that there are complex inter-temporal elements involved in answering the question of 'blessing or curse'. Additionally, there is the impossibility of knowing the implicit counterpoint: How well would the country have done in the absence of oil? Therefore, economists have focused on a simpler, precise criterion, namely, aggregative economic growth: Does mineral abundance retard growth? While there is much evidence to support this (most recently Sachs and Warner 1995),[5] there are also many problems with this conclusion.

- *Causality*. While many authors claim that resource abundance causes poor growth performance the causality could be reversed. Resource abundance is usually defined in terms of GDP. Thus, since all less developed economies initially are dependent on primary products, only those with low growth and otherwise poor economic performance remain dependent. In other words, low growth is the cause of dependence on resources (i.e. by definition, resource abundance) and not vice versa.
- The results depend crucially on the time period chosen: pre-1970 the results are reversed with mineral abundance affecting growth positively while the later period seems to support the pessimistic view. As Stevens (2003) notes, however, the literature does not seem to support a firm conclusion for the overall period since the Second World War. It is also obvious that in periods of price booms mineral based economies grow faster, whereas negative growth dominates periods when prices are falling.
- Manzano and Rigobon (2001) directly tackle the question of causality by introducing a third factor correlated with low growth and the oil boom,

namely, debt overhang. Thus, controlling for debt they find that oil does not retard growth. Their conclusion would seem to suggest that the fault of the 1970s and 1980s lay not so much in oil production *per se* but rather in the over-estimate of future revenue[6] which led to over-borrowing.

- It is often difficult to compare the conclusions of different empirical tests as they use differing definitions of resource abundance with some emphasizing the abundance of minerals while others use other measures including the abundance of arable land (for example, Auty 2001).

Thus, on the basis of the current literature it is not possible to reach any firm conclusion. In any case, as argued above, to conclude that oil (or mineral abundance in general) is a curse one would have to go beyond just looking at average growth rates. Therefore, rather than dwelling on the blessing/curse question it is probably more productive to analyze the impact of oil revenue and thus identify its possible deleterious effects in order to avoid them. It is to this that we now turn.

Dutch disease

The Dutch disease[7] is the term given to the malady associated with the appreciation of the real exchange rate. Although the term is now often used broadly to describe the fallout from a real appreciation from any cause (for example, a capital inflow), it was originally and is still most frequently, used in relation to these effects when they result from the production and export of oil and gas. To understand this is helpful to consider two key characteristics of most oil exporting countries, particularly developing ones. First, the oil industry is an enclave in the sense that it employs few domestic factors of production (importantly, labour) and exports all but a negligible part of its output; and, second, the central government 'owns' the oil and gas reserves. This means that practically all the rent deriving from oil and gas (i.e. the revenue that is not paid to capital or labour) accrues to the central government. The impact of the rents on the domestic economy thus depends almost entirely on fiscal policy: that is, on how fiscal policy responds to the revenue and how this in turn influences the overall economy.[8] There is also the related question of how oil rents influence the behaviour of the government in terms of efficiency, governance and in provoking conflict. This latter element is discussed below.

Oil and the real exchange rate

The main symptom of Dutch disease is the loss of competitiveness of the non-oil sectors of the economy. The real exchange rate is a measure of an economy's 'competitiveness' in international markets. In models of non-traded and traded goods it is defined as the price of traded goods in terms of non-traded goods. In aggregative (macroeconomic models) it is defined as the price of foreign goods relative to home-produced goods. The domestic price of foreign goods is given by the nominal exchange rate (E) multiplied by the price of imported goods. The real exchange rate is therefore, $E*P_m/P_h$. Or, in the traded/non-traded version it is:

$E*P_T/P_n$ (where the numerator and denominator stand for traded and non-traded prices, respectively.) A relative rise in the numerator is called a real depreciation (i.e. of the currency) and vice versa. (The terminology can be confusing giving rise to the seeming anomaly that 'down is up'. That is, a real *appreciation* is a *fall* in the real exchange rate.) A rising relative price of home or non-traded goods means that exports will fall as resources are drawn to producing non-traded goods. In the composite good model, as the price of the domestically produced good rises so export demand will fall. This is the familiar fall in competitiveness, which is the subject of much discussion in the exchange-rate economics literature. One of the consequences of an oil windfall is, other things being equal, a real appreciation. The mechanism is as follows: the windfall brings a rise in income, some of which will be spent on home produced or non-traded goods. If the economy is at its natural rate of employment then this will cause some rise in home goods prices relative to import prices, which are determined internationally, or non-traded goods prices relative to traded. Employment is maintained as more home goods are consumed domestically and non-oil exports fall and imports rise. Overall, consumption has risen as the increase in imports is financed by the rise in oil revenue.[9]

The above describes the case where trade is balanced. This will not always be the case. Briefly, where there is a current account surplus then domestic saving exceeds investment. This can be interpreted as some of the windfall being saved abroad. This will have the effect of sterilizing or offsetting part of the real appreciation. However, when the income on the saving is repatriated then the resulting flows will have the same effect as the oil windfall on the real exchange rate. In the case of oil revenue, such an increase in saving abroad may be due to the government. (For example, the government may save some revenue in an oil fund or may reduce foreign debt.) It can also be understood in terms of inter-temporal allocation in the sense that more saving means shifting some of the consumption benefits of the windfall from the present to the future. Thus, the real appreciation can be understood to a large extent as a symptom resulting from enjoying the benefits of the windfall: if it occurs contemporaneously then the benefits are enjoyed in the present; if the benefits are postponed, possibly for future generations, then real appreciation will occur later.

There are two cases where real appreciation will not occur contemporaneously with the windfall. The first occurs when the windfall is spent entirely on imports. In that case the net inflows on the balance of payments will be exactly matched by the outflows and the real exchange rate will not change. Alternatively, one could view this as a case where none of the additional income is spent on home goods and so home goods prices do not change. Consumption will increase by the amount of the additional imports, which is exactly equal to the windfall. This is obviously an extreme case where the marginal propensity to import is equal to one, which greatly restricts its applicability. In fact, in most oil exporting countries the boom is usually accompanied by a sharp rise in domestically produced (and non-traded) goods and services such as residential housing. However, it does illustrate the potential benefits from oil or other foreign transfers from a growth perspective

34

(which will be expanded on below). In an economy with a high propensity to import, a small addition to income will result in a relatively large increase in imports. To finance the additional imports, exports must rise and so the real exchange rate must depreciate to achieve this. This can only be brought about by a reduction in consumption of the domestic good. An inflow of oil revenue or other transfers such as international aid helps prevent or reduce the 'sacrifice' in terms of consumption that accompanies the growth in income. Thus, the benefits can be seen as preventing the real depreciation that would otherwise be required.

The second case arises when the government sterilizes all the revenue by saving it offshore. Then the inflow of revenue is offset by an equal outflow representing the increase in the government's net foreign assets (or, equivalently, the reduction in net liabilities.) This is an extreme example of the inter-temporal allocation described above. However, in the case of complete sterilization there is no contemporaneous benefit from the windfall. When the income from the foreign assets is repatriated then the real exchange rate will appreciate. Again, this is an example of benefits postponed.[10]

The inescapable conclusion from the above would seem to be that the real appreciation is an intrinsic part of the absorption of the oil revenue. The real exchange rate can be sterilized perhaps indefinitely,[11] but only at the cost of postponing, perhaps indefinitely, any benefit from the income. Some of the harmful effects of the real appreciation, often referred to as Dutch disease, will be addressed below. However, the point to be emphasized here is that the real appreciation *per se* is not the source of the problem and, indeed, is unavoidable if any benefit is to be derived from the oil.

Growth. We noted above that the resource curse thesis claims that mineral abundant economies grow at a slower rate than resource poor ones. However, it is not clear why Dutch disease, that is the real exchange rate appreciation and the decline of the non-oil tradables sector, should affect growth. In other words, as usually described, the costs of the oil boom in terms of restructuring the economy are static rather than dynamic. Why should the decline of the traditional sector alter the key elements affecting per capita growth, namely, the pace of capital accumulation, and technological progress?[12] From a macroeconomic perspective, it is not obvious why the real exchange appreciation and the resulting transfer of factors of production from declining sectors to booming ones should translate into poor long-run economic performance rather than remaining once-and-for-all adjustments. The following are some of the explanations offered in the literature:

- *De-industrialization.* It is often argued that the manufacturing sector produces positive dynamic external effects (Matsuyama 1992) which stimulate faster growth, for example, 'learning by doing.' Thus, the social marginal product of capital in manufactures is higher than its market rate because it also results in human capital accumulation. The real appreciation therefore, not only causes a one-off adjustment but also has long-run effects by slowing growth via the reduction in the spillovers from learning by doing. However, there is not much empirical evidence to support the view either that the manufacturing

35

sector stimulates 'learning by doing' more than other sectors, or, that manufacturing suffers disproportionately from the real appreciation.[13] In fact, in most developing countries the manufacturing sector is initially relatively small and so the traded sector that takes the biggest hit is usually agriculture. Thus, the 'competitiveness' of the industrial sector after the windfall is really no different from that of any other developing country, with or without resource abundance. Indeed, in many cases despite the overall decline in traded goods, manufacturing often actually increased perhaps as a result of free trade agreements and/or rising world demand and prices (Neary and van Wijbergen 1986).

- *Linkages*. It is often claimed that because the mineral sector has few 'linkages' to the rest of the economy it does not stimulate growth and development.[14] However, it is not clear why the linkages of sectors stimulated by the increased demand due to mineral boom should be less important than any other. If linkages are important why does the growth of the non-traded sector not lead to growth and development?[15]

The conclusion from the above is that the risks to beneficial long-run performance of oil exporters should focus on the following elements:

- *Volatility*: the foregoing argued that the real appreciation *per se* (Dutch disease) was not an adequate explanation for the deleterious effects of oil. However, the real exchange rate may play a role if it is volatile. Thus, if oil revenue itself is volatile, which is likely because oil prices are volatile, then revenues will be volatile. If the revenues are absorbed in the domestic economy then the turbulence will spill over to the real exchange rate leading to a boom–bust cycle. This has the effect of increasing uncertainty in the non-oil export (or traded goods sector) and so may result in an increasing risk premium on investment in that sector. This would lead to lower investment and lower growth. As argued above, the government can sterilize the real exchange rate effect by saving part of the windfall offshore. The question of how much to save is, of course, a very complex one. A fairly rough guideline can be derived from consumer theory. That is, the government should save abroad the 'transitory' component of the windfall and spend only the 'permanent' part.[16] This will not prevent the real appreciation but can help smooth or stabilize it over time. This is also sometimes referred to as de-linking current expenditure from current revenue and thus preventing pro-cyclical fiscal behaviour.[17]
- *Exhaustibility*: oil is an exhaustible resource. Most of the countries surveyed in Chapter 1 face a fairly short time horizon. Therefore, even in the absence of volatility the oil revenue is a windfall in the sense of its being transitory. Again, as in the case of volatility, expenditure smoothing will contribute to the orderly movement of the real exchange rate. However, if the other deleterious effects of the rents are present then the non-oil sector will not grow as needed and as the oil nears depletion the economy will require painful adjustment.

- *Governance*: in addition to the problems of an unstable fiscal policy the concentration of the revenues in government may lead to the over-extension of government and the evolution of numerous other behavioural maladies. This is not so much a resource curse but rather a 'governance curse'.
  - Even with the best of intentions the quality of investment may deteriorate. A government-initiated investment boom is likely to exceed its implementation capacity and lead to waste and inefficiency. Moreover, the government will often undertake investment in productive ventures. These investments, not disciplined by the rigors of the financial sector, often end up draining the fiscal authority. This can also have the effect of crowding out the financial sector and therefore retarding its development.
  - Rent-seeking and corruption are also typically associated with mineral-dependent governments. It is important to distinguish between the two: the former can be entirely legitimate and part and parcel of any democratic regime, but a drain on scarce resources nevertheless. When government is the booming sector there are large incentives for private citizens to invest time and money to get a part of the rents. Policies to minimize the risk of resource curse should take this into account.
  - It is often argued (Collier and Hoefler 2000) that mineral- (and particularly oil-) based economies are prone to internecine conflict.[18] Mineral revenue concentrated in the central government thus provide the incentives and the means for waging conflict.

An aside on fiscal policy

Privatization of the oil sector is unlikely in developing countries. The government will therefore remain the recipient of the oil rents and so fiscal policy will be at the centre of policies to minimize the risk of turning the resource blessing into a curse. In this regard, two issues are worth considering: the choice confronting government to save abroad or domestically; and the importance of the overall fiscal stance.

Saving: domestic or foreign? Some insight into the first question can be derived from open economy macroeconomic models that assume perfect international capital mobility, or fully integrated capital markets (i.e. Mundell–Flemming–Dornbusch type models). While this assumption may be a bit of a stretch for most developing countries it is, nevertheless, an interesting special case. Where capital is perfectly mobile then domestic saving and investment will not necessarily be equal and the real rate of interest in a small economy will be exogenous and equal to the international rate. In the simplest case where investment is determined by the real rate of interest then, since the oil windfall does not affect the rate of interest, investment and hence growth, will not change. In this case, the increase in saving due to the windfall will not cause domestic growth to accelerate. But if saving has increased there will be an excess of saving over investment; that is, a surplus on the current account of the balance of payments. In other words, the effect of the windfall is to make the country a net saver. The resulting capital outflow sterilizes the real appreciation in the same way as if the government had saved all or part of the revenue abroad. While this may be an extreme assumption, it illustrates the possibility that in some circumstances saving the revenue domestically and abroad are equivalent. Thus, if the government is the recipient of the rent and it saves all or part of the revenue domestically it will put pressure on domestic interest rates to fall. This will cause a capital outflow and reverse the initial real appreciation caused by the windfall. The outcome for domestic disposable income will be similar in the two cases: instead of income rising because of increased domestic growth, it will rise due to the earnings on foreign investments.[19]

In the case where capital markets are not fully integrated, and in the poorer countries the degree of capital mobility is likely to be quite low, if some of the windfall revenue is saved domestically – either by the government or by the private sector – growth will increase. As explained above, with low capital mobility the rise in saving will lower real interest rates and therefore raise investment. Is domestic saving therefore preferable to saving abroad? On the one hand, by saving abroad the government can moderate the loss of competitiveness due to the real exchange rate. On the other hand, the increase in productivity due to investment also offsets the loss of competitiveness from the real appreciation. While domestic saving will not address the volatility of the exchange rate it may help offset its harmful effects on domestic investment: lowering the real interest rate counters the effect on investment of the increased risk premium.[20] Government saving here is defined as the net acquisition of assets: financial or physical assets (investment). In deciding on investment versus other forms of saving the policy-makers need to introduce into the equation the social rate of return on public sector investment. The government therefore faces a typical portfolio-choice problem and in most cases a diversified portfolio (i.e. in this case some balance between saving at home, abroad and in infrastructure investment) will be optimal.

Fiscal policy: the importance of fiscal policy has been stressed because the government is the conduit of the oil rents to the rest of the economy. However, the fungibility of government funds needs to be taken into account when assessing the fiscal impact of an oil windfall. Thus, the impact of additional government revenue is determined by the overall fiscal stance and not just by the disposition of the oil funds themselves. It is the *net* acquisition of assets that determines the fiscal stance. Thus a government can deposit a given amount in a revenue management fund but if at the same time it borrows to finance spending by an even greater amount then, in fact, it will be increasing its liabilities. Actually, in such a case the government would be borrowing funds to deposit in the oil revenue fund. Therefore, a revenue management tool such as an oil fund needs to be complemented by restraints on spending; possibly, by a fiscal rule or some other formal mechanism.

Conclusion

This chapter has examined the so-called resource curse argument. It has concluded that the question of 'blessing or curse' is not well defined and, further, that the literature has not really addressed it in an appropriate way. When the question is narrowly defined to focus on the growth performance of resource-abundant economies, unambiguous conclusions are not yet evident. The chapter also argued that the Dutch disease argument boils down to two key elements: volatility and exhaustibility. The antidote to Dutch disease therefore lies in some form of expenditure smoothing. Since the fiscal authority is the main and sometimes almost exclusive recipient of the rents, responsibility for smoothing rests with fiscal policy. Additionally, the potentially corrupting influence of oil revenue on governments may constitute the key risk. There is no panacea for the 'governance curse'. Transparency is a necessary component of the policy mix needed to address the governance problem. It is unlikely to be sufficient. Policy-makers need to avoid addressing the problems of adjustment with policies that encourage rent seeking and corruption; for example, many industrial and trade policies to protect tradable sectors. Government also needs to be mindful of the unwanted consequences of good intentions such as the crowding out of the private sector from investment and the financial sector. Thus governments can avoid over-extending themselves by focusing on the provision of public goods such as infrastructure, health and education, and providing a rational regulatory framework. In short, the government can do best by doing what seems to work best in any development context, with or without resource abundance.

Notes

1 This is also the conclusion of Stevens (2003) in his survey.
2 This seems to have begun with Gelb *et al.* (1988) and has been repeated often since then.
3 For example, assume oil revenue begins to flow in the current period and that non-oil GDP continues to grow at, say, 2% per annum in real per capita terms. Then in 36 years time, non-oil domestic product will have doubled. Even if the oil is exhausted at that time the cohorts born 36 years hence will enjoy an income twice that of the current generation which has not yet begun to enjoy the benefits of the oil. While 2% is far from stellar growth performance, future generations can hardly claim to be cursed.
4 We can look at this in another way. New oil production (call it the 'windfall') increases income. The post-windfall economy is a richer economy. Comparing before and after is therefore akin to comparing a richer and poorer economy. The richer economy grows from a larger base and may grow at a slower rate. The poorer economy, growing from a smaller base may grow at a faster rate and yet convergence to the richer may not occur for a very long time. Thus, consumption and income are higher in the richer economy for the relevant time period even though it grows at a slower rate.
5 A comprehensive survey of the literature and an illuminating commentary is given by Stevens (2003). This section will therefore look only briefly at some critical elements arising from the literature. Stevens does not, however, mention the Manzono/Rigobon critique of Sachs/Warner, which is noted below.
6 High oil prices tend to lead to oil price optimism particularly insofar as governments are concerned. (Although, of course, the lenders are equally at fault.)

7 The term seems to have been coined by *The Economist* in the 1970s and refers to the effects on the Dutch economy of the discovery of natural gas in the North Sea (Corden 1984).

8 Oil/gas output is part of GDP. However, given the above characteristics its impact on the economy is most similar to that of a transfer. Oil revenue is therefore often compared to other transfers such as factor remittances (wages, profits and interest) and international aid. Since remittances are transfers to the private sector their impact does not depend directly on the government. Alternatively, aid flows usually go directly to government and so the comparison to oil flows is more appropriate.

9 In the aggregative model, an exogenously caused increase in exports (for example, caused by a rise in foreign income) will raise export prices and therefore the price of home goods. Export supply may be expected to rise in response to the higher prices but at the cost of lower consumption of the home produced good. Consumption of the relatively cheaper imports will rise. Thus, the improvement in the terms of trade is clearly welfare enhancing and, unlike the case of foreign transfers, there is no apparent downside in terms of loss of produced exports.

10 Complete sterilization results from a 'bird in hand' investment strategy. That is, all the oil revenue is saved and only income from the investment assets is consumed.

11 It is questionable for how long sterilization can be achieved. In other words, what amount of foreign assets can an economy accumulate or for how long can a surplus be sustained. For example, if the conventional wisdom about China is correct then it would seem that the answer is 'quite a long time'. If, in fact, the Chinese currency is undervalued then it would seem to be deliberately pursuing an export-led growth strategy at the expense of current consumption. The benefits of this strategy for future generations depend to a large extent on maintaining the value of its foreign investments. One country's surplus is only as stable as the rest of the world's deficit and if the imbalances are corrected by real currency revaluations then the accumulating countries will suffer a loss.

12 In fact, it quite possible that capital accumulation will quicken. If the marginal propensity to save is positive, then the additional income due to the windfall will increase saving and, therefore, investment. This result would be predicted by a Keynesian-type model where the marginal propensities to save and consume from income are constant. As noted above, in models where saving is based on permanent income or life-cycle theories, then it is possible that overall saving could decline. However, this is not to say that this is likely but rather just that it is possible. We shall argue below, however, that this kind of expenditure smoothing addresses the key element of Dutch disease, which is volatility.

13 For a summary of the arguments for and against, see Stevens (2003: 12–13).

14 This argument is usually associated with the work of Prebisch (1950, 1964) and Singer (1950).

15 Also associated with the work of Prebisch and Singer is the argument that mineral-based economies have suffered because of the secular decline of the terms of trade of commodities relative to industrial goods. This argument has been largely discredited and is beyond the scope of this chapter. However, it should be evident that the declining terms of trade argument sits uneasily with the Dutch disease argument. If the real exchange rate appreciates when the terms of trade improve and this leads to de-industrialization, then declining terms of trade should lead to a real depreciation and the growth of industry. Thus, the Prebisch-Singer and Dutch disease views cannot both be correct.

16 In the introductory section to this chapter, it was argued that if the private sector were the recipient of the revenue it may take into account the expected future income from oil in making its saving/consumption decisions. Thus, the permanent income hypothesis (a natural precursor to rational expectations theory) would predict that if the windfall went directly to households they would consume only that part that

they perceived as permanent and would save the transitory amount. Consumption would increase only by the amount that the windfall added to permanent or expected income.

17 In fact, since government is the conduit of the revenue to the economy, if government expenditure is linked to current revenue, then it is the government that initiates the boom-bust cycle. It is therefore not so much that fiscal policy is pro-cyclical but rather that fiscal policy is the source of the cycles.

18 This view has been challenged by Hausmann and Rigobon (2003) who argue that a government flush with oil revenue should be able to co-opt potential opponents by payoffs rather than coercion. This is unpersuasive: government based on payoffs seems to be inviting trouble by advertising the financial advantages of holding power.

19 If there is perfect arbitrage then the rates of return will be equal.

20 In an economy with a strong financial sector the need to address the volatility issue is reduced because the financial sector provides instruments for private sector hedging. Additionally, a developed financial sector will raise the efficiency of investment and tip the scales more toward domestic saving rather than offshore.

Part II

MACROECONOMIC LINKS AND FISCAL DECENTRALIZATION

4

NOMINAL AND REAL EXCHANGE RATES IN KAZAKHSTAN

Any sign of Dutch disease?

Balázs Égert and Carol S. Leonard

This chapter investigates evidence of Dutch disease in Kazakhstan. We assess effects of increasing oil prices on the nominal and real exchange rates of the Kazakh economy. We rely on variants of the monetary approach to the exchange rate to explore the relationship, using a range of empirical real exchange rate models. The estimation results show a possible relationship between the rise in the price of oil and an appreciation of the dollar exchange rate of oil and non-oil sectors. However, the appreciation only influences the real effective exchange rate calculated for the whole economy, and it has no systematic effect on the non-oil manufacturing sector. We conclude that thus far, the Kazakh economy has not been affected much by Dutch disease, at least in regard to the competitiveness of non-oil manufacturing.

Introduction

Most economists hold that long-term economic growth in developing countries can be negatively affected by abundant natural resources. Sachs and Warner (1995) show that natural resources can lead to higher macroeconomic volatility and lower long-term economic growth due to the hollowing out of the non-oil manufacturing sector. Avoiding this result is of paramount importance for oil producing economies, including emerging market economics in the Commonwealth of Independent States (CIS).

We examine evidence of the current potential for Dutch disease in the Kazakh economy. Most research on Dutch disease in transition economies has been carried out on panel data (Kronenberg 2004; Papyrakis and Gerlagh 2004; Davoodi 2005). Kutan and Wyzan (2005) break out of this pattern and account for country-specific features of the Kazakh economy, while preparing their policy recommendations. However, Kutan and Wyzan (2005) draw on a fairly narrow concept of Dutch disease. The impact of oil prices on the real exchange rate is assessed by a simple real exchange rate model using the Balassa–Samuelson effect (for instance the CPI-to-PPI ratio) and the real price of oil as explanatory variables.

In this chapter, we extend the characteristic analysis by looking at the impact of oil prices first on the nominal exchange rate and then on the real exchange rate. We use variants of the monetary model augmented with oil prices. Having established the relationship between oil prices and the nominal exchange rate, we use a variety of real exchange rate models to study the effect of oil prices on the real exchange rate. Our control variables include variables such as the productivity differential, the relative price of non-tradable goods to tradable goods, public debt to GDP ratio, public expenditure as a share of GDP, the openness ratio and the terms of trade. We also distinguish between the real exchange rate of the whole economy and the real exchange rate of the non-oil manufacturing sector. This enables us to obtain a clear picture regarding the change in the competitiveness of non-oil manufacturing in the wake of oil price changes.

The rest of the chapter is structured as follows. The next section, 'The price of oil and the exchange rate', describes our nominal and real exchange rate models. The third section, 'Data and estimation issues' deals with data and econometric issues, while the fourth section, 'Estimation results' presents the estimation results. The final section is the conclusion.

The price of oil and the exchange rate

As indicated in the introduction, we employ two approaches which help us to understand the relationship that links the price of oil and the exchange rate in a generalized framework. We first use the monetary model to establish any possible link between oil prices and the nominal exchange rate. We then rely on alternative real exchange rate models that help us to establish the connection between oil prices and the overall and sectoral real exchange rate.

The nominal exchange rate

The standard monetary model

The monetary model has been widely used for industrialised countries in the past to explain observed movements of the nominal exchange rate and also to forecast exchange rates (Groen 2000).[1] The baseline version of the monetary model relies on a standard money demand function of the following form in the domestic and foreign economies:

$$m_t^D - p_t = \alpha_1 \cdot y_t - \alpha_2 \cdot i_t \tag{1}$$

$$m_t^{D*} - p_t^* = \alpha_1^* \cdot y_t^* - \alpha_2^* \cdot i_t^* \tag{1'}$$

where m_t^D, p_t, and i_t are money demand, domestic prices, income and the interest rate, respectively, with small letters denoting log-transformed variables. The asterisk refers to the foreign economy. Expressing p_t from equation (1) and constructing the difference between the domestic and foreign equations yields the inflation differential between the home and the foreign economies as shown in equation (2):

$$p_t - p_t^* = m_t^D - m_t^{D*} - \alpha_1 \left(y_t - y_t^* \right) + \alpha_2 \left(i_t - i_t^* \right) \tag{2}$$

where it is assumed that $\alpha_1 = \alpha_1^*$ and $\alpha_2 = \alpha_2^*$. The assumption of purchasing power parity (PPP) to hold for the whole economy $\left(e_t = p_t - p_t^* \right)$ helps us express the nominal exchange rate as a function of money demand, income and interest differential across the home and foreign economies:

$$e_t = m_t^D - m_t^{D*} - \alpha_1 \left(y_t - y_t^* \right) + \alpha_2 \left(i_t - i_t^* \right) \tag{3}$$

where e_t is the nominal exchange rate, expressed as units of domestic currency units over one unit of foreign currency.[2]

The Balassa–Samuelson augmented monetary model

One strong assumption of the standard monetary model is that PPP holds for the economy as a whole, i.e. the real exchange rate is stable over time. However, according to the well-known Balassa–Samuelson effect, the real exchange rate may appreciate systematically because of the impact of productivity gains in the open sector on the relative price of non-tradables. This can be shown by decomposing prices into tradable and non-tradable prices:

$$p_t = \phi \cdot p_t^T + \left(1 - \phi\right) p_t^{NT} \tag{4}$$

where ϕ is the share of tradable goods in the price index, and T and NT refer to the tradable and the market-based non-tradable sector, respectively. Using equation (4) makes it possible to break down the overall real exchange rate into two components: (a) the real exchange rate of the open sector, and (b) the differential of the relative price of non-tradable goods between the domestic and foreign economies:

$$\underbrace{e + p_t^* - p_t}_{\text{overall real exchange rate}} = \overbrace{e + p_t^{T*} - p_t^T}^{\text{real exchange rate for tradables}} - (1 - \phi)\underbrace{\left(\left(p_t^{NT} - p_t^T \right) - \left(p_t^{NT*} - p_t^{T*} \right) \right)}_{\text{relative price differential}} \tag{5}$$

where $\phi = \phi^*$. The Balassa–Samuelson effect predicts that an increase in productivity in the open sector $\left(a_t^T \right)$ exceeding that in the sheltered sector $\left(a_t^{NT} \right)$ leads to a rise in the price of non-tradable goods $\left(p_t^{NT} - p_t^T \right)$ due to the wage equalisation process across sectors: the real exchange rate will appreciate if the productivity differential in the domestic economy is higher than the one in the

47

foreign economy $\left(\left(a_t^T - a_t^{NT}\right) - \left(a_t^{T*} - a_t^{NT*}\right) > 0\right)$ and provided PPP holds for tradables:

$$e + p_t^* - p_t = \left(e + p_t^{T*} - p_t^T\right) - (1 - \phi)\left(\left(a_t^T - a_t^{NT}\right) - \left(a_t^{T*} - a_t^{NT*}\right)\right) \tag{5'}$$

This trend appreciation driven by productivity gains, usually thought to be a feature of catching-up economies, can be also transposed to the standard monetary model. Substituting equation (2) in the left-hand side of equation (5') gives equation (6) after some rearrangement. The Balassa–Samuelson augmented monetary model[3] such as shown in equation (7) can subsequently be derived easily under the assumption that PPP holds for the open sector $\left(e + p_t^T - p_t^{T*}\right)$:[4]

$$p_t^T - p_t^{T*} = m_t^D - m_t^{D*} - \alpha_1\left(y_t - y_t^*\right) + \alpha_2\left(i_t - i_t^*\right) - (1 - \phi) \tag{6}$$
$$\left(\left(a_t^T - a_t^{NT}\right) - \left(a_t^{T*} - a_t^{NT*}\right)\right)$$

$$e_t = m_t^D - m_t^{D*} - \alpha_1\left(y_t - y_t^*\right) + \alpha_2\left(i_t - i_t^*\right) - (1 - \phi) \tag{7}$$
$$\left(\left(a_t^T - a_t^{NT}\right) - \left(a_t^{T*} - a_t^{NT*}\right)\right)$$

The monetary model augmented with oil prices

If we think of the implications of Dutch disease on the nominal exchange rate, according to which an increase (decrease) in the oil price $\left(p_t^{OIL}\right)$ causes the nominal exchange rate to appreciate (depreciate), it seems reasonable to add the oil price to the standard and to the Balassa–Samuelson augmented monetary model:

$$e_t = m_t^D - m_t^{D*} - \alpha_1\left(y_t - y_t^*\right) + \alpha_2\left(i_t - i_t^*\right) - p_t^{OIL} \tag{8}$$

$$e_t = m_t^D - m_t^{D*} - \alpha_1\left(y_t - y_t^*\right) + \alpha_2\left(i_t - i_t^*\right) - (1 - \phi) \tag{8'}$$
$$\left(\left(a_t^T - a_t^{NT}\right) - \left(a_t^{T*} - a_t^{NT*}\right)\right) - p_t^{OIL}$$

Testable equations

For empirical tests of the monetary model, it is crucial to assume that money demand equals money supply at each moment, i.e. continuous equilibrium at the money market $\left(m_t^D = \overset{S}{t}\right)$. This is how data on money supply can be used. As we are primarily interested in the effect of oil prices on the exchange rate, the standard and two variants of the Balassa–Samuelson augmented monetary models (with relative productivity and with relative prices) completed with oil prices are employed.

$$e_t = f\left(\left(m_t^S \overset{+}{-} \overset{S*}{t}\right); \left(y_t \overset{-}{-} y_t^*\right); \left(i_t \overset{+}{-} i_t^*\right); \left(p_t^{\overline{OIL}}\right)\right) \tag{9}$$

$$e_t = f\left(\left(m_t^{S\;+} - {}_t^{S*}\right); \left(y_t\; \overset{-}{-}\; y_t^*\right); \left(i_t\; \overset{+}{-}\; i_t^*\right); \left(a_t^T - a_t^{NT}\right) - \left(a_t^{T*} - a_t^{NT*}\right); \left(p_t^{\overset{-}{OIL}}\right)\right) \quad (10)$$

$$e_t = f\left(\left(m_t^{S\;+} - {}_t^{S*}\right); \left(y_t\; \overset{-}{-}\; y_t^*\right); \left(i_t\; \overset{+}{-}\; i_t^*\right); \left(p_t^T - p_t^{NT}\right) - \left(p_t^{T*} - p_t^{NT*}\right); \left(p_t^{\overset{-}{OIL}}\right)\right) \quad (10')$$

An increase in relative money supply and the interest differential is expected to lead to a depreciation (positive sign), while an increase in relative income, relative productivity, the price of oil and total oil revenues are assumed to cause an appreciation of the exchange rate (negative sign).

The real exchange rate

Productivity and the Balassa–Samuelson effect

The decomposition of the real exchange rate (q_t) into the real exchange rate of the open sector q_t^T and into the ratio of relative prices in the home economy and abroad such as in equation (5), restated in equation (11) below is a useful starting point:

$$q_t = q_t^T - (1-\phi) \cdot \left(\left(a_t^T - a_t^{NT}\right) - \left(a_t^{T*} - a_t^{NT*}\right)\right) \quad (11)$$

where a denotes average labour productivity in the open and sheltered sectors. As already mentioned, a widely accepted explanation for the failure of PPP in catching-up economies is the much-cited Balassa–Samuelson effect, attributing effects to productivity in the tradables sector. However, New Open Economy Macroeconomics (NOEM) models show that higher productivity growth in the open sector can also have an effect on the real exchange rate through tradable prices (see, for example, MacDonald and Ricci 2002; Benigno and Thoenissen 2003). In particular, productivity gains in the tradable sector can lead to a depreciation of the real exchange rate of the open sector via the terms of trade channel. The overall effect of productivity on the real exchange rate depends on whether or not the depreciation of the open sector's real exchange rate is higher than the real appreciation induced by the Balassa–Samuelson effect. In transition economies, the open sector's real exchange rate may exhibit a trend appreciation because of rapid shifts in the quality of the produced goods – a result of economic transformation. These quality changes in the CPI can go undetected by the statistical offices and thus would show up in higher inflation rates. In addition, goods may contain a non-tradable component including local inputs, the price of which is a function of the domestic wage level. If the overall wage level increases because of economic catching-up, the prices of goods will also increase. This leads to a positive inflation differential for tradable goods and leads to a real appreciation of the real exchange rate (Égert et al. 2003). As a result, the sign on productivity is ambiguous, as it may be either positive or negative.

A unifying framework

The risk adjusted real interest parity relationship, which has been used extensively in the literature (Faruqee 1995; MacDonald 1998a, 1998b) provides a convenient general framework for modelling the relationship between the real exchange rate and economic fundamentals (other than productivity). The real interest parity condition can be written as follows:

$$\Delta q_{t+k}^e = r_{t,t+k}^e - r_{t,t+k}^{*e} + \lambda_t \tag{12}$$

where Δq_{t+k}^e is the difference between the real exchange rate expected in t for $t+k \left(q_{t,t+k}^e \right)$ and the observed real exchange rate in period $t \left(q_t \right)$, $r_{t,t+k}^e = i_t - \Delta p_{t+k}^e$ and $r_{t,t+k}^{*e} = i_t^* - \Delta p_{t+k}^{*e}$ represent the domestic and foreign ex ante real interest rates and λ_t is the time-varying risk premium. The real exchange rate can be expressed from equation (12) after some manipulation:

$$q_t = q_{t,t+k}^e - \left(r_{t,t+k}^e - r_{t,t+k}^{*e} \right) - \lambda_t \tag{13}$$

If $q_{t,t+k}^e$ is the result of the expected values of the economic fundamentals $\left(\bar{x}_{t,t+k}^e \right)$, assuming rational expectations leads to equation (15):

$$q_t = \bar{x}_{t,t+k}^e - \left(r_{t,t+k}^e - r_{t,t+k}^{*e} \right) - \lambda_t \tag{14}$$

$$q_t = \bar{x}_t - \left(r_t - r_t^* \right) - \lambda_t \tag{15}$$

where the vector of long-run fundamentals may contain, in addition to productivity (the relative price of non-tradables), public debt, public consumption, openness, terms of trade or real oil prices. The time varying risk premium can be approximated by public or foreign debt. Higher debt is reflected in an increase in the risk premium, which leads to a real depreciation. Finally, the real interest differential can be viewed as a medium-term factor. The real price of oil (and the oil revenue variable) is expected to have a negative sign, i.e. an increase in this variable leads to a real appreciation. The same applies to the public expenditure and the terms of trade variable. By contrast, an increase in openness is assumed to be related to a depreciation of the real exchange rate (positive sign). For more discussion on the variables, see, for example, MacDonald 1998a, 1998b.

Testable equations

Our estimated equations for the real exchange rate (q_t), use a number of specifications. Our baseline specification contains productivity (prod) and, alternatively, relative prices, as they turn out to be a very robust variable in empirical testing, and it includes the real price of oil (roil), the variable of interest for us. Additionally, a number of macroeconomic variables are also used, including the public debt to

GDP ratio (pdebt), the public expenditure to GDP ratio (exp), openness (open) and terms of trade (tot):

$$q_t = f\left(\overset{-/+}{prod_t}/\ \overset{-}{rel_t}, \overset{-}{roil_t}/\ \overset{-}{revoil_t} \right) \tag{16}$$

$$q_t = f\left(\overset{-/+}{prod_t}/\ \overset{-}{rel_t}, \overset{-}{roil_t}/\ \overset{-}{revoil_t}, \overset{+}{pdebt_t} \right) \tag{17}$$

$$q_t = f\left(\overset{-/+}{prod_t}/\ \overset{-}{rel_t}, \overset{-}{roil_t}/\ \overset{-}{revoil_t}, \overset{-}{\exp_t} \right) \tag{18}$$

$$q_t = f\left(\overset{-/+}{prod_t}/\ \overset{-}{rel_t}, \overset{-}{roil_t}/\ \overset{-}{revoil_t}, \overset{+}{open_t} \right) \tag{19}$$

$$q_t = f\left(\overset{-/+}{prod_t}/\ \overset{-}{rel_t}, \overset{-}{roil_t}/\ \overset{-}{revoil_t}, \overset{-}{tot_t} \right) \tag{20}$$

Data and estimation issues

Data description

Our dataset comprises monthly observations for the period running from January 1994 to September 2005. Nominal exchange rates are period averages. Nominal GDP data are annualized and interpolated linearly from quarterly to monthly frequency. Industrial production data are nominal quarterly data interpolated to monthly frequency and deflated by the PPI for Kazakhstan. M2 is used for money supply. For short-term interest rates, money market rates are used for Kazakhstan, treasury bill rates for the US economy and three-month money market rates for the euro area and Russia.

For the real exchange rate models, productivity is obtained using industrial production divided by employment in industry or manufacturing. As data is not available for services, productivity in this sector is assumed to be equal to zero in all four economies. If productivity gains are comparable in the four economies, this zero growth assumption has little effect on the variable. The non-oil PPI is constructed on the basis of the PPI series for food processing; the textile and sewing industry; the chemical industry; rubber and plastic products; and machinery and equipment. As no weights are available, an arithmetic average is taken. The openness ratio is computed as exports and imports of goods over nominal GDP. Public debt is the cumulated government deficit over GDP. The price of Ural crude is used for the price of oil. The data are drawn from Datastream. The two exceptions are the terms of trade and exports and imports of goods, which are obtained directly from the Statistical Agency of the Republic of Kazakhstan.

The effective variables are computed as the weighted average of the three series (US, euro area and Russia) based on constant weights derived from foreign trade shares.

51

BALÁZS ÉGERT AND CAROL S. LEONARD

Econometric methods

Standard unit root and stationarity tests are used: the augmented Dickey–Fuller (ADF), Phillips–Perron (PP) and the Elliott–Rothenberg–Stock (ERS) point optimal unit root tests and the Kwiatkowski, Phillips, Schmidt, and Shin (KPSS) stationarity test. In some cases, the tests provide with conflicting results. However, they never indicate unambiguously that the series are stationary in level. This is why we conclude that the series are I(1). The Appendix at the end of this chapter gives the results.

As the series turn out to be I(1) for the periods studied, we implement three alternative cointegration techniques described below. Such an approach enables us to check whether possible cointegration findings are sensitive to the estimation technique. The starting point is the Engle–Granger residual-based cointegration method, according to which Y_t and $X_{i,t}$ are cointegrated if the residuals obtained from equation (21) are stationary:

$$Y_t = \beta_0 + \sum_{i=1}^{n}\beta_i X_{i,t} + \varepsilon_t \tag{21}$$

Stationary of the residuals ε_i can be tested by applying the ADF unit root test without constant and trend. Since equation (21) does not account for potential endogeneity of the right-hand side variable, the dynamic ordinary least squares (DOLS) introduced by Stock and Watson (1993) is also employed. DOLS estimates account for the endogeneity of the regressors and for serial correlation in the residuals in equation (21) by incorporating lags and leads of the regressors in first differences as in equation (22):

$$Y_t = \beta_0 + \sum_{i=1}^{n}\beta_i X_{i,t} + \sum_{i=1}^{n}\sum_{j=-k_1}^{k_2} \gamma_{i,j}\Delta X_{i,t-j} + \varepsilon_t \tag{22}$$

where k_1 and k_2 denote, respectively, leads and lags. The length of leads and lags is determined on the basis of the Schwarz, Akaike and Hannan-Quinn information criteria. The presence of cointegration is assessed upon stationarity of the residuals obtained from the long-term relationship, analogously to the Engle–Granger approach (see equation 21).

An alternative framework for testing for cointegration is provided by the bounds testing approach proposed by Pesaran *et al.* (2001). This approach, which allows the mixture of I(0) and I(1) variables is based on the error correction form of the ARDL model given in equation (23), where the dependent variable in first differences is regressed on the lagged values of the dependent and independent variables in levels and first differences.

$$\Delta Y_t = \beta_0 + p\left(Y_{t-1} + \sum_{i=1}^{n}\beta_i X_{i,t-1}\right) + \sum_{j=1}^{l_1}\eta_j\Delta Y_{t-1} + \sum_{i=1}^{n}\sum_{j=0}^{l_2}\gamma_{i,j}\Delta X_{i,t-j} + \varepsilon_t \tag{23}$$

To detect the presence of cointegrating relationships, Pesaran *et al.* (2001) implement conventional F-tests, where the null of $H_0 : \rho = \beta_1 = \ldots \beta_n = 0$ is tested against the alternative hypothesis of $H_1 : \rho \neq \beta_1 \neq 0, \ldots, \beta_n \neq 0$. Pesaran *et al.* (2001)

tabulate two sets of critical values, one for the case when all variables are I(1), i.e. upper bound critical values, and another one for when all variables are I(0), i.e. lower bound critical values. Critical values are provided for five different models, of which specification (3) with unrestricted intercept and no trend will be used in our study. If the test statistic is higher than the upper bound critical value, the null of no cointegration is rejected in favour of the presence of cointegration. On the other hand, an F-statistic lower than the lower bound critical value implies the absence of cointegration. In the event that the calculated F-statistic lies between the two critical values, there is no clear indication of the absence or existence of a cointegration relationship.

The error correction representation of equations (21) and (22) is also estimated to obtain the error correction term. The error correction terms obtained for equations (21), (22) and (23) are used in addition to the formal tests of cointegration. If formal tests indicate the presence of cointegration and if the error correction term is statistically significant and negative but not lower than -1, we take this as strong evidence for cointegration. If no formal cointegration can be established but the error correction term is statistically significant and is lower than zero but not lower than -1, we interpret it as weak evidence for cointegration.

Initial undervaluation

Before jumping to the model estimations, it is important to make sure that no major initial undervaluation is observed for Kazakhstan at the earlier stages of the transition process. Maeso-Fernandez *et al.* (2005) pointed out that in the presence of an initial undervaluation of the real exchange rate, the estimated coefficients and the constant term in the real exchange rate equation could be biased because if the initial undervaluation was corrected by a relative steady adjustment process to equilibrium, the observed movement of the real exchange rate is to some extent driven by this adjustment and not by changes in the fundamentals. In other words, a given change in a given fundamental could possibly lead to an over-proportionate change of the real exchange rate due to the adjustment process. An even worse situation would be when real exchange rate movements are completely disconnected from the development of the fundamentals in an adjustment process to equilibrium.

A simple first check for the presence of initial undervaluation consists in looking at cross-sectional data. More precisely, the level of the real exchange rate[5] can be regressed on GDP per capita in Purchasing Power Standards (PPS) against the US dollar. The fitted value of the real exchange rate for Kazakhstan gives us the level of the real exchange rate, which would be consistent with the country's level of development (measured by GDP per capita) when considering the average relationship for 169 countries (Figure 4.1). The comparison of the fitted value with the observed real exchange rate in level gives the size and the duration of a possible initial undervaluation.

As shown in Figure 4.2, there seems to be a large initial undervaluation in 1994. This was corrected for very quickly, followed by another, rather prolonged

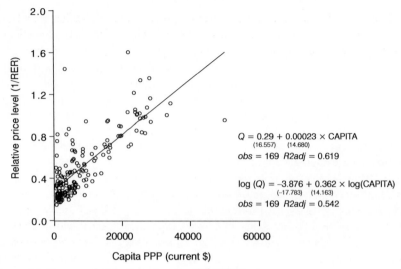

$Q = 0.29 + 0.00023 \times \text{CAPITA}$
        (16.557)   (14.680)
$obs = 169 \quad R2adj = 0.619$

$\log (Q) = -3.876 + 0.362 \times \log(\text{CAPITA})$
            (-17.783)   (14.163)
$obs = 169 \quad R2adj = 0.542$

Figure 4.1 Cross-sectional regression; Q=f(CAPITA)

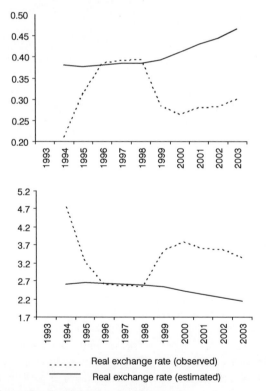

.... Real exchange rate (observed)

―――― Real exchange rate (estimated)

Figure 4.2 The observed and estimated real exchange rate

Note: The real exchange rate on the graph on the left is expressed as foreign currency/NCU whereas it is defined as NCU/foreign currency in the graph on the right.

and stable undervaluation period. Although initial undervaluation might pose problem from 1994 to 1998 for the econometric estimations, there appears to be no long-lasting and steadily declining undervaluation.

Estimation results

The nominal exchange rate

The cointegration analysis is carried out for the entire period (1994/5 to 2005) where a dummy capturing the Russian crisis period from September 1998 to June 1999 is employed. The post-Russian crisis period (1999 to 2005) is then analyzed separately, which also helps to deal with the problem of a possible initial undervaluation. The estimation results witness a substantial instability of the monetary model as the coefficient estimates are either statistically insignificant or have the wrong sign for most of the variables for the whole period (these results are not reported here). Therefore, we need to be cautious about the analysis of the coefficient estimates of the oil price variable. As a matter of fact, the oil price variable is either insignificant or has a positive sign. A positive sign indicates that an increase (decrease) in oil prices is linked to a nominal depreciation (appreciation).

When it comes to the sub-period running from 1999 to mid-2005, the monetary model exhibits more stability even though the results are not particularly robust against different estimation methods. However, despite the fact that the variables are occasionally insignificant, the main variables such as relative income, relative money supply and the interest differential have the expected sign. By contrast, the productivity differential and the relative price variables usually have an unexpected positive sign. This, indeed, indicates that increases in productivity in the open sector are not associated with a rise in relative prices and with an appreciation of the exchange rate as the Balassa-Samuelson effect predicts. Regarding the oil price variable, it enters systematically the estimation equations with a negative sign, indicating that an increase in the price of oil results in an appreciation of the exchange rate.

The real exchange rate

This section focuses on the results obtained for the real exchange rate based on the PPI and the real exchange rate deflated by means of the non-oil PPI. Because the results for the second sub-period are more robust than those obtained for the entire sample period, only the former are reported in Table 4.2. Let us now start analysing the oil variable. Generally, this variable has a negative significant effect on the overall (oil and non-oil) real exchange rate *vis-à-vis* the dollar. This means that oil price increases relate to an appreciation of the dollar real exchange rate. For the real effective exchange rate for which only non-oil PPI is considered, the results are also interesting because an increase in oil prices is usually found to be linked to a real depreciation. All this indicates that the appreciation of the

Table 4.1 Estimation results – monetary model

| | June 1999 – July 2005 | | | | | |
| | Effective exchange rate | | | Dollar exchange rate | | |
	EG	DOLS	BTA	EG	DOLS	BTA
COINT	**−3.586(0)**	**−4.864**(1)**	**−1.567**	**−4.195 (0)**	**−4.525**(0)**	**−2.777**
ECT	**−0.154****	**−0.197*****	**−0.32*****	**−0.068****	**−0.189*****	**−0.115*****
c	3.692***	3.785***	3.733***	5.653***	5.632***	5.652***
$y-y^*$	−0.095	−0.816***	−0.115	−0.611***	−0.593***	−0.34
$m-m^*$	0.078***	0.344***	0.082	0.335***	0.324***	0.149
$i-i^*$	0.035***	0.083***	0.034**	0.027**	0.023**	0.002
poil	−0.056***	−0.041	−0.065**	−0.129***	−0.122***	−0.136
COINT	**−3.57 (0)**	**−5.989**(0)**	**−0.385**	**−4.464 (0)**	**−7.307**(0)**	**−1.785**
ECT	**−0.159****	**−0.205*****	**−0.332*****	**−0.073****	**−0.136*****	**−0.121*****
c	3.689***	4.329***	4.03***	5.733***	6.663***	5.973***
$y-y^*$	−0.095	−0.824***	−0.167	−0.589***	−0.654	−0.405
$m-m^*$	0.077***	0.446***	0.16**	0.328***	0.432	0.214
$i-i^*$	0.035***	0.104***	0.043***	0.035***	0.066***	0.003
rel	0.006	−0.646**	−0.385*	−0.228	−1.665***	−0.287
poil	−0.055**	−0.234***	−0.169***	−0.166***	−0.508***	−0.245*
COINT	**−3.864(0)**	**−3.226 (2)**	**−1.184**	**−4.109 (0)**	**−5.517**(0)**	**−2.195**
ECT	**−0.168****	**−0.054*****	**−0.349*****	**−0.065**	**−0.224*****	**−0.114*****
c	3.594***	4.481***	3.69***	5.342***	5.288***	5.695***
$y-y^*$	0.004	−1.737***	−0.072	−0.355***	−0.236*	−0.375
$m-m^*$	−0.006	0.892***	0.047	0.099	0.018	0.177
$i-i^*$	0.039***	0.139***	0.036**	0.033***	0.03***	0.001
prod	0.199***	0.191*	0.075	0.562***	0.642***	−0.075
poil	−0.055***	−0.289***	−0.063**	−0.122***	−0.125***	−0.135

Notes: EG, DOLS and BTA denote the Engle–Granger, Dynamic OLS and the bounds testing approach. The row COINT reports the residual-based cointegration tests for EG and DOLS (lag length in parentheses) and the F-test for BTA. The row ECT contains the error correction term from the error correction representations. *,** and *** denote statistical significance at the 10%, 5% and 1% levels, respectively. The lag length is selected using the Schwarz information criterion (SIC). If cointegration is not found when using SIC, results from the Akaike and Hannan-Quinn information criterion are also looked at (A, H). c, prod and poil denote the constant term, the productivity differential and the dollar price of Ural crude.

real exchange rate against the dollar is linked to the appreciation of the nominal exchange rate. Nonetheless, the appreciation of the nominal effective exchange rate is not large and prolonged enough to show up in statistically significant and negative coefficient estimates for the non-oil sector.

Regarding the overall quality of the real exchange rate models, the real exchange rate models are slightly more robust than those for the monetary model because the

Table 4.2 Estimation results for the PPI-based real exchange rate, 1999–2005

	Non-oil effective exchange rate			Overall dollar exchange rate		
COINT	**–3.259 (0)**	**–5.374** (0)**	**0.891**	**–5.56** (0)**	**–7.972** (0)**	**1.338**
ECT	**–0.064**	**0.042**	**–0.099****	**–0.134***	**–0.127***	**–0.083***
c	–0.162***	–0.144***	0.034	0.274***	0.31***	0.077
prod	0.758***	0.731***	0.476	–0.362***	–0.345***	0.095
poil	0.067**	0.075**	0.02	–0.42***	–0.526***	–0.781**
COINT	**–2.214 (0)**	**–7.359*** (1)**	**0.709**	**–5.447*** (0)**	**–8.008*** (0)**	**–0.059**
ECT	**–0.103****	**0.085**	**–0.155****	**–0.156***	**–0.167***	**–0.081**
C	0.38***	0.369***	0.872***	–0.07	–0.194	–0.545
prod	0.168*	0.168*	–0.51	–0.001	0.217	0.802
poil	0.046**	0.065***	0.041	–0.427***	–0.567***	–0.895**
def	2.18***	2.1***	3.247***	–1.45**	–1.978***	–2.461
COINT	**–3.149 (0)**	**–5.449*** (0)**	**0.242**	**–5.739*** (0)**	**–7.846*** (0)**	**4.982****
ECT	**–0.044**	**0.056**	**–0.091****	**–0.144***	**–0.145***	**–0.178****
C	0.195	0.163	0.204	–0.763	–2.166***	–1.115
prod	0.721***	0.7***	0.349	–0.251**	–0.009	0.206
poil	0.07**	0.076**	0.04	–0.436***	–0.677***	–0.79***
exp	0.226	0.197	0.064	–0.657**	–1.554***	–0.773
COINT	**–3.493 (0)**	**–5.775*** (0)**	**1.98**	**–5.383*** (0)**	**–8.402*** (0)**	**5.121****
ECT	**–0.063**	**0.067***	**–0.124****	**–0.123****	**–0.148***	**–0.16****
C	–0.32***	–0.897***	–0.737**	0.163	0.673***	0.825**
prod	0.726***	0.706***	0.31	–0.382***	–0.156*	0.272
poil	0.098***	0.264***	0.191	–0.398***	–0.662***	–0.953***
open	–0.108	–0.464***	–0.524**	–0.075	0.277***	0.505**
D						
COINT	**–4.371*** (0)**	**–7.495*** (0)**	**–0.773**	**–4.831*** (0)**	**–8.181*** (0)**	**3.421a**
ECT	**–0.071**	**0.108***	**–0.096***	**–0.114****	**–0.112****	**–0.142****
C	–0.178***	–0.251***	0.166	0.226***	0.304***	0.078
prod	0.36***	–0.282*	–0.401	–0.763***	–0.268	0.499
poil	0.188***	0.517***	0.241	–0.261***	–0.557***	–0.937***
tot	–0.252***	–0.656***	–0.354	–0.29***	0.04	0.218

Notes: See Table 4.1.

explanatory variables other than the oil price have a significant effect on the real exchange rate. The signs mostly meet our expectations. The productivity variable deserves special attention because it is usually positively signed. This means that the Balassa-Samuelson effect can be dismissed for Kazakhstan.

Conclusion

This study analyzed the impact of oil prices on the nominal and real exchange rates in Kazakhstan in order to determine whether or not economic evidence for Dutch disease is present. It turns out that the real exchange rate of the open sector has been appreciating during the last couple of years chiefly due to the appreciation of the nominal exchange rate. Our econometric estimations based on the monetary model of the exchange rate provide us with some indication that the rise in the oil price might be linked with an appreciation of the exchange rate.

The real exchange rate models render this picture a bit more nuanced in that an increase in the oil price variable leads to a real appreciation of the exchange rate in both the oil-sector and non-oil manufacturing sectors. Nevertheless, this appreciation goes through only partially for the effective exchange rate: while the overall real exchange rate of the open sector appreciates following a rise in the oil variable, the real exchange rate does not follow the same pattern for the non-oil manufacturing. This suggests that the appreciation of the real exchange rate against the dollar is associated with an appreciation of the nominal exchange rate. However, the appreciation of the nominal effective exchange rate is not large enough and prolonged enough to have a statistically significant effect on the non-oil sector's real effective exchange rate.

Overall, our results suggest that the real exchange rate of the non-oil manufacturing sector has until now not suffered negative effects of oil price increases. This should, however, be of only temporary relief to economic policy-makers in Kazakhstan because in the event that the price of oil remains high, or increases further, nominal and real exchange rates in the future will continue to appreciate by putting pressure on non-oil manufacturing.

Appendix

Table A4.1 Variables for the monetary model, effective benchmark, 1995–2005

	ADF-trend	ADF-const	PP-trend	PP-const	KPSS-trend	KPSS-const	ERS-trend	ERS-const
	Levels							
*y–y**	−1.36	−0.04	−2.44	−1.16	0.23***	1.21***	24.44	210.52
*i–i**	−3.39*	−3.7***	−3.38*	−3.62***	0.19**	0.86***	54.67	110.37
*ip–ip**	−6.69***	−1.88	−2.76	−0.85	0.33***	0.79***	153.64	32.00
*m–m**	−1.34	0.56	−1.54	0.42	0.23***	1.24***	23.73	162.90
prod	−3.03	−0.73	−2.78	−0.45	0.17**	1.28***	18.72	15.79
rel	−2.94	−2.86*	−3.53**	−3.23**	0.10	0.72**	24.26	42.01
oil_ural	−1.96	−0.74	−2.35	−0.96	0.14*	0.99***	10.36	17.62
	1st diff							
*y–y**	−8.59***	−8.21***	−8.63***	−8.19***	0.24***	0.61**	6.8*	7.71
*i–i**	−10.33***	−10.2***	−10.33***	−10.23***	0.12	0.33*	1.74***	0.96***
*ip–ip**	−19.85***	−17.97***	−17.69***	−15.71***	0.15**	0.58**	27.97	24.36
*m–m**	−12.63***	−12.48***	−12.49***	−12.41***	0.06	0.17*	2.19***	0.96***
prod	−18.34***	−17.8***	−16.38***	−15.92***	0.16**	0.23*	21.11	20.57
rel	−9.89***	−9.93***	−10.32***	−10.35***	0.10	0.1*	1.67***	0.62***
oil_ural	−10.38***	−10.38***	−10.34***	−10.35***	0.06	0.11*	1.41***	0.43***
	2nd diff							
*y–y**	−8.75***	−8.73***	−43.57***	−40.12***	0.13*	0.3*	2.07***	1.91***
*i–i**	−11.27***	−11.31***	−96.8***	−94.84***	0.10	0.12*	0.01***	0***
*ip–ip**	−7.9***	−7.81***	−108.41***	−93.1***	0.14*	0.26*	3813.88	3599.39
*m–m**	−13.27***	−13.33***	−32.18***	−32.34***	0.03	0.03	1.26***	0.52***
prod	−8.23***	−8.17***	−212.02***	−116.83***	0.15**	0.29*	4099.00	3956.38
rel	−11.08***	−11.13***	−32.4***	−32.53***	0.02	0.02	0.02***	0.01***
oil_ural	−10.12***	−10.15***	−64.35***	−64.59***	0.15**	0.16*	3.14***	1.02***

Notes: ADF, PP; KPPS and ERS are the Augmented Dickey–Fuller, the Phillips–Perron, the Kwiatowski–Phillips–Schmidt–Shin and the Elliott–Rothenberg–Stock point optimal unit root tests, respectively, for the case including only a constant (-const) and a constant + a trend (-trend). The lag length is chosen using the Schwarz information criterion for the ADF and ERS tests and the Newey West kernel estimator for the PP and KPSS tests. *, ** and *** denote the rejection of the null hypothesis. For the ADF, PP and ERS tests, the null hypothesis is the presence of a unit root, whereas for the KPSS tests, the null hypothesis is stationarity.

Table A4.2 Variables for the monetary model, effective benchmark, 1999–2005

	ADF-trend	ADF-const	PP-trend	PP-const	KPSS-trend	KPSS-const	ERS-trend	ERS-const
Levels								
y–y*	–2.45	0.20	–3.08	–0.70	0.16**	1.2***	7.39	302.63
i–i*	–1.29	–1.24	–1.47	–1.40	0.18**	0.25*	32.64	24.11
ip–ip*	–5.54***	–0.52	–5.67***	–0.35	0.06	1.22***	5.12**	151.02
m–m*	–2.25	–0.85	–2.07	–0.90	0.18**	1.2***	19.87	414.39
prod	–2.50	–2.07	–2.16	–2.22	0.23***	1***	29.02	80.32
rel	–1.74	–1.61	–1.89	–1.74	0.12*	0.23*	24.71	28.75
oil_ural	–2.71	–2.05	–3.44*	–2.35	0.13*	0.86***	15.18	41.81
1st diff								
y–y*	–4.08**	–4.42***	–11.94***	–12.12***	0.09	0.08*	16.90	3.45*
i–i*	–9.81***	–9.91***	–9.67***	–9.75***	0.14*	0.14*	2.56***	0.86***
ip–ip*	–8.79***	–8.85***	–14.16***	–14.29***	0.06	0.06*	5.05**	3.44*
m–m*	–10.2***	–10.25***	–10.36***	–10.4***	0.08	0.12*	4.17**	2.33**
prod	–9.01***	–8.75***	–12.63***	–12.02***	0.07	0.21*	3.93***	2.36**
rel	–8.02***	–7.02***	–8.02***	–7.01***	0.09	0.86***	5.49**	5.64
oil_ural	–8.53***	–8.54***	–8.53***	–8.54***	0.17**	0.2*	2.51***	0.89***
2nd diff								
y–y*	–11.31***	–11.24***	–28.32***	–25.95***	0.22***	0.42*	7.26	6.02
i–i*	–10.02***	–10.06***	–31.24***	–31.11***	0.34***	0.39*	0.23***	0.14***
ip–ip*	–7.43***	–7.49***	–46.76***	–47.11***	0.14*	0.15*	3624.51	2744.61
m–m*	–9.99***	–9.92***	–39.79***	–41.19***	0.15**	0.23*	0.46***	0.1***
prod	–7.92***	–7.97***	–48.28***	–46.99***	0.12*	0.14*	4171.62	3210.03
rel	–7.41***	–7.35***	–22.3***	–20.94***	0.08	0.18*	220.05	60.50
oil_ural	–8.02***	–8.07***	–30.45***	–33.77***	0.08	0.12*	17.65	11.22

Notes: See Table A4.1.

Table A4.3 Variables for the real exchange rate models, effective benchmark, 1995–2005

	ADF-trend	ADF-const	PP-trend	PP-const	KPSS-trend	KPSS-const	ERS-trend	ERS-const
Levels								
q(cpi)	−3.44**	−3.54***	−2.61	−2.8*	0.24***	0.25*	11.15	9.31
q(ppi)	−3.87**	−4.3***	−3.82**	−4.14***	0.21**	0.62**	60.32	90.04
prod	−3.03	−0.73	−2.78	−0.45	0.17**	1.28***	18.72	15.79
rel	−2.94	−2.86*	−3.53**	−3.23**	0.10	0.72**	24.26	42.01
roil	−1.97	−1.07	−2.37	−1.47	0.15*	0.75***	10.35	10.82
open	−2.92	−1.90	−2.13	−1.74	0.09	0.55**	0.98***	1.28***
pdebt	−2.49	−2.52	−0.59	−0.83	0.3***	0.31*	17.36	0.66***
exp	−4.05***	−3.76***	−2.10	−2.11	0.12	0.14*	2.44***	0.66***
tot	−1.46	−2.44	−1.69	−1.70	0.26***	1.15***	18.12	46.17
1st diff								
q(cpi)	−6.21***	−6.17***	−5.13***	−5.18***	0.06	0.2*	1.9***	0.52***
q(ppi)	−8.08***	−7.98***	−8.22***	−8***	0.09	0.22*	1.57***	0.43***
prod	−17.81***	−17.39***	−16.08***	−15.71***	0.16**	0.21*	20.84	21.07
rel	−8.96***	−8.97***	−8.98***	−8.96***	0.08	0.09*	1.52***	0.45***
roil	−15.71***	−15.72***	−15.98***	−16.05***	0.06	0.13*	1.48***	0.42***
open	−2.58	−2.54	−4.19***	−4.14***	0.06	0.09*	14.92	5.51
pdebt	−2.17	−1.28	−5.14***	−5.69***	0.11	0.47**	72.91	42.78
exp	−3.36*	−3.39**	−4.47***	−4.53***	0.07	0.06*	1.36***	0.99***
tot	−15.7***	−15.41***	−21.41***	−16.59***	0.09	0.3*	6.58*	4.98
2nd diff								
q(cpi)	−8.58***	−8.49***	−20.73***	−21.04***	0.2**	0.2*	40.70	25.65
q(ppi)	−8.81***	−8.84***	−45.99***	−46.3***	0.16**	0.16*	0***	0***
prod	−8.28***	−8.2***	−101.11***	−85.47***	0.14*	0.25*	4118.70	3896.24
rel	11.32***	−11.13***	−56.39***	−54.6***	0.11	0.13*	5.14**	1.97**
roil	−13.61***	−13.67***	−53.99***	−55.66***	0.13*	0.13*	1.74***	0.85***
open	−10.07***	−10.13***	−18.5***	−17.26***	0.15*	0.28*	377.97	101.87
pdebt	−10.7***	−10.69***	−17.6***	−17.2***	0.11	0.19*	608.47	157.52
exp	−7.85***	−7.86***	−20.52***	−20.7***	0.25***	0.32*	12.52	3.28*
tot	−8.84***	−8.87***	−108.38***	−97.44***	0.12*	0.27*	447.02	359.68

Notes: See Table A4.1.

Table A4.4 Variables for the real exchange rate models, effective benchmark, 1999–2005

	ADFtrend	ADF-const	PP-trend	PP-const	KPSS-trend	KPSS-const	ERS-trend	ERS-const
	Levels							
q(cpi)	−3.93**	−5.28***	−3.72**	−4.48***	0.2**	0.6**	453.27	467.98
q(ppi)	−1.79	−2.45	−1.91	−2.62*	0.22**	0.35*	31.89	20.97
prod	−2.50	−2.07	−2.16	−2.22	0.23***	1***	29.02	80.32
rel	−1.74	−1.61	−1.89	−1.74	0.12*	0.23*	24.71	28.75
roil	−2.73	−2.22	−3.47**	−2.6*	0.13*	0.75***	15.09	34.06
open	−3.13	−3.21**	−2.31	−2.37	0.12	0.19*	8.39	10.36
pdebt	−2.66	−1.11	−2.35	−0.84	0.18**	1.13***	0.04***	140.49
exp	−4.57***	−4.42***	−3.78**	−3.61***	0.07	0.14*	9.16	4.05*
tot	−1.95	−2.42	−1.74	−2.35	0.25***	0.56**	13.26	7.61
	1st diff							
q(cpi)	−9.01***	−4.43***	−6.2***	−5.82***	0.10	0.37*	0.43***	0.65***
q(ppi)	−7.95***	−7.57***	−7.95***	−7.59***	0.06	0.37*	2.45***	0.81***
prod	−8.6***	−11.16***	−12.89***	−11.68***	0.07	0.25*	4.5**	4.12*
rel	−7.57***	−7.63***	−7.58***	−7.64***	0.14*	0.14*	2.84***	1.2***
roil	−13.25***	−13.31***	−13.44***	−13.5***	0.15**	0.16*	3.5***	1.5***
open	−2.52	−2.38	−3.37*	−3.56***	0.10	0.12*	41.37	14.16
pdebt	−2.91	−3.12**	−4.86***	−4.84***	0.06	0.07*	17.20	7.46
exp	−2.63	−2.39	−3.28*	−2.93**	0.12	0.31*	8.58	7.09
tot	−10.87***	−10.65***	−11.93***	−10.95***	0.07	0.37*	3.55***	2.44**
	2nd diff							
q(cpi)	−5.48***	−5.49***	−23.62***	−23.97***	0.14*	0.16*	84.80	19.20
q(ppi)	−9.97***	−10.04***	−27.39***	−27.64***	0.05	0.11*	2.09***	1.12***
prod	−7.61***	−7.66***	−81.16***	−76.57***	0.28***	0.31*	3684.49	2808.65
rel	−7.64***	−10.6***	−60.57***	−42.11***	0.15**	0.29*	6.64*	0.77***
roil	−9.66***	−9.69***	−39.34***	−39.53***	0.18**	0.28*	2.75***	0.84***
open	−7.7***	−7.75***	−13.85***	−14.18***	0.15**	0.19*	927.44	323.37
pdebt	−8.25***	−8.17***	−17.35***	−15.28***	0.19**	0.22*	2125.27	1338.97
exp	−8.59***	−8.65***	−19.88***	−19.8***	0.5***	0.5***	0.02***	0***
tot	−8.47***	−8.45***	−50.33***	−46.9***	0.5***	0.5**	128.62	88.97

Notes: See Table A4.1.

Notes

1 This revival comes after the seminal paper of Meese and Rogoff (1983) which showed that a random walk outperforms exchange rate models (among others the monetary model) in forecasting exchange rates.

2 This implies that an increase (decrease) in the exchange rate is a depreciation (appreciation) of the domestic currency *vis-à-vis* the foreign currency.

3 It was first proposed by Clements and Frankel (1980) and applied recently to transition economies by Crespo-Cuaresma *et al.* (2005a, 2005b).

4 Some cautionary notes should be addressed here when applying the monetary model to transition economies mainly because of the fragility of some of the strong underlying assumptions. The first assumption is the existence of a stable money demand function. Although this issue is not uncontroversial for industrialised countries, the stability of the money demand function is probably too strong a hypothesis for transition economies with multiple changes in the real economy and in the monetary policy framework. Second, PPP fails not only for the overall real exchange rate but also for the real exchange rate of the open sector (crucial for establishing the relationship between the exchange rate and the money demand) as documented in, for example, Égert *et al.* (2006). Finally, the homogeneity imposed to some of the elasticities in different versions of the monetary model may fail in practice. For instance, Knell and Stix (2003) emphasise systematic cross-country differences in the α_1 and α_2 terms (hence, $\alpha_1 \neq \alpha_1^*$ and $\alpha_2 \neq \alpha_2^*$). The same applies to ϕ and ϕ^* given that the share of non-tradable goods in the consumer price index is considerably lower in developing countries (around 25% in Kazakhstan in 2005) as compared to industrialised countries (around 45% in the euro area).

5 Based on absolute price level data.

5

RESOURCE REVENUE AND FISCAL SUSTAINABILITY IN KAZAKHSTAN

Peter Lohmus and Anna Ter-Martirosyan

Introduction

Oil output and the associated fiscal revenue in Kazakhstan have increased sharply in recent years. More than one third of total government revenue was derived from the oil sector in 2005, compared to only 6 per cent in 1999.[1] Although the overall budget has remained in surplus, pressures to increase public expenditure have intensified. Recently, the government of Kazakhstan has taken steps to redesign the fiscal strategy for managing the country's oil wealth.

This chapter analyses challenges for conducting fiscal policies in a resource rich economy. First, it reviews recent oil wealth management, as well as prospects for oil production and oil revenue in Kazakhstan. Then, it presents a formal framework to assess whether fiscal policies to manage oil wealth have been sustainable in the long run. Further, the rules governing the National Fund of Kazakhstan (NFRK) – the vehicle for saving part of the oil income for future generations – are discussed. Finally, some general conclusions are presented.

Management of oil wealth in Kazakhstan

In 2005, the output of oil and gas condensate reached almost 62 million metric tons (about 1.3 million barrels per day (mb/d)), increasing more than two-fold since 1999 (29.4 million metric tons). Oil-related activity is estimated to account for about 30 per cent of the country's nominal GDP and more than 60 per cent of its export earnings (Table 5.1).

Oil production in Kazakhstan is expected to rise much further over the long term. At present, proven oil reserves in Kazakhstan have reached 35 billion barrels. However, total reserves are estimated to be higher (at around 50 billion barrels to 60 billion barrels) although industry and official estimates vary. Under the current official scenario, oil production is expected to double by the beginning of the next decade, and triple over the next 10–15 years, reaching 3.5 mb/d). Most of this output increase would come from offshore fields in the North Caspian region, notably from the Kashagan field – the largest field outside the Middle East and the fifth largest field in the world.[2] This level of production would place

Table 5.1 Oil production and revenue, Kazakhstan, 1999–2006

	1999	2000	2001	2002	2003	2004	2005
Oil production (milion metric tons)	29.4	35.4	39.3	47.3	51.3	59.4	61.9
Oil export revenue to total export revenue (in %)	35.5	46.8	48.9	50.1	53.1	55.4	61.5
Government oil revenue (in % of GDP)	2.2	3.3	6.6	4.4	6.0	7.0	10.6

Sources: Ministry of Finance of the Republic of Kazakhstan and IMF staff estimates.

Kazakhstan among the world's top 10 crude oil exporters, on a level comparable to Iran, Mexico, Norway and Venezuela. Production volumes are then projected to moderate to around 2.5 mb/d by 2030 (Figure 5.1).

The growth in oil revenue (supported by the recent surge in oil prices) has been remarkable, although future growth is associated with some uncertainties. Oil revenue has increased from $0.4 billion in 1999 to $6.0 billion in 2005. The government's oil revenue is expected to grow further to an annual average of about $16 billion during the peak production period from 2015 to 2030.[3] However, the country's oil wealth is associated with significant uncertainties. Since most of the oil earnings will come in the distant future, several potential obstacles (such as inadequate transport capacity, environmental considerations or technological challenges associated with off-shore drilling) may restrain the realization of the full production potential.[4] Also, the production projections depend critically on continued sizable foreign investments, which are subject to exogenous shocks.

Higher oil revenue, together with the prospect of a further substantial rise in the future, has permitted a rapid expansion of public spending and led to an increase in the non-oil deficit (Figure 5.2). Since 2001, average annual growth in expenditure has persistently exceeded growth in GDP (Figure 5.3). An increased share of public spending was used for social spending and financing investment in the infrastructure in Kazakhstan. Not all of the oil revenue has been spent; a

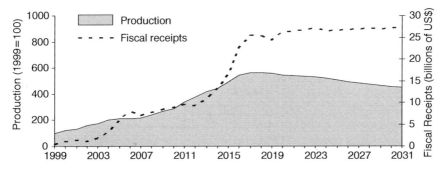

Figure 5.1 Medium-term petroleum outlook

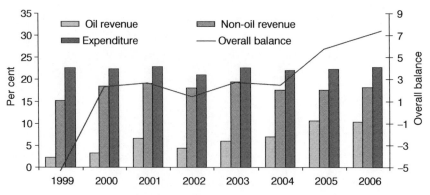

Figure 5.2 Non-oil fiscal position (% of GDP)

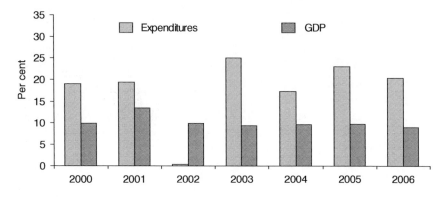

Figure 5.3 Real growth (%)

substantial part of it was saved in the national oil fund of Kazakhstan. In assessing whether the government's fiscal policies have been sustainable in the long run, one needs to study the range of fiscal rules applicable for a resource rich economy.

The sustainable non-oil deficit path

Since revenue from oil is volatile and exhaustible, an assessment of fiscal sustainability is a challenge. Decisions about spending oil revenue have to be based on assumptions about oil prices, extracting costs and the time horizon during which exhaustible resources may be depleted. Since most assumptions are likely to be subject to frequent revisions, estimates of the sustainable deficit path need to be updated regularly. In addition, the 'optimal' fiscal policy that addresses these challenges would not necessarily be the same across oil countries. Among other factors, this policy will depend on the initial fiscal policy stance, the time horizon of oil depletion, the level of dependency on oil revenue and the initial net financial wealth of the government.

A range of fiscal rules to manage natural resource wealth have been discussed in the literature. These rules address a variety of trade-offs with regard to expenditure dynamics and intergenerational oil wealth distribution. One extreme is the bird-in-hand rule, where only the interest earned on accumulated financial assets originating from oil revenue is used for consumption. In this case, the bulk of oil revenue is saved in the early part of the oil-extraction cycle, but at the expense of foregone spending with potentially high social and/or economic returns. The other extreme is a rule where all oil revenue is spent, while keeping the overall budget balanced. In this case, fiscal spending is subject to a high degree of volatility, which may lead to undesirable outcomes, and oil wealth is depleted over time. Constant expenditure rules (where the government maintains a constant real expenditure stream) and the Permanent Income Hypothesis (PIH) rule are examples of intermediate rules.[5]

The PIH provides a rule for setting long-term fiscal policy and is the most heavily used assumption in studies of economies with significant natural resources. It imposes fiscal discipline on the government by requiring that the government's total net wealth (its permanent income) forms the basis for its fiscal policy rather than current resources available to it. The total wealth is defined as a sum of financial and non-financial wealth. Oil wealth, the value of oil in the ground at the beginning of period t, W_t, is defined as present value of cash tax revenue from the oil sector. Hence:

$$W_t = \sum_{j=0}^{T} \frac{O_{t+j}}{\prod_{j=0}^{T}\left(1+i_{t+j}\right)\left(1+i_t\right)^{-1}}$$

where O_t denotes tax revenue from oil extracted during time t, T is the period when oil reserves are depleted, and i_t is the per period nominal interest rate which is assumed to vary over time. Optimal consumption in the period t, C_t^o, which is equivalent to the non-oil deficit, can be defined as:

$$C_t^o = \frac{\left(1+i_{t+1}\right)-\left(1+n_t\right)\left(1+\pi_t\right)}{\left(1+i_{t+1}\right)}W_t$$

where n_t and π_t are population growth and inflation in period t, respectively.[6] Roughly, this translates into spending the present discounted value of oil wealth multiplied by the expected rate of earning from this wealth (adjusted for the projected rate of population growth). Over time, as the economy grows, the sustainable non-oil deficit will narrow in relation to GDP.[7]

Maintaining oil wealth per capita at a constant level means that future genera-tions would benefit from oil reserves to the same extent as current generations. If the country consumes more than what is dictated by the PIH, then oil wealth would decline faster and the current generation would naturally receive a higher share of wealth than future generations. Conversely, consuming less than the level indicated by the PIH implies that the current generation is saving more and leaving more oil wealth to future generations. It should be noted that some depletion of oil wealth may be appropriate as economic development proceeds and living standards improve. Therefore the appropriate deficit path could be higher in the short term that the one implied by the pure PIH.

Key assumptions regarding future oil production, prices, and other variables are required to assess the sustainable non-oil deficit path. An illustrative baseline scenario presented for Kazakhstan in Figure 5.4 is based on *World Economic Outlook* (October 2006) assumptions for 2006–10 and IMF staff projections for 2011–31. The main underlying assumptions are presented in Table 5.2. Oil production is estimated to peak at 3.5 mb/d in 2017–18, while oil prices are projected to stay at about $60 per barrel until 2020, remaining constant in real terms thereafter. According to this scenario, the non-oil deficit that maintains oil wealth in real per capita terms is equivalent to 6 per cent to 7 per cent of GDP in the short term, and declines markedly relative to GDP over the long term.[8]

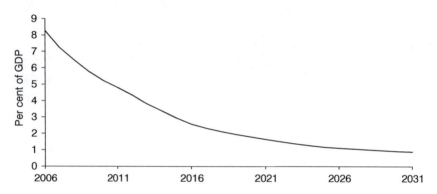

Figure 5.4 Sustainable non-oil deficit implied by PIH[1] (% of GDP)

Note: 1 Non-oil deficit that would maintain oil wealth in real per capita terms.

Table 5.2 Assumptions underlying the PIH

	2006	2007	2008	2009	2010	2015	2020	2030	2040	2049
Oil production (in million bp/d)	1.4	1.5	1.6	1.9	2.1	3.1	3.4	2.8	1.2	0.6
Government oil revenues (in billions of tenge)	997	857	928	1,004	1,051	1,800	2,496	2,220	931	382
6-m LIBOR on US$ (in %)	5.05	5.62	5.62	5.62	5.62	5.62	5.62	5.62	5.62	5.62
World inflation rate, CPI (in %)	2.3	2.1	2.1	2.1	2.2	2.0	2.0	2.0	2.0	2.0

However, the estimated sustainable path is highly sensitive to changes in the assumptions on oil prices and interest rates. For example, a permanent decrease in the oil price by 20 per cent (relative to the baseline) would reduce the average sustainable non-oil deficit for 2006–10 by about 1.3 per cent of GDP (Figure 5.5). Similarly, permanent decline in the nominal discount rates by 50 basis points would result in about 0.8 per cent reduction in sustainable non-oil deficit for the same period (Figure 5.6).

Comparing the actual non-oil deficit path with PIH baseline estimates shows that Kazakhstan has been prudent with its oil wealth. The non-oil deficit (although increasing over time) was below the projected PIH path by more than 2 per cent in 2005–6. Moreover, Kazakhstan's saving from its current oil revenue has been considerably higher than in many other oil-producing countries, despite the fact that the bulk of the oil production for Kazakhstan is expected in the future

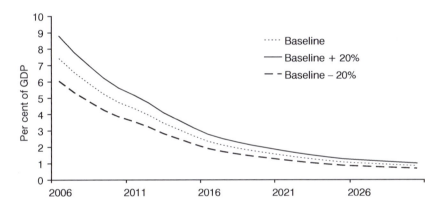

Figure 5.5 Sustainable non-oil deficit (PIH) under different oil price scenarios (% of GDP)

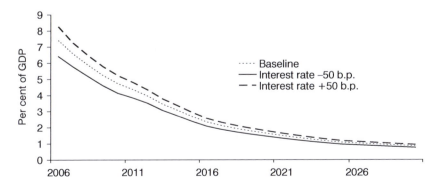

Figure 5.6 Sustainable non-oil deficit (PIH) under different interest rate scenarios (% of GDP)

(Figure5.7). The ratio of the overall fiscal surplus to oil revenue (the share of oil revenue saved) was over 50 per cent in 2005.

The National Fund of the Republic of Kazakhstan

The NFRK was established in 2001 to reduce the economic impact of volatile oil prices and to serve as a vehicle for saving part of the oil income for future generations. Since the NFRK was established, about 50 per cent of the revenue from the oil sector, including one-off bonus payments, has been saved and the NFRK has accumulated over $14 billion in assets (Figure 5.8).[9]

Before July 2006, the rules governing the NFRK had been rather complex and changed over time, and NFRK had not been integrated into the budget.[10] Flows to the fund consisted of a 'savings' component equal to 10 per cent of budgeted baseline revenue from the designated companies, which was invariant to oil price

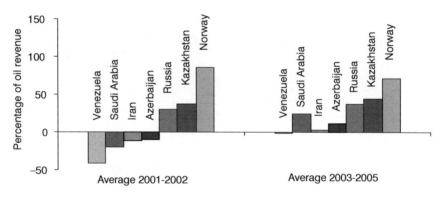

Figure 5.7 Overall balance (% of oil revenue)

Source: National authorities and IMF.

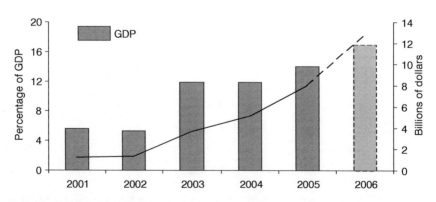

Figure 5.8 Balance of NFRK

changes, and a 'stabilization' component. The latter included all revenue from the designated companies in excess of receipts that would have been realized at a reference oil price, which remained fixed at $19 a barrel. The government had also allocated privatization receipts, special bonus payments, and royalties from certain natural resource companies to the fund. All NFRK assets were invested abroad.

In September 2005 the president approved a new decree defining a medium-term framework for the accumulation and use of assets of the NFRK.[11] The new rules came into effect from July 2006. Under the new framework, the principal tasks of NFRK are defined as follows: to support macroeconomic stability by removing excess petrodollars from the economy and to curb pressure on the tenge's exchange rate and inflation. All enterprises in the oil sector that are engaged in the extraction and/or sale of crude oil and gas condensate are included in the list of contributors into NFRK. Moreover, all payments from the oil sector to the republican budget (not only revenue in excess of the budgeted oil price) are to be allocated to the National Fund.

The NFRK is directly integrated with the budget. Under the new framework, a guaranteed transfer from the NFRK to the budget (G_0) is earmarked solely for the financing of spending under budget development programs that provide for investment in projects that will also be used by future generations. This transfer is defined as a constant amount plus a portion of NFRK assets for the previous period.

$$G_0 = A + b \cdot NFRK_{t-1} \cdot e,$$

where A represents the fixed amount (in tenge), b represents the coefficient corresponding to the average investment income for a specific period, $NFRK_{t-1}$ represents the National Fund's assets at the beginning of the financial year; and e represents the exchange rate of the tenge against the dollar. Constant A and coefficient b are established by a legislative act of the Republic of Kazakhstan for a three-year period and are not subject to change during the given period.[12] The 'development budget' is a key component of the government's programs to increase the longer-term capacity and productivity of the economy, and is in broad terms equal to public capital spending. In this way, the portion of oil revenue to be spent (broadly equivalent to the non-oil deficit less government borrowing[13]) is used to enhance the economy's longer-term capacity. Amounts of guaranteed NFRK transfers to the budget in 2007–9 are fixed at 302, 341 and 337 tenge billion, respectively, which on average represents about 2.5 per cent of projected GDP for the same period.

The 'A plus b' model can be related to the PIH model described in the previous section, since variable b is set equal to the expected average annual return on NFRK assets over the long term and A could be derived based on some optimal non-oil deficit in the short term. In the early stages, the A term is expected to dominate, In the long term, as the NFRK balance grows, this would result in a steady reduction of the non-oil deficit in relation to GDP, consistent with the declining path of the sustainable deficit based on a PIH framework. Of course, sufficient flexibility would need to be retained to be able to alter the formula if oil prices or production prospects change substantially.

Conclusions

Given the prospects for oil production and fiscal oil revenue, Kazakhstan can sustain non-oil deficits of over 6 per cent of GDP in the short term without reducing the value of oil wealth. However, the sustainable deficit will decline markedly in relation to GDP over the longer term. Moreover, as the analysis illustrates, the sustainable path is very sensitive to unanticipated developments in oil prices, production, reserves, and key macroeconomic variables. The new rules for NFRK will help in the design and implementation of the medium-term budget strategy, but the new mechanism will not automatically instill budget discipline. In order to ensure that the budgetary position remains sustainable, the fiscal strategy guiding the use of oil revenue should retain sufficient flexibility to respond to major changes in expectations regarding the value of future oil earnings.

Notes

1 Oil revenue includes the sum of taxes collected from the oil sector, royalties, bonuses, and payments from production-sharing agreements.
2 Under some scenarios, the Kashagan off-shore field alone may have reserves amounting to more than 50 billion barrels. See Mathieu (2004) for a more comprehensive discussion.
3 It should be noted that oil extraction and transportation costs in Kazakhstan (up to $12 a barrel) are higher than in some other countries, especially in the Middle East, and consequently oil revenue is somewhat lower.
4 For instance, the introduction of the first phase of the Kashagan off-shore oil field (the largest in the Caspian Sea) was recently postponed till 2010.
5 See, for example, Wakeman-Linn et al. (2004) for a discussion of alternative fiscal rules.
6 For a more detailed derivation, see Davoodi (2002).
7 The return on financial assets is treated as interest income and not included as oil revenue. See, for example, the discussion in Barnett and Ossowski (2003).
8 The actual non-oil deficit has widened but remained well within the estimated sustainable level for the short term.
9 By way of comparison in 2005, the Norwegian Petroleum Fund (established in 1990), and the State Oil Fund of Azerbaijan (established in 1999) have accumulated assets of $207 billion and $1.4 billion, respectively.
10 The number of designated oil companies in the natural resources sector, whose fiscal payments were subject to transfer to the NFRK, had been changed several times.
11 President Decree No. 1641, 1 September 2005.
12 The decree also incorporates other rules to ensure that NFRK will not be depleted. The amount of the guaranteed transfer should not exceed one-third of the National Fund's assets. In addition, the level of budget deficit financing through government borrowing is limited to no more than 1% of GDP on an average annual basis for a five-year period.
13 The non-oil deficit concept is broader as oil revenue defined in NFRK excludes the oil-related taxes for local governments.

6

FISCAL DECENTRALIZATION IN CENTRALIZED STATES

Central Asian patterns[1]

Natalie Leschenko and Manuela Troschke

In the resource-based Central Asian countries Kazakhstan, Turkmenistan and Uzbekistan the budget revenue accruing from natural resource production is growing at a rapid pace. At the same time, increasing inequality in terms of regional economic development and of household incomes in oil and non-oil regions can be observed (Najman *et al.* in Chapter 7; Luecke and Trofimenko in Chapter 8). These developments indicate shortcomings of fiscal policy and of fiscal decentralization, which should correct regional imbalances instead of aggravating them.

The Central Asian countries constitute a special case, because political centralization is accompanied by centralized administration of resource rents and weak governance structures at local levels. However, fiscal decentralization is on the reform agenda. Following minor reforms of the fiscal sphere, new Budget Laws came into force in Turkmenistan in 1996, Uzbekistan in 2001, and Kazakhstan in 2005. Recently, these laws have been supplemented by laws on administrative decentralization, and soon they shall be followed by increased voter control at local levels. At the same time, democracy scores for all these countries show a clear downward trend and the economic dependency on revenue accrued in natural resource production grows. This casts doubt on the political willingness to transfer rights to the local level and the voters.

Under these circumstances, can fiscal decentralization in Central Asia be an efficient solution to fiscal and administrative problems? Do we observe real fiscal decentralization in these countries? How far do the Central Asia states follow the successful model of fiscal decentralsation in centralized China? To answer these questions, we analyze the quality of progress towards fiscal decentralization in Kazakhstan, Uzbekistan and Turkmenistan. The first two sections start with insights from the theoretical and empirical literature. The third section provides an overview on fiscal decentralization and major reforms in the three countries. The fourth section analyzes expenditure assignment. The fifth section describes the pace of revenue sharing and assignment. The effectiveness of the solution of vertical and horizontal imbalances is discussed in the sixth section. The final section draws conclusions.

Theoretical considerations

Traditional economic theory generally is in favour of administrative and fiscal decentralization. Underlying assumptions of the traditional models include a benevolent state and benevolent state agents, factor mobility and skilled human capital at the local level – conditions that will hardly be met in the Central Asian transitional economies.

Second generation theories of decentralization come closer to Central Asian reality and question the benevolence of government officials. They focus on the incentives created by decentralization. The seminal papers of Weingast (1995), Qian and Weingast (1997) and Qian and Roland (1998) on 'Market preserving federalism' apply advances in the new theory of the firm to questions of decentralization. They argue that the appropriate decentralization of information and authority will limit the 'state predation' problem (North 1990) by setting positive incentives for individuals to take risk and make effort today. On the other hand, appropriate decentralization will reduce the 'soft budget constraint' problem (Kornai 1986) by setting negative incentives for officials for bailing out inefficient projects or firms. In both cases, the credibility of the central government's commitment to the local level plays a decisive role. High transaction costs for central government intervention, for example, the political costs of 'confiscating' local tax revenue above the planned level, will be essential for this credibility. The experience of fiscal decentralization in China illustrates incentive mechanisms through decentralization.

Based on both strands of the theory, a growing albeit contradictory literature discusses the effects of decentralization on corruption and overall governance. Both indicators rank comparatively low for Central Asian countries and might improve via mechanisms of decentralization. If 'voting with their feet' can take place, decentralization will induce less corruption (Breton 1996). In contrast, Shleifer and Vishny (1993) argue that, based on the theory of industrial organization, decentralization may lead to a cumulative overgrazing of the bribe base if the central government is too weak to control and punish lower levels of government. Tanzi (1995) adds that, from a political economy perspective, that decentralization under limited political competition causes a mutual dependence between local elites and inhabitants, which leads to an aggravation of corruption on the local level if decentralization is not controlled.

The discussion of effects on overall governance is similar. If local politicians are punished by voters in cases of mismanagement, fiscal decentralization is expected to improve overall governance (Seabright 1995; Persson and Tabellini 2000). This is rejected by Blanchard and Shleifer (2000), who point out the risks of local capture of political power (the buying of political decisions by business and individuals) resulting from the proximity of the involved parties. Contrasting Russia and China in a small model, the authors argue for strong political control and even political centralization accompanying decentralization in countries with weak democratic institutions. This argument is based mainly on Riker (1964), who argued that the strength of the national party system is more important for controlling local politicians than administrative regulations or constitutional arrangements. Hence, in the centralized states of Central Asia, we should generally expect fiscal decentralization to influence positively corruption and governance.

The empirical literature on the effects of decentralization produced highly mixed results. Relating decentralization to growth, cross-country studies in general support the existence of the positive effects of fiscal decentralization (Huther and Shah 1996). Studies examining developing countries find no links between decentralization and growth (Woller and Philipps 1998), and some even report a slightly negative relationship (Davoodi and Zou 1998). Single-country studies for China show positive (Lin and Liu 2000) as well as negative (Zhang and Zou 1998) relationships.

Regarding corruption and governance, one finds more consistent results in cross-country-studies. Fisman and Gatti (2002) observe a strong negative relationship between fiscal decentralization in government expenditure and corruption. However, corruption and governance deteriorate if the reliance on the local revenue base exceeds a certain level, local capture being the most probable explanation (de Mello and Barenstein 2001). These somewhat contradictory results illustrate the problems of measuring fiscal decentralization, discussed by Ebel and Yilmaz (2002). Linking fiscal decentralization and political institutions by testing Rikers theory, Enikopolov and Zhuravskaya (2003) find that weak parties worsen the effect of fiscal decentralization. Most interesting, their results show positive effects of centrally appointed versus locally elected local politicians on overall growth and quality of government.

Empirical research on fiscal decentralization in post-soviet transition countries so far is restricted to Russia and an empirical testing of the incentive-mechanisms. Using panel data from 2118 Russian municipalities, Slinko (2002) shows that regional disparities increased with fiscal decentralization, because delayed enterprise restructuring and lacking market institutions hampered the positive results of better incentives at the local level. Timofeev (2002) tests this effect of decentralization on soft budget constraints of local enterprises using panel data of 72 Russian regions from 1995 to 1997. His results demonstrate that only retained taxes lead to less subventions, whereas decentralization via increased transfers or shared taxes worsens soft budget constraints substantially. Desai *et al.* (2005) extend this relationship to regional growth indicators using a comparable data set and produce similar results. Resource-rich rentier regions as well as extremely poor regions are identified as vulnerable because of their 'unearned income streams' which limit the positive possible effects of fiscal decentralization. On the other hand, Zhuravskaya (2000), using Russian panel data from 1992 to 1997, shows that expansions of the local tax base were almost entirely offset by reduced central transfers in the following year. This ratchet effect clearly creates no incentives on the local level.

Several conclusions can be drawn for our analysis of fiscal decentralization. First, the assumptions of traditional theories are too restrictive. Decentralization per se cannot guarantee positive effects, as empirical studies show. Second, according to a new theory, it is the appropriate design of decentralization that matters. Incentives mechanisms will work only if information and authority are transferred to local levels and the credibility of the central government is sufficient. Empirical evidence, especially from Russia, illustrates some pitfalls of fiscal decentralization. Hence we should consider not only quantitative indicators, but the quality of decentralization. Third, if strong democratic institutions and high factor mobility are missing, fiscal decentralization should be accompanied by strong political control to induce a positive influence on growth and governance indicators. Centralized states *per se* are not harmful to the merits of fiscal decentralization, as the example of China demonstrates.

First insights

An international comparison of decentralization indicators (Figure 6.1) may lead to the conclusion that fiscal decentralization in Turkmenistan, Kazakhstan and Uzbekistan is comparable with OECD countries. In 2001 the expenditure of local budgets of Turkmenistan, Kazakhstan and Uzbekistan was 10 per cent, 12 per cent, and 15 per cent of GDP, respectively, which is comparable with OECD countries whose average weight of local budgets in GDP at this time was 14.9 per cent. The weight of local budget revenue without transfers in the consolidated budget for 2001 in Turkmenistan was 29 per cent, which is slightly below the OECD average indicator of that year (32 per cent).

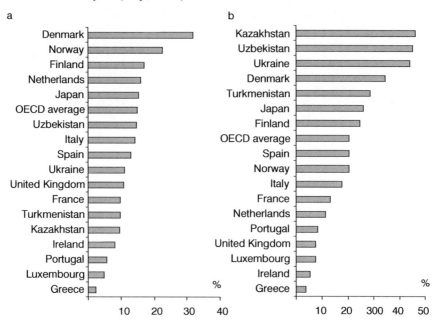

Figure 6.1 International comparison of fiscal decentralization*

Source: OECD Economic Outlook 2004: Fiscal relations across levels of government; Ministries of Finance (MoF) of Turkmenistan, Kazakhstan, Uzbekistan, Ukraine, own calculations.

Note: * Revenue and expenditure were taken net of intergovernmental transfers.

On the expenditure side, the picture of high indicators of fiscal decentralization is valid for the whole period of fiscal reforms in all three countries (Table 6.1). In Kazakhstan, during fiscal reforms the weight of local expenditure in GDP increased from 7 per cent in 1997 to 11 per cent in 2004. Turkmenistan's ratio of local expenditure, 10 per cent in 2003, remained nearly unchanged in comparison to 1995. Uzbekistan's local expenditure to GDP ratio decreased gradually from 18 per cent in 1997 to 14 per cent in 2004. The importance of local government expenditure in total state expenditure has even increased in Kazakhstan and Turkmenistan in comparison to the 1990s (up to 49 per cent and 51 per cent respectively), while for Uzbekistan the weight of local budget expenditure in total state expenditure varied from 51 per cent to 56 per cent between 1997 and 2004.

On the revenue side, signs of increasing fiscal centralization can be found. In Kazakhstan local budget revenue without central transfers decreased from 47 per cent of the state budget in 2001 to 36 per cent in 2004. For Uzbekistan this ratio also decreased, from 45 per cent in 2001 to 43 per cent in 2004, although it remained far above the OECD average. For all three countries, after 1999 any decline in the

Table 6.1 Major indicators of fiscal decentralization in Central Asia

	1995	1997	1998	1999	2000	2001	2002	2003	2004
Weight of State (consolidated) budget expenditures in GDP									
Kazakhstan	26	20	22	23	23	23	21	22	22
Turkmenistan	20	–	–	–	24	22	17	19	–
Uzbekistan	33	32	33	31	29	27	26	25	26
Weight of local expenditures in GDP									
Kazakhstan	–	7	9	11	12	12	10	11	11
Turkmenistan	9	–	–	–	11	10	9	10	–
Uzbekistan	–	18	17	17	15	15	14	13	14
Weight of local expenditures w/o transfers in GDP									
Kazakhstan	–	5	7	9	10	11	8	8	8
Turkmenistan	7	–	–	–	6	6	5	5	–
Uzbekistan	–	15	13	15	13	12	12	10	12
Weight of local expenditures in state budget									
Kazakhstan	–	34	41	46	50	52	48	48	49
Turkmenistan	43	–	–	–	47	45	49	51	–
Uzbekistan	–	56	51	54	52	55	55	53	55
Weight of local revenues w/o transfers in state budget									
Kazakhstan	–	23	36	47	44	47	36	38	36
Turkmenistan	35	–	–	–	26	29	27	29	–
Uzbekistan	–	55	48	51	45	45	45	41	43

Source: Own calculations based on data from World Development Indicators 2005, Ministry of Finance of Kazakhstan, Turkmenmillichasabat (2005) and Nuritdinov (2005).

level of local budget funding other than transfer revenue was compensated for by a rise in intergovernmental transfers. This development may be explained by the fact that centrally assigned tasks have been transferred to the local level, but it also implies more limited responsibilities and a lack of autonomy for the regions.

In Central Asia these widely accepted measures of fiscal decentralization do not tell the true story. As further analysis will show, de facto levels of fiscal decentralization in all three countries are considerably lower than in the OECD area. A highly autocratic governance manner, non-transparency of fiscal operations, and discretionary distribution of revenue are only some of the reasons for qualitative distortion of the usual decentralization indicators.

The existence of extra-budgetary centralized funds mostly fed by resource rents adds a substantial quantitative distortion to the indicators. There are two reasons why this distortion will not be corrected here. First, the amounts of extra-budgetary funds can be estimated in Kazakhstan and, less reliably, in Uzbekistan, but have to be guessed in Turkmenistan. Second, we aim at a qualitative evaluation of fiscal decentralization. In the case of centralized funds, mostly under direct presidential control, the legal influence of local levels on their spending is zero, whereas the real influence based on personal ties, lobbying, extortion or bribing is hard to access.

Characterizing the starting points

The collapse of the USSR led to a substantial worsening of the fiscal situation in the countries under consideration. During Soviet times, Turkmenistan, Uzbekistan and Kazakhstan received substantial transfers from Moscow.[2] After the break-up of the Soviet Union these transfer-dependent countries had to cope with the simultaneous collapse of incomes caused by transformation recession, and the unexpected need to finance expenditure stemming from the crash of the labour market and social systems.[3] The fiscal imbalances led to debt accumulation, non-payments in the state sector and the accumulation of tax arrears, especially in value-added tax (VAT). Inefficient and not legalized institutional arrangements were established, such as mutual settlements between different tiers of government together with tax offsets, and such practices imposed a heavy burden on future fiscal reforms.

All former Soviet Union countries inherited the Soviet system of intergovern-mental financing, often named the 'Russian doll' model. The relationships between Moscow and the 15 republics were taken as a model and replicated in the republics at all levels of the government. The negative elements of this system include a lack of local autonomy, a poor legislative basis of fiscal transactions, a high level of intended non-transparency and excessive equalization between regions. The budgetary process and public administration were conducted within the framework of dual subordination of central and local governments and a general uncertainty concerning the responsibilities of different tiers. Although the expenditure assignment seemed appropriate, it lacked explicit rules for implementation. Expenditure needs were determined by the application of quantitative norms that were not oriented towards ex-post audit and thus hampered local autonomy.

Local governments also had little autonomy on the revenue side. Revenue-formation of local levels was mainly based on shared revenue from turnover, enterprise profit tax (ENPT) and progressive personal income tax (PIT) collected directly from state-owned enterprises according to the registration principle.[4] The latter source of revenue was dwarfed by the wage ceilings essential for revenue collection due to the high share of public sector in the economies.

Different kinds of direct and indirect subsidies, provided on an ad-hoc gap-filling basis and supplemented by soft budget constraints and mutual settlements, served to solve issues of vertical and horizontal imbalances. During budgeting, the original amounts were cut according to the revealed revenue capacity of the regions. This made it impossible for local governments to plan and execute their budgets efficiently. Due to the lack of legislative provisions, bargaining became an integral part of the budget process. The outcome to a great extent depended on the political influence of the head of a particular oblast and his personal ties to the upper levels of the government. In general, the system of tax-sharing, subsidies and transfers was non-transparent, incompatible with the principles of predictability and stability, and created an adverse incentive structure at the local level.

Current status and reforms of administrative and fiscal decentralization

Kazakhstan

The Constitution of the Republic of Kazakhstan adopted in 1995 laid the foundations for administrative reforms. It defines Kazakhstan as a unitary state, with a strong position for the president and two Houses of Parliament. The local administration consists of elected local self-administrative bodies, *Maslikhates*, who should represent the interests of the population and define measures that are necessary to defend these interests, and of presidentially appointed local executive bodies, *Akimates*, responsible for the social and economic development of the respective territory and subordinate to state organs. *Akyms* could be dismissed by a two-thirds majority of the *Maslikhat*. In practice, the country lacks democracy and law enforcement. President Nazarbayev has headed the country since independence and strengthened his power via frequent amendments to the Constitution. The legislative provisions that allow the execution of local government de facto are not applied.[5] The *Maslikhates* function without their own budgets and enjoy no fiscal autonomy.

The administrative territory of Kazakhstan is divided into three tiers: 14 oblasts plus two cities with special status (Astana and Almaty), 160 regions and 79 cities that have the status of a region, and villages (200 villages and 2,150 village districts). Local budgets and the budget of the Republic function independently and after consolidation represent the state budget. De jure, all administrative tiers are involved into the process of budgeting. De facto and de jure the local governments lack the power to set up their budgets. The Ministry of Finance determines revenue and expenditure of the budget by applying norms for expenditure. The local budgets are formally to be approved by the respective *Maslikhates* once the republic level budget is approved and the volume of intergovernmental transfers is set. Local budgets execution reports are to be published quarterly in the press. An auditing commission of the local *Maslikhat* should have control over the execution of the local budget.

The country has undertaken several measures to strengthen the power of local levels via legislation. Major acts concerning these questions are the laws 'On the budget system' (1991) and 'On local representative and executive bodies of Republic of Kazakhstan' (1993). These laws empowered local representatives to decide on sub-national budgets and to control the use of their funds. They announced sub-national budgets as independent and prohibited the interference of the higher governmental levels. In fact, the laws failed to define the division of tasks between oblast and rayon levels as well as between the centre and the regions. According to the 1995 Constitution, within two years the law on local self-governance should have been adopted, but the legislative loophole has not yet been filled and the law is still in the drafting process. Other major legislative acts aiming at decentralization were the laws 'On the system of local representative and executive bodies under the circumstances of administrative and territorial settings' and 'On the budget system' (1996). At the same time, the president was successful in further strengthening his central power with the approval of the Order 'On the governance of the Republic of Kazakhstan' that had the power of a constitutional law. Only in 2001 was the law 'On local state administration in the Republic of Kazakhstan' adopted, and this set major definitions, tasks, requirements and limitations for local representative and local state executive bodies. In the same year, in 28 districts experimental elections of *Akyms* took place (Public Policy Research Center 2004). Until now, however, formal decentralization is countervailed by the centralization of power at the presidential and ministerial level.

The history of fiscal reforms is comparable to that of administrative reforms. The year 1995 saw a major tax reform towards international standards with the adoption of the law 'On taxes and non-tax payments' (1995). The number of taxes was reduced from 50 to 11. The law also changed the major tax rates and defined local taxes. But once again the central government retained substantial power in setting these local taxes, and the independence of local budgets did not increase to a substantial level. The law 'On the budget system' (1999) brought several innovations for intergovernmental relations. First, the law provided the legislative basis for the division of tasks among different levels of government. Second, the local budgets have been assigned significant new revenue sources in the form of a social tax. Third, more responsibilities were pushed down to the local level. Fourth, extra-budgetary funds were incorporated into the budget. Fifth, the system of positive transfers and withdrawals was introduced. The new Tax Code 2002 and the Budget Code 2004 once again reformed local revenue and modified local borrowing regulations. The Budget Code clarified rules of local budget drafting, established a unified budget classification, and explicitly assigned tasks among the second and third levels of government. The law contains provisions that favour more openness and transparency of public finance. Transfers were defined for the period of three years (instead of one), and the principle of one tax for one budget was set. Extra-budgetary funds no longer exist. However, the oil-stabilization fund, established in 2001 and fed by rents from natural resource extraction, continues to grow to substantial amounts and constitutes a shift towards the centralization of financial resources (Kalyuzhnova 2006).

Turkmenistan

According to the Constitution, Turkmenistan is defined as a democratic and presidential republic. De jure the power is divided into executive, legislative represented by the *Khalk Maslakhaty* (people's council) and judicial. On the local level, the executive powers rest in the hands of the *hyakims*, who are assigned and dismissed by the president.[6] Local self-governance is carried out by the so-called *Gengeshes* (people's councils), elected for a term of five years and governed by the *Archyn* (mayor), who is elected by and accountable to the members of *Gengesh*. The *Gengesh* should define the major guidelines of social and economic development, approve the budget and the report on its execution, supervize the local tax administration, etc. The relations and division of responsibilities between *hyakims* and *Gengeshes* are defined by legislation. *De facto* the local councils enjoy no autonomy or decision-making authority; President-for-life Niyazov concentrates power in an autocratic manner upon himself.

The territory of Turkmenistan is divided into five oblasts (velayats), and further into rayons and etraps. The budgetary system of Turkmenistan is represented by the Republican budget that formerly also incorporated the state-targeted funds and local budgets. The *Gengeshes* are also allowed to create extra-budgetary funds. Local budgets include the budgets of oblast level, the budgets of cities of republic subordination, the budgets of rayons, and the budgets of cities of rayon subordination, settlements and villages.

The legislative basis for the administrative decentralization was mainly elabora-ted in the mid-1990s. The laws 'On the Cabinet of Ministers of Turkmenistan' (1995) and 'On Hyakims' (1995) define the foundations of these bodies and set their areas of responsibility and relations with the other government bodies. However, the legislation fails to define the procedure of responsibilities assignment. The constitutional base for local self-governance (the law 'On Gengesh') was developed only in 2003. In spite of formal administrative decentralization, a process of *de facto* administrative centralization can be observed. Local hyakims are appointed and dismissed by the president over short periods of time, with and without reasonable explanations. In these circumstances, competition among regions and incentives at the local level do not play a role. The effective legislation contains provisions that do not form grounds for local government independence.[7]

As in Kazakhstan, fiscal decentralization has been on the reform agenda for several years. During 1991 to 1993 major shared taxes such as VAT, PIT and ENPT were introduced and reformed. A resolution of the president established an exhaustive list of local taxes. The law 'On the budget system' was introduced in 1996, but its provisions poorly addressed the issues of fiscal decentralization.

Its contribution to the clarity of tasks was very moderate. The problem of vertical imbalance was addressed with non-transparent methods, such as revenue sharing and non-formula based transfers. The tax reform of 2000 allowed a reduction in the number of local taxes with little revenue potential. This decision became law only in 2004 with the approval of the Tax Code 2004. For the local budgets, these reforms implied only a marginal increase in revenue autonomy and hence did not contribute to predictability and stability of local revenue.

The existence of extra-budgetary funds aggravates the de facto centralization of the fiscal sphere. Although in 1994 all extra-budgetary funds were incorporated into the budget, in the years 1996 to 2000 Turkmenistan developed a complicated system of state-purpose funds.[8] Although these funds once again became part of the consolidated budget in 1998, they are governed in a non-democratic manner solely depending upon decisions of the president. In addition to these official funds, several unofficial and unreported presidential funds serve the purpose of accumulating rents from resource extraction. The amount of these funds might even exceed the official budget.

Uzbekistan

The administrative reforms in Uzbekistan started with the adoption of the Constitution (1992), which defined three branches of power and three administrative tiers. As in the other Central Asian countries, the president has been provided with substantial competence. The structure and responsibilities of local governments are fixed in the law 'On local State governance' (1993). In 1996 the president undertook some steps towards re-concentration and eliminated the administrations of cities of district subordination. The state representative body in oblasts, rayons and cities is the council of people's deputies headed by the *hokim*; both have a nominal term of five years. Oblast-level *hokims* and the *hokim* of Tashkent city are assigned and dismissed by the president, *hokims* of rayons and cities are assigned and dismissed by higher-level *hokims*. In practice, *hokims* at all levels do not stay in power the whole term, but depend on presidential ad-hoc decisions. In 1995, President Karimov was successful in strengthening his power and prolonging his presidential term from five to seven years. Due to political turmoil and outbreaks of violence in the capital and the Ferghana valley in recent years, in spite of further decentralization measures, a substantial tightening of political control and concentration of power can be observed. The local governors or *hokims* are in fact part of the system of the president.

Uzbekistan is divided into 12 provinces, the city of Tashkent and the autonomous republic of Karakalpakstan. The system of local state executive bodies includes oblast, rayon and city *hokimiyats*. The budgetary structure is represented by independently functioning local and republican budgets, the budget of the republic of Karakalpakstan and state-targeted funds. The local budgets also include budgets of rayons, cities and oblasts. Budgets of rayons include rayon budgets and budgets of rayons of city subordination. The consolidated state budget is prepared by the Ministry of Finance based on norms of expenditure and approved by the

Parliament. After the state budget is centrally approved, the respective *hokimiyats* and other key spending units are informed about major parameters of the budget. The representative local governmental bodies approve the local budget and report on their execution. The structure of fiscal decentralization implies a dual link between local governmental bodies and central financial bodies. *Mahallas* serve as a link between the state and the recipients of aid.

Since 1996 little attention has been paid to administrative decentralization. The only exception relates to the 1999 law on local self-governance of citizens that increased the formal role of the *mahallas*. They became responsible for the delivery of allowances to non-working mothers of children under two years of age and foodstuff to single pensioners. However, the *mahallas* have no access to autonomous financial resources. During 2002 to 2004 attempts towards governmental reforms were undertaken. In 2002, the president made a commitment to the Parliament (*Oliy Majlis*) aimed at de-concentration and gradual transfer of central powers and functions to lower state bodies and citizens' self-governance. However, the latter has not yet brought about any concrete results.[9] In 2003 some re-concentration took place via incorporation of the urban district into the respective city *hokimiyat*. In 2003, the law 'On the Cabinet of Ministers of the Republic of Uzbekistan' was adopted. Uzbekistan took substantial steps towards reducing the number of government officials and this also had implications for the structure of local representative bodies. Currently, Uzbekistan is on its way towards setting up a treasury, which would enable a certain element of control of the fiscal process.

Reforms in the fiscal sphere have been substantial. The mid-nineties were the times of establishing the tax system. The Tax Code (1997) and the structure of the tax service (1997) were set up. The Tax Code defined the list of local taxes and made the Cabinet of Ministers responsible for developing procedures for the calculation of local taxes and fees and their payment into the budget. Two important revenue sources (property tax and land tax) were defined as local taxes. At the time that the law 'On the Budget system' (1999) replaced the soviet-time law 'On the budgetary right of Republic of Uzbekistan and local councils of workers of the Republic of Uzbekistan', major budgetary reforms were started. The legislative base for formation, allocation and execution of budgets, and a (not sufficiently detailed) assignment of tasks to local government was set up. However, this law mainly concerned the state and republic level budgets, and provisions on the local budgets were scarce. Only the 2001 order of the Cabinet of Ministers of Uzbekistan stated more detailed rules on the procedure of the compilation and the implementation of the state budget, as well as on the consideration of local budgets. Provisions in relation to an external budget audit were set up in 2002.

Summary

To sum up, three facts characterize the decentralization process in the countries under consideration. First, administrative and fiscal decentralization proceeded at different rates, the latter progressing quicker. Second, provision and implementation of laws concerning decentralization differ a lot. Due to the lack of democracy in the administrative sphere this gap in the administrative sphere is wider than in the fiscal sphere.[10] Third, local self-governance as an element of political decentralization in spite of distinctive laws does not play a role. From these three facts, it can be concluded that decentralization in the fiscal sphere in all countries is hampered by lack of administrative decentralization. As long as local budgets are compiled on centrally defined parameters and not on actual costs and local needs, fiscal decentralization is merely formal.

Analysis of expenditure assignment

A proper expenditure assignment is the first step for efficient decentralization. Clear assignment of governmental tasks avoids a populist-inspired discretion of local authorities. In general, the expenditure assignment for an efficient provision of public services should correspond to the principles of subsidiarity, territorial equivalency, economies of scale and the consideration of externalities.

In centralized states a political reluctance to assign tasks to the local level is inherent. Tasks with higher autonomy in spending, for example, carrying out of economic activities, tend to stay with the central government. Tasks with little spending autonomy like health, education and social protection can be transferred to the local level without losing control over spending, especially if their volumes depend on centrally set standards.

Kazakhstan

The legislative basis of expenditure assignment in Kazakhstan was brought about by the budget reform of 1999 (see Leschenko and Troschke 2006: Annex I, Table I.1). Previously, the division of tasks at the local level was not defined; the structure of expenditure at the lower level was subject to frequent changes and bargaining. For instance, in some oblasts schools were financed from the oblast budget while in others they were financed from the rayons' budget (Mahmutova 2003: 5). In 1999, the general clarification of assignment rules and budget transparency was improved by the incorporation of extra-budgetary funds that had previously obscured fiscal decision-making at all levels. The responsibilities of local budgets have been expanded. According to the principle of territorial equivalency, local governments became responsible for tasks like the construction and maintenance of roads and streets of local importance. However, from the perspective of the effectiveness of fiscal decentralization, some changes in the budget reform were debatable. For instance, as a result of the reform, the local government became responsible for provision of unemployment benefits and targeted social assistance payments, imposing a high administrative and fiscal burden on poorer regions.

The structure of local expenditure in 1998 shows that the general principles of subsidiarity were upheld even before the reform (Table 6.2). National tasks such as defence and general public services were mainly assigned to the central government. The share of economic affairs tasks (for example, the fuel and energy

84

Table 6.2 Share of local expenditure in the consolidated budget, Kazakhstan* (%)

	1998	1999	2000	2001	2002	2003	2004
General public services	21	31	30	30	28	32	26
Defense	14	17	20	18	18	15	17
Public order and justice	25	23	24	22	21	19	21
Education	78	83	84	81	86	88	88
Health-Care	70	81	86	78	83	83	82
Social protection	84*	12	12	16	18	17	15
Utilities	100	100	100	100	100	100	98
Culture	45	74	73	68	64	62	65
Fuel and energy sector						14	43
Agriculture and hunting	19	17	23	14	13	16	13
Industrial construction	68	10	7	21	24	64	50
Transport	–	71	58	41	29	32	33
Other	34	39	71	54	83	73	53
Debt service		1	1	2	2	3	3
Total expenditures	41	46	50	52	48	48	49

Source: Own calculations based on data from the Ministry of Finance of the Republic of Kazakhstan.

Note: * The calculations do not take into account extra-budgetary funds.

sector, agriculture) assigned to the local budgets seems substantial, but its weight in total local expenditure is tiny, which means local budgets do not have room for manoeuvre in this sphere. During the period 1998 to 2004, the role of local budgets in financing education and health care increased from 78 per cent to 88 per cent and from 70 per cent to 80 per cent, respectively. The share of social protection tasks financed at the expense of local budgets fell from 29 per cent in 1998 to 7 per cent in 2004. After 1998, when the extra-budgetary funds were eliminated, the Republican (Central) budget had to finance all the pensions on a pay-as-you-go system, as well as categorical benefits and social allowances, while local budgets had to finance poverty-related social assistance payments.

The legislation that regulated intergovernmental relations was upgraded in 2005 with the approval of the new Budget Code. The latter provides a more detailed assignment of tasks assignment (for example, it listed all types of social welfare payments that should be financed at the expense of local budgets). More importantly, the Budget Code of Kazakhstan defined the redistribution of tasks at lower than oblast levels of government such as rayons, cities, and re-assigned more social aid provisions to the central level of the government.

Table 6.3 Structure of local budget expenditure, Kazakhstan* (%)

	1998	1999	2000	2001	2002	2003	2004
General public services	4	4	3	4	3	5	4
Defense	2	1	1	1	2	2	2
Public order and justice	5	4	4	4	4	4	4
Education	35	30	23	22	28	28	27
Healthcare	12	17	15	12	16	16	18
Social protection	29	9	7	8	10	9	7
Utilities	3	3	7	8	7	7	11
Culture	3	4	4	3	4	4	5
Fuel and energy sector	–	–	–	–	–	–	1
Agriculture and hunting	1	1	1	1	1	1	1
Industrial construction	1	–	–	–	–	1	–
Transport	–	4	7	5	4	6	6
Other	5	5	7	8	8	6	4
Debt service	–	–	–	–	–	–	–

Source: Own calculations based on data from the Ministry of Finance of the Republic of Kazakhstan.

Note: * The total expenditure is net of transfers.

Uzbekistan

Uzbekistan so far shows little progress concerning the legal assignment of tasks among different budget levels according to the principles of clarity and subsidiarity (Center for Economic Research 2004: 17; Leschenko and Troschke 2006: Annex I, Table I.2 a and b). The provisions of the budget legislation enforced in 1999 failed to assign several tasks even at the centre-oblast level, and even in relation to tasks like defence and public order (Nuritdinov 2005: 16). The expenditure of authorities below the oblast levels is still not assigned at all. In general, the budget reform implied an extension of local government responsibilities. The responsibility for some social aid provision was transferred down from the central to the local level. This aid is financed out of district budgets and administered through the *mahallas* to guarantee optimal targeting. Although this aim seems to have been reached (Coudouel and Marnie 1999), in autocratic states the system obviously bears the risk of setting wrong incentives at the local level and is reportedly misused for political control (Human Rights Watch 2003).

As stated earlier, the weight of local expenditure in the consolidated budget of Uzbekistan is quite high and has varied from 51 per cent to 56 per cent for the period 1996 to 2004, and was 54 per cent in 2004 (Table 6.4). Disaggregated data corroborate the assumption that, despite high indicators of decentralization, local levels in fact do not have substantial financial scope for own policies. The share of social sphere expenditure financed from local budgets, that includes education,

Table 6.4 Share of local expenditure in consolidated budget, Uzbekistan* (%)

	1996	1997	1998	1999	2000	2001	2002	2003	2004
Total expenditures	53	56	51	54	52	55	55	53	54
Social sphere**	79	80	77	79	79	84	83	83	84
Social protection	61	75	69	70	75	74	78	75	88
Economic expenditures	51	37	30	38	40	52	50	39	23
Financing centrally planned investments	53	59	52	50	59	58	59	61	68
Maintenance of state government bodies and local bodies	3	4	3	4	3	3	4	4	2
Other expenditures	11	13	12	13	10	11	10	11	10

Source: Own calculations based on data from Nutridinov (2005).

Notes: *The calculation does not take into account extra-budgetary funds. **Includes education, healthcare, social welfare, culture and sport expenditure.

healthcare, social welfare, culture and sport, rose from 79 per cent in 1996 to 84 per cent in 2004. Its weight in local expenditure in the same period increased from 51 per cent to 63 per cent (Table 6.5). The same trend can be observed for social protection. Eighty-eight per cent of all social protection expenditure has been pushed down from the central level to the regions. In sum, three quarters of all local budget expenditure is spent on social measures, which have to be provided according to centrally set laws and instructions. Adding the 16 per cent for the execution of centrally planned investments, almost 90 per cent of the local budgets are administered centrally.

Table 6.5 Structure of local budget expenditure, Uzbekistan* (%)

	1996	1997	1998	1999	2000	2001	2002	2003	2004
Social sphere**	51	51	54	56	54	57	57	60	63
Total expenditures	100	100	100	100	100	100	100	100	100
Social protection	13	13	12	12	11	10	11	11	11
Economic expenditures	12	8	10	8	7	8	8	9	6
Financing centrally planned investments	20	24	21	20	23	19	19	15	16
Maintenance of state government bodies and local bodies	0	0	0	0	0	0	0	0	0
Other expenditures	4	4	4	4	5	5	5	5	5

Source: Own calculations based on data from Nutridinov (2005).

Note: * The calculations do not take into account extra-budgetary funds. ** Includes education, healthcare, social welfare, culture and sport expenditure.

On the other side, during the transition process many tasks of executing economic affairs formerly assigned to the regions have been shifted to the central level. The level of total economic affairs expenditure financed from the state budget remains high, but the share of economic affairs expenditure financed from the local budgets of Uzbekistan decreased from 51 per cent to 23 per cent from 1996 to 2004. The share of funds spent for these purposes out of the local budgets decreased from 24 per cent in 1997 to 6 per cent in 2004. Because disaggregated data under this budget heading are not accessible, it is impossible to state whether these shifts stem from a real centralization of tasks or from privatization and/or reduced soft budget constraints.

Turkmenistan

In Turkmenistan, the 1996 law 'On the budget system' provides only a broad and insufficiently detailed division of tasks between the central and the oblast level. Furthermore, the centralization of production tasks (for commercial purposes) and construction implies that government intervention into business and local needs is highly undesirable. Loopholes in the legislation related to the division of financial responsibilities at levels lower than oblasts result in situations when expenditure assigned to the local level (especially oblast-rayon level) is, in fact, defined by the higher-level governmental tiers and subject to frequent changes and bargaining.

In general, Turkmenistan shows a similar picture of high quantitative decentralization indicators without de facto decentralization. While the weight of local expenditure in the consolidated budget fell from 77 per cent in 1991 to 43 per cent in 1995, it revived to 51 per cent in 2003 (Table 6.6). During this

Table 6.6 Share of local expenditure in consolidated budget, Turkmenistan (%)

	1991	1995	2000	2001	2002	2003
TOTAL	77	43	47	45	49	51
Financing economic affairs	22	34	0	1	1	1
Education*	73	82	90	89	89	89
Culture	50	41	39	44	40	44
Healthcare	86	79	80	79	80	80
Utilities**	98	n/a	100	100	100	100
Social provision	1	1	–	–	–	–
Government	57	16	7	8	9	8
Defense	–	–	–	–	–	–
Public order	–	–	7	7	7	2

Source: Own calculations based on data from Turkmenmillichasbat (2005).

Note: * Contrary to classification effective in Turkmenistan, education expenditure include payment of stipends. ** Utility expenditure was excluded from economic affairs expenditure.

period, the local budgets were assigned higher shares of education expenditure and health care. Expenditure for financing utility functions of Turkmenistan was 100 per cent assigned to the local level. As water and natural gas in Turkmenistan are distributed to the population at no cost, this increases the dependency of the local budgets on centralized transfers and does not constitute decentralization. As in Uzbekistan, the assigning of social tasks to the local level was accompanied by a centralizing of economic affairs tasks. The share of economic affairs expenditure assigned to the local level declined from 22 per cent in 1991 to mere 1 per cent in 2003 (Turkmenmillichasbat 2005: 23). Since there has been almost no privatization of state enterprises, for Turkmenistan this shift can be explained only by centralization of formerly locally financed affairs. The structure of local budget expenditure shows respective changes for the period of independence (Table 6.7). Social services provision including education and healthcare became the priority of local budgets. While the share of local education expenditure was 17 per cent in 1991, it reached 31 per cent in 1995 and 51 per cent in 2003. Healthcare expenditure consumed nearly 23 per cent of local budgets in 2000 to 2003. The weight of local economic expenditure approached zero.

Overview

From a comparative perspective, at the beginning of independence all countries under consideration lacked explicit legislative provisions that defined the division of responsibilities. In spite of this, the de facto expenditure assignment to the local governments was generally in line with decentralization principles. During the reform years, against the background of Turkmenistan and Uzbekistan,

Table 6.7 Structure of local budget expenditure, Turkmenistan (%)

	1991	1995	2000	2001	2002	2003
Financing economic affairs**	11	5	0	0	0	0
Education*	17	31	53	52	49	51
Culture	1	1	2	2	2	2
Healthcare	10	17	23	23	22	22
Utilities	4	27	16	17	17	17
Social provision	0	1	1	1	1	1
Government	1	2	3	3	3	3
Public order	–	–	1	1	1	0
Other	56	16	0	0	5	4
TOTAL	100	100	100	100	100	100

Source: Own calculations based on data from Turkmenmillichasbat (2005).

Note: * Contrary to classification effective in Turkmenistan, education expenditure include payment of stipends. ** Utility expenditure was excluded from economic affairs expenditure.

Kazakhstan's reforms became the most prominent. Thanks to the Budget Code approved in 2004, Kazakhstan is now closest to a clear assignment of tasks at all levels, while the division of tasks in Turkmenistan and Uzbekistan remains unclear at levels lower than oblast level. However, in all three countries the reform of tasks assignment lacks clarity and economic justification. Local budgets especially in Uzbekistan and Turkmenistan became heavily burdened with the financing of social tasks, whereas economic affairs financing keeps on decreasing. Without some autonomy in spending, incentive mechanisms will not work.

Is there spending autonomy at the local level?

In all three countries expenditure autonomy is limited in a number of ways. Norms and regulations issued by the central government are aggravated by unfunded mandates. Expenditure limits are set at the central level in all three countries. In Uzbekistan, each distinct local budget request has to refer directly to a particular article of an official act as a justification for the expenditure. In Kazakhstan the provisions establishing expenditure limits became even stricter. The Budget Code of Kazakhstan that came into force in 2005 requires all expenditure of all programs and of all levels of budgets to be based on the limits of expenditure (RGP Institute for Economic Research 2005: 25). These limits are to be approved by the budget commissions and are to be taken into account while composing the budget. Thus, one could not expect local governments freedom to define expenditure.

For further examination of this question we look at the regional (oblast) variation of per capita expenditure according to the functional classification of expenditure. A high variation may reflect the ability of local governments to set their own preferences and to conduct economic policy according to their own needs. It may also reflect differences in the quality of local governance and administrative efficiency.

For Kazakhstan the coefficient of variation shows rather low rates in 1998, which more than tripled during reforms (Table 6.8). This was mostly due to the introduction of official withdrawals, which became necessary as growing revenue from resource extraction had led to serious regional disparities. The regional per capita variation of expenditure in Turkmenistan (Table 6.9) and Uzbekistan (Table 6.10) remained fairly stable. Most interestingly, the largest contribution to the variability in all countries stems from the smallest budget categories (for example, financing tasks from economic affairs). Relatively high per capita expenditure variations in the general public services seem to depend more on the number of administrative units[11] rather than on the quality of services delivered. Comparatively low levels of per capita expenditure variation at the oblast level in all countries can be observed in the most important categories such as education and healthcare, suggesting unified priorities and little spending autonomy.

This analysis hints at the important role of centrally set minimum expenditure requirements for education and healthcare sectors. The extremely scarce financial resources seem to be redistributed to the other sectors as a residual. Further analyses will show along what lines this redistribution is organized.

Table 6.8 Coefficient of variation of local per capita expenditure, Kazakhstan*

	1998	2002	2003	2004	
Total	0.22	0.76	0.69	0.60	
General public services	0.29	0.32	1.12	0.33	
Defence		0.42	0.48	0.31	0.40
Public order and justice	0.44	0.38	0.33	0.35	
Education		0.27	0.29	0.25	0.26
Healthcare	0.34	0.33	0.30	0.24	
Social welfare	0.22	0.31	0.29	0.20	
Utilities		0.62	2.06	1.55	0.97
Culture		0.32	0.69	0.61	0.49
Fuel and energy complex	–	–	3.87	3.09	
Agriculture and forestry	0.75	0.61	0.41	0.33	
Industry		1.22	1.75	2.11	1.51
Transport		–	0.83	0.94	1.05
Other		1.43	0.69	0.92	0.68
Debt servicing	2.24	2.35	2.93	2.71	
Official transfers	–	2.17	2.10	2.17	

Source: Own calculations based on data from the Ministry of Finance of the Republic of Kazakhstan.

Notes: The calculation of the coefficient is based on data on categorical local per capita expenditure by oblast. * The calculations do not taking into account Astana city due to its exceptional status.

Table 6.9 Coefficient of variation of local per capita expenditure, Turkmenistan

	2001	2002	2003
Total	0.21	0.15	0.20
General public services	0.30	0.23	0.35
Public and social services	0.17	0.14	0.16
Education	0.07	0.13	0.10
Healthcare	0.26	0.25	0.24
Social	0.22	0.28	0.24
Utilities	0.95	0.83	0.92
Culture	0.43	0.39	0.42
Economic affairs	1.40	1.92	1.40
Transfers	1.08	2.45	2.27

Source: Own calculations based on data from Turkmenmillichasbat (2005).

Table 6.10 Coefficient of variation of local per capita expenditure, Uzbekistan*

	1996	1997	1998	1999	2000	2001	2002	2003	2004
Total	0.14	0.15	0.15	0.13	0.13	0.10	0.12	0.12	0.13
Social sphere	0.10	0.12	0.11	0.11	0.11	0.11	0.12	0.11	0.13
Social protection	0.16	0.09	0.22	0.15	0.15	0.16	0.17	0.19	0.20
Economic expenditures	0.46	0.43	0.46	0.44	0.46	0.40	0.47	0.44	0.48
Financing centrally planned investments	0.68	0.70	0.51	0.36	0.29	0.41	0.33	0.24	0.26
Maintenance of state government bodies and local bodies	0.36	0.29	0.32	0.30	0.35	0.25	0.25	0.28	0.43
Other expenditures	0.32	0.48	0.36	0.37	0.37	0.36	0.52	0.25	0.34

Source: Own calculations based on data from Nutridinov (2005).

Note: * The calculations do not take into account Tashkent city due to its exceptional status.

This suggests that the influence of centrally set limits is significant, whereas the budgetary autonomy of local governments in all three countries is generally as limited as expected.

Analysis of revenue assignment and sharing

According to conventional wisdom, the core for local revenue should consist of easily administered taxes with an immobile tax base, a predictable revenue yield and visible sub-national government liabilities. Local governments should have access to genuine local revenue that is compatible with their responsibilities and they should have the right to define the tax base/rate within the limits established. Taxes that are redistributive in nature have important economies of scale, are sensitive to cyclical fluctuations, and/or unevenly distributed such as VAT and ENPT should be centralized. The progressive PIT performs redistribution functions and in the presence of high regional disparities may exacerbate the difference in the quality of public services provided locally. Rents from natural resource extraction are generally treated as payment for ownership; in the countries under consideration these resources constitute national wealth and the rents should be assigned to the central level.

If revenue is assigned to create incentive effects at the local level, a certain share of ENPT and PIT should remain at the local level. This makes local governments interested in creating a business-friendly environment and promoting local growth. However, long-term credibility of the central government's commitment not to withdraw unexpected surpluses from the local level is essential to make incentive mechanisms work. For nations rich in point-source natural resources (resources extracted from a narrow geographic and economic base) this commitment creates a trade-off between the promotion of local growth and growing regional disparities.

Kazakhstan

In Kazakhstan the pre-reform tax legislation enforced more than 50 taxes. In 1995 their number was cut to 11 and so-called 'regulatory' (shared) and local taxes were defined. The list of local taxes included property tax, vehicle owner tax, land tax and several kinds of non-tax revenue. These genuine local taxes provided the potential for a small revenue base. The sub-national governments had no power to set the tax rates even for local taxes (with the exception of land tax). With the enforcement of the Tax Code in 2002, the local administrations acquired the right to raise the standard rates of local taxes set by the Tax Code by up to 50 per cent and to set their own rates for fines and administrative sanctions (Leschenko and Troschke 2006: Appendix II.1). This genuine local revenue, over which the local government had some degree of discretion, funded slightly more than 10 per cent of local budgets. Thus, local tax autonomy stayed limited.

As a result of the small genuine local tax base, the lion's share of local revenue is through the shared taxes VAT (including VAT on imports) and ENPT (Table 6.11). In 1995 the assignment of tax revenue among regions became based on operational indicators of an enterprise (depending on the part of the wage bill of the enterprise directed to a particular region, the assets location, etc.) replacing the original principle based on the administrative subordination of the enterprise.

Table 6.11 Structure of local revenue, Kazakhstan* (%)

	1998	1999	2000	2001	2002	2003	2004
EPT	14	13	26	20	0	0	0
VAT	8	4	4	2	3	2	1
PIT	17	16	16	17	20	19	16
Excises	8	2	1	1	6	4	4
Social tax	0	31	25	32	35	33	28
Privatization and operations with capital*	0	0	0	1	1	1	2
Non-tax revenues	9	5	3	4	1	1	2
Other tax revenues	19	15	10	10	14	13	12
Transfers	27	15	14	12	20	26	35
Total	100	100	100	100	100	100	100

Source: Own calculations based on the data from the Kazakhstan Ministry of Finance.

Note: * The receipts from the sale of fixed capital in Kazakhstan are represented by revenue from the sale of state property, the sale of goods from the state material reserve and the sale of non-tangible assets owned by the government.

Thus the accountability of local budgets grew, and incentives for the promotion of enterprise development might have resulted. However, due to yearly changes in the assigned shares, the predictability at the local level has been low.

The 1999 reforms brought major changes in the assignment of shared taxes. The assigned shares of taxes had been fixed in the annual Budget Laws and were unified for all regions. The introduction of the so-called 'social tax', which is in fact a payroll tax and is contributed to by the local employers, began to provide nearly 30 per cent of funding for local budgets. As a tax paid by enterprises this set positive incentives at the locallevel, but its design as a central tax which is assigned to the local budgets makes it a financing source dependent on decisions taken centrally. By and by all vulnerable taxes were assigned to the central level, for example VAT (in 1997) and ENPT (in 2002) previously collected by the local budgets began to flow to the central level. The tendency to centralize was reinforced by the redirection of 50 per cent of excises to the central level. The weight of progressive PIT in local revenue increased from 16 per cent in 1999 to 20 per cent in 2002, but the tax reform of 2004 replaced the progressive PIT with a 10 per cent flat rate and thus contributed to the reduction of its weight in local revenue to 16 per cent. A mere administrative feature concerning the shared taxes adds to the dependency of the local budgets on the centre – all shared taxes collected at the local level have to be 100 per cent directed to the centre, and only afterwards are they redirected to the regions. In times of high inflation, this process deprived the regions of already earned revenue.

In contrast to the standard arguments of tax assignment among different tiers, after 1999 we find many unified redistributive taxes on the local level. Due to growing differences in the revenue capacities of the regions, this led to an increase of revenue disparities and horizontal imbalances between the regions. Consequently, the weight of transfers in local revenue, which had decreased from 27 per cent in 1998 to 15 per cent in 1999, rose considerably and reached 35 per cent in 2004.

According to the Budget Code 2004, above-plan revenue collected at the local level cannot be withdrawn by the centre and stay at the local level, which enjoys spending autonomy. However, interviews with local *hokims* revealed that spending autonomy for this revenue in reality is very limited because it has to be spent on underfunded and unfunded mandates.

Turkmenistan

In Turkmenistan, the genuine local taxes have a low revenue potential and constitute only a negligibly small share of local revenue. Since 1993 Turkmenistan has had 17(!) local taxes with little revenue potential. Only in 2000 was the number of local taxes cut to five (advertisement tax, targeted duty for developing territories of cities, settlements, and villages, duty that paid by the owners of car parks, duty for sale of cars, and duty from dog keepers). Their share in total local revenue constituted about 3 per cent in 2001 to 2003 (Table 6.12).

Table 6.12 Structure of local revenue, Turkmenistan (%)

	1995	2000	2001	2002	2003
VAT	17	20	20	16	15
EPT	20	10	10	9	9
Property tax	1	4	5	5	3
PIT	8	17	17	18	21
Local taxes		2	3	3	3
Non-tax revenues	1	1	1	1	1
Transfers	23	45	40	45	45
Other revenues	30	2	3	2	3
Total	100	100	100	100	100

Source: Own calculations based on data from Turkmenmillichasbat (2005).

Excess orifut tax assigned to local governments, according to the place of registration and local governments' shares of the valueadded tax remained revenue of crucial importance for sub-national budgets. A part of local revenue comes in the form of a royalty for natural resource extraction. The assigned shares depend on the regional fiscal capacity and are set on a yearly basis. Reportedly they can be changed even during the fiscal year on an *ad hoc* basis. Revenue above the planned level is withdrawn by the centre. This design of shared taxes does not create incentives on the local level. In 1995, the shares of ENPT and VAT in local revenue were 37 per cent. Although the importance of this revenue diminished to 24 per cent in 2003, its role in local budget funding still remained substantial.

The tax reform of 1997 highlights the dependency of local budgets on centrally taken decisions. It brought about the increase of the VAT rate from 18 per cent to 20 per cent and a two-stage decrease in the ENPT rate from 37 per cent in 1996 to 35 per cent in 1998. It also changed the flat rate 8 per cent PIT to an eight-level progressive PIT with rates from 8 per cent to 25 per cent. Thus, the share of PIT in local budget funding rose from 8 per cent in 1995 to 21 per cent in 2003. With the approval of the Tax Code 2004, the progressive rates for the eight levels were replaced with a flat 10 per cent rate, making local revenue shrink anew. Additionally, the centralized wage setting in the huge public sector of Turkmenistan makes PIT an almost exogenous parameter for local budgets.[12] Above-plan revenue cannot be withdrawn by the center and stay at the local level, which has autonomy on spending the revenue (Turkmenmillichasbat 2005: 5). However, no such cases are reported so far, because in case of unexpected revenue the level of assigned expenditure is raised during the fiscal year.

A structure of local revenue that leaves nearly 95 per cent for shared revenue and official transfers suggests that the role of the genuine local revenue in funding local budgets in Turkmenistan is negligible. Regions are fully dependent on centrally set limits and central financing. The assignment of transfers (positive transfers and subsidies) is used to balance local budgets.

Uzbekistan

In Uzbekistan we find a broader tax base for genuine local revenue. The adoption of the Tax Code 1997 allowed the share of genuine local revenues in local budgets to increase from 11 per cent in 1997 to 18 per cent in 1999 (Nuritdinov 2005: 30). In 1999 property tax and land tax were defined as local, making the share of genuine local taxes rise to 20 per cent for 2000 to 2003. New taxes including property, infrastructure development and environmental taxes became more important. However, the legislative provisions of local taxes were not workable in terms of fiscal decentralization. Some of the 'local' tax rates and bases were defined centrally. The Cabinet of Ministers defines the rates of land tax and property tax each year with the approval of the yearly budget law. Furthermore, the latter had substantial administration costs thus its net revenue approached zero (Nuritdinov 2005: 25).

The role of shared taxes in local budget financing in Uzbekistan decreased steadily (Table 6.13). The share of ENPT and VAT was 52 per cent of local revenue in 1995, and it fell to 23 per cent in 2003. Tax rates other than VAT and PIT were

Table 6.13 Structure of local revenue, Uzbekistan* (%)

	1995	1996	1997	1998	1999	2000	2001	2002	2003
VAT	19.7	16.1	24.3	21.0	17.1	20.4	18.3	18.9	15.8
EPT	32.0	29.6	20.8	13.3	0	12.7	8.6	7.5	6.9
Entrepreneurial activity	0.7	0.1	1.3	2.1	2.6	3.6	4.0	3.4	2.6
PIT	13.5	15.5	21.4	13.6	19.0	14.9	14.4	14.0	14.2
Property tax physical persons	0.3	0	0	0.8	0.9	1.0	0.9	0.5	0.6
Property tax legal persons	5.2	2.9	4.0	4.7	4.8	6.4	4.7	2.9	5.3
Excise tax	8.7	4.8	14.1	16.3	17.5	19.5	12.1	10.6	10.0
Environmental tax	0	1.1	4.4	4.4	3.8	4.8	4.1	4.2	5.0
State duty	1.2	1.0	1.4	1.0	0.9	1.0	0.7	0.6	1.7
Land tax	5.9	0.3	6.3	6.9	7.5	7.3	5.4	3.7	3.7
Infrastructure development	1.8	1.6	0.3	2.0	1.8	2.5	2.4	3.9	3.3
Water tax	0.7	0.6	0.6	1.0	0.7	1.1	0.7	0.6	0.7
Duties and non-tax revenues	3.9	2.7	2.6	5.1	4.8	9.5	7.9	11.4	11.2
Transfers	3.0	14.1	18.8	22.2	10.6	17.1	16.9	18.6	21.1
Total*	97.0	90.0	120.0	114.0	92.0	122.0	101.0	101.0	102.0

Source: Own calculations based on data from Nuritdinov (2005).

Note: * These officially reported data are obviously inconsistent in some queues. Therefore care has to be taken in the interpretation of single lines.

approved each year in the budget resolution, for example, the ENPT rate declined gradually each year from 35 per cent in 1998 to 18 per cent in 2004. The lowest and highest PIT levels decreased in 2001 from 15 to 12 times the minimum wage and from 40 to 36 times the minimum wage respectively. In 2004, the lowest and highest PIT levels equaled 13 and 30 times the minimum wage.[13] Thus, the contribution of progressive PIT increased from 14 per cent in 1995 up to 19 per cent in 1999 (four levels for rather high rates of 15 per cent to 40 per cent), then fell to the initial level of 13 per cent in 2004. These frequent changes in the tax legislation, added to frequent changes in the assigned revenue shares (Table 6.15), made the contribution of shared taxes unpredictable for the regions.

The centre provides only weak commitments concerning above-plan revenue. Although this revenue may need to be withdrawn by the centre, at the same time the local level has no spending autonomy for additional revenue, and spending has to be agreed with the upper levels. In practice, in case of above-plan revenue the level of centrally planned expenditure is raised during the fiscal year (Nuritdinov 2005: 41). Clearly this mechanism does not create incentives to raise local tax revenue.

In Turkmenistan and Uzbekistan the assignment of shared taxes so far has not been unified, i.e. different regions receive different shares of these taxes. Local administrations de jure have influence upon this process, but de facto can use personal connections to push their interests at higher levels. That leads to the question of whether centrally assigned taxes in fact served the role of equalizing intergovernmental transfers or whether they have been used for political ends (either gratification or punishment of local rulers). The negative correlation between regional GDP and assigned shares corroborates the equalizing assumption: higher shares are assigned to less-developed regions (Tables 6.14 and 6.15).

Table 6.14 Revenue shares for centrally assigned taxes, Turkmenistan*

Velayat	2001			2002			2003		
	EPT (%)	VAT (%)	Per capita revenues (m manat)	EPT (%)	VAT (%)	Per capita revenues (m manat)	EPT (%)	VAT (%)	Per capita revenues (m manat)
Ahalskiy	80	80	0.6	80	80	0.7	80	80	0.9
Ashhabad	31	31	2.1	14	14	3.0	25	25	2.2
Marykskiy	80	80	0.7	80	80	0.7	80	80	0.9
Dashoguzskiy	80	80	0.6	80	80	0.6	80	80	0.9
Balkanskiy	49	49	1.4	20	20	1.6	41	41	2.5
Lebapskiy	80	80	0.6	80	80	0.8	80	80	1.0
Correlation	−99	−99		−94	−94		−92	−92	

Source: Own calculations based on data from Turkmenmillichasbat.

Note: * Correlations for shares of central taxes assigned to the oblast and GDP per capita in the oblast in the respective year.

Table 6.15 Revenue shares for centrally assigned taxes, Uzbekistan*

Veloyat	2001				2002			
	VAT	EPT	PIT	GDP per capita	VAT	EPT	PIT	GDP per capita
Karakalpakstan republic	100	100	100	0.41	100	100	100	0.38
Andijanskaya	100	100	100	0.87	100	100	100	0.82
Buharskaya	23	20	50	1.01	32	20	50	1.06
Djizzakskaya	100	100	100	0.64	100	100	100	0.68
Kashkadaryinskaya	69	64	100	0.77	100	99	100	0.78
Navoinskaya	58	54	50	1.36	72	54	50	1.54
Namanganskaya	100	100	100	0.61	100	100	100	0.59
Samarkandskaya	100	100	100	0.69	100	100	100	0.69
Surhandarjinskaya	100	100	100	0.76	100	100	100	0.76
Syrdarjinskaya	100	100	100	0.85	100	100	100	0.78
Tashkentskaya	56	51	50	1.04	61	56	50	1.05
Fergananskaya	39	34	100	0.85	80	65	100	0.84
Horezmskaya	100	100	100	0.75	100	100	100	0.71
Tashkent	14	10	16	1.75	6	6	17	1.62
Correlation*	−76	−75	−89		−80	−82	−89	

Source: own calculations; Nuriev (2003: 11, 22).

Note: * Correlations for shares of central taxes assigned to the oblast and GDP per capita in the oblast in the respective year.

Summary

In a comparative view, despite high quantitative decentralization indicators in all three countries, at least 85 per cent to 90 per cent of local budget revenue depends on decisions taken by the central government. Genuine local taxes, although introduced by all countries, play a minor role in financing and depend on centrally set rules. A common feature of all three countries is the substantial reliance on revenue-sharing mechanisms. This situation is undesirable in terms of fiscal decentralization, since heavy reliance on variable taxes affected by frequent changes of the central tax policy exposes the local budgets to uncertainty and poor predictability of fiscal flows. This implies a lack of fiscal choice depriving local government of accountability and incentives. By and by, the countries approved provisions that allowed sub-national governments to keep the revenue received above the plan. However, due to underfunding and/or limited spending autonomy de facto no incentives arose from these provisions.

Intergovernmental transfers/grants

The two major dimensions of intergovernmental transfers include vertical (central versus local government) and horizontal (units of the same levels of government) imbalances. The system of transfers should ensure not only the correction of vertical/horizontal imbalances, but also the predictability, understandability and timeliness of local budgeting. Strict and democratically legitimized rules of transfer assignment should leave no room for corruption and illegal negotiation processes. Stability in transfer setting is a prerequisite for incentive creation at the local level. If, in the case of donor regions, additional revenue is completely withdrawn by the centre or, in the case of receiving regions, deficit-covering by automatic central transfers is anticipated, then no incentives are created.

Inherited from the Soviet system, the intergovernmental transfers at the early stages of transition in Kazakhstan ('*subsidies*'),[14] Turkmenistan ('*positive transfers*') and Uzbekistan ('*subsidies*') represented either general-purpose or targeted intergovernmental grants. The vertical imbalance was solved with the help of gap-filling intergovernmental transfers that could be negotiated during the fiscal year. The amount of the transfers has been fixed every budget year anew. The system of transfers was supplemented with a mutual offset mechanism and soft budget constraints set by the central budgets, especially in Turkmenistan and Uzbekistan. Although the early budget reforms pushed the countries to distinguish between general-purpose and targeted grants, equalization transfers were still not formula-based and did not account for regional particularities, such as changes in population numbers. Even today, no clear mechanisms of targeted funds allocation have been set up. The calculation of 'needed expenditure' is still based on extrapolation or on last year's expenditure. Standards and norms for cost calculation in service provision are missing, which creates a high risk for underfunded mandates at the local level.

Regional disparities

The need for intergovernmental transfers stems from differences in the regional fiscal capacities. In the resource-based economies of Central Asia these disparities are mostly based on the uneven geographic distribution of the natural resources.

Kazakhstan

In Kazakhstan the disparities of per capita regional fiscal capacities have intensified since the development of the country's oil reserves accelerated after 1998. High average per capita income figures characterize those areas where oil was extracted, while the corresponding figures for the other regions remained very low. The regions of Jambyl, Almaty, South Kazakhstan, North Kazakhstan and Akmola remain constantly poor. In 1998 the GDP per capita in Atyraurskaya oblast was five times higher than in Jambylskaya oblast. Until 2004, the regional disparities driven by the oil boom increased further; the coefficient of variation

99

Table 6.16 GDP per capita by oblast, Kazakhstan (indexes)

	1998	1999	2000	2001	2002	2003	2004
Kazakhstan	1.00	1.00	1.00	1.00	1.00	1.00	1.00
Akmola	0.53	0.73	0.61	0.64	0.64	0.56	0.58
Aktyubinsk	1.17	1.02	1.00	1.00	1.13	1.08	1.20
Almaty	0.54	0.48	0.45	0.48	0.48	0.43	0.42
Atyrau	2.08	2.38	3.42	3.33	3.72	4.05	4.18
East Kazakhstan	1.09	1.03	0.90	0.85	0.78	0.72	0.74
Jambyl	0.41	0.36	0.33	0.31	0.36	0.35	0.35
West Kazakhstan	0.85	0.96	1.16	1.21	1.40	1.20	1.28
Karaganda	1.18	1.25	1.21	1.10	1.03	1.03	1.04
Kzyl-Orda	1.05	1.01	0.95	0.85	0.76	0.79	0.81
Kostanai	0.57	0.49	0.55	0.56	0.79	0.71	0.81
Mangystau	1.68	2.05	2.47	2.26	2.84	2.18	2.38
Pavlodar	1.49	1.13	1.23	1.23	1.10	1.15	1.23
North Kazakhstan	0.75	0.75	0.58	0.68	0.60	0.55	0.59
South Kazakhstan	0.44	0.45	0.49	0.50	0.44	0.42	0.38
Almaty City	2.39	2.34	2.03	2.26	2.02	2.32	1.88
Astana	1.44	1.81	1.82	1.73	1.76	2.05	2.03
Min	0.41	0.36	0.33	0.31	0.36	0.35	0.35
Max	2.08	2.38	3.42	3.33	3.72	4.05	4.18
Difference	5.10	6.58	10.42	10.79	10.28	11.64	12.04
Coefficient of variation	0.52	0.57	0.69	0.68	0.74	0.79	0.78

Source: Own calculations based on data from the Statistical Ccommittee of Kazakhstan.

of GDP per capita increased from 0.52 to 0.78, while the difference between minimum and maximum GDP per capita climbed to 12.

Uzbekistan

Regional disparities in Uzbekistan are less severe, but show the same trend. In Uzbekistan, natural resource extraction so far contributes only a minor part to the regional disparities. The major source of regional disparities is the distorted industrial structure inherited from the Soviet Union, which created some industrial giants located in strategically selected regions. Thus the oblasts Buhara, Navoi,

Tashkent and Tashkent city remain above the national average. The development of Tashkent city is defined by its status as capital, the oblast Navoi is a centre of gold and uranium mines. Oil and gas production so far are dispersed throughout the country, and the same is true for the agrarian sector. The autonomous republic of Karakalpakstan and the oblast of Horezm are burdened with the Aral Sea problems. The oblast Suhardarjo located at the Afghan border has only limited access to transport infrastructure and the densely populated oblast Ferghana lacks land resources.

During transition, the increasing importance of the extracting industry against the background of a declining manufacturing industry became the driving force of the uneven regional development. From 1997 to 2004 the coefficient of variation of regional disparities increased from 0.31 in 1997 to 0.46 in 2004. With natural

Table 6.17 GDP per capita by oblast, Uzbekistan (indexes)

	1997	1998	1999	2001	2002	2003	2004
Uzbekistan	1.00	1.00	1.00	1.00	1.00	1.00	1.00
Karakalpakstan republic	0.53	0.53	0.58	0.41	0.38	0.42	0.42
Andijanskaya	0.79	0.79	0.87	0.87	0.82	0.76	0.74
Buharskaya	0.93	0.95	1.19	1.01	1.06	1.11	1.08
Djizzakskaya	0.66	0.63	0.66	0.64	0.68	0.80	0.77
Kashkadaryinskaya	0.92	0.78	0.74	0.77	0.78	0.74	0.75
Navoinskaya	1.14	1.10	1.22	1.36	1.54	1.66	1.70
Namanganskaya	0.65	0.55	0.59	0.61	0.59	0.60	0.45
Samarkandskaya	0.64	0.68	0.72	0.69	0.69	0.64	0.60
Surhandarjinskaya	0.60	0.66	0.70	0.76	0.76	0.69	0.66
Syrdarjinskaya	0.82	0.81	0.86	0.85	0.78	0.78	0.77
Tashkentskaya	0.94	0.93	0.93	1.04	1.05	1.01	1.03
Ferganskaya	0.93	0.87	0.90	0.85	0.84	0.79	0.76
Horezmskaya	0.92	0.88	0.97	0.75	0.71	0.69	0.67
Tashkent	1.57	1.59	1.65	1.75	1.62	1.67	1.68
Max	1.57	0.59	1.65	1.75	1.62	1.67	1.70
Min	0.53	0.53	0.58	0.41	0.38	0.42	0.42
Difference	2.95	2.08	2.11	3.30	4.03	3.92	4.02
Coefficient of variation	0.31	0.32	0.33	0.38	0.39	0.42	0.46

Source: Nuritdinov (2005).

resource extraction gathering pace in the coming years, regional disparities will increase further, following the Kazakh path.

Turkmenistan

With respect to Turkmenistan, limitations on regional GDP data allow only an approximation of regional disparities. Here we use fiscal capacity, i.e. major revenue assigned to the local budgets (for simplicity we assume that 100 per cent of revenue is collected by the local budgets) without transfers, as a proxy for disparities. Over the past decade, the regional development in Turkmenistan has been driven by gas extraction activity, mainly concentrated in the Amu Darya Basin and near the Caspian Sea. The gas sector enterprise became a major contributor to Turkmenistan's consolidated budget (47 per cent in 2003 and 34 per cent in 2004).[15] Unfortunately, the revenue of local budgets is not perfect in relation to the economic development of the respective regions. Major taxes assigned to the local budgets are paid centrally, still based on the registration principle of the big enterprises like 'Turkmengaz', 'Turkmenneftegaz' and 'Turkmenneft'. Thus, although Maryyskiy and Akhalskiy velayats are the places where the natural gas is extracted, the revenue flows into Ashgabad and Balkanskiy local budgets. The tax from the use of minerals is collected mainly to the Akhalskiy and Balkanskiy velayats.

There are significant disparities in the distribution of per capita revenue that are sometimes inversely correlated with expenditure needs. The largest expenditure needs are in Lepubskiy, Maryyskiy and Dashoguzskiy velayats due to the high number of administrative units and population density. Furthermore, the expenditure needs of Lepubskiy and Dashuguzkiy velayat are growing at faster rates.[16] At the same time, the highest local fiscal revenue per capita are in Ashgabad and Balkanskiy velayat, while the fiscal capacities of Maryyskiy, Dashoguzskiy and Lepubskiy velayats are limited (Table 6.18).

Vertical imbalances

For the period under consideration, the indicators of vertical balance (shares of all local revenue net of transfer to local expenditure) in Uzbekistan and Kazakhstan were comparatively lower than in Turkmenistan.[17] All three countries have exhibited an improvement of this indicator during recent years (Table 6.19). Most interestingly, this process was accompanied by a further increase in regional disparities. The latter had the highest magnitude in Kazakhstan. More narrow definitions of vertical imbalance, like the mismatch between genuine local revenue and expenditure, demonstrate very substantial imbalances for all three countries. Taking into account the level of genuine local revenue available to the local governments, the vertical balances of Uzbekistan will be around 0.15, for Turkmenistan it would be close to 0.05. Recent tax innovations (2002) in Kazakhstan allowed it to reach a level of approximately 0.14.

Table 6.18 Local revenue by oblast, Turkmenistan (thousand manat per capita)

	2001			2002			2003		
	EPT	VAT	Other revenue	EPT	VAT	Other revenue	EPT	VAT	Other revenue
Akhal	89	235	299	71	167	425	71	167	686
Ashgabad	631	988	463	1,406	1,173	470	516	839	812
Maryyskiy	45	128	551	46	124	482	34	123	736
Dashoguzskiy	29	69	516	27	79	512	23	90	744
Balkanskiy	223	607	528	366	684	604	674	986	798
Lepubskiy	9	34	526	33	79	646	115	198	735
Total	129	260	490	246	295	523	170	304	745
Variations	1.39	1.10	0.19	1.68	1.17	0.16	1.18	1.00	0.06
Min	9	34	299	27	79	425	23	90	686
Max	631	988	551	1,406	1,173	646	674	986	812
Max/Min	73	29	2	51	15	2	30	11	1

Source: Turkmenmillichasbat (2005).

Note: Other revenue does not include transfers; data limitation does not allow us to analyze horizontal imbalances with ex-ante fiscal revenue.

Table 6.19 Vertical imbalance structure

	1991	1995	1998	1999	2000	2001	2002	2003	2004
Turkmenistan	0.50*	n/a	n/a	n/a	0.55	0.65	0.56	0.55	n/a
Uzbekistan	n/a	0.89	0.74	0.87	0.81	0.83	0.82	0.80	0.80
Kazakhstan	n/a	n/a	0.71	0.86	0.89	0.88	0.80	0.76	0.64

Source: Own calculations based on the data of Ministries of Finance of Kazakhstan, Uzbekistan and Turkmenistan.

Note: * Turkmenmillichasbat (2005: 27).

Kazakhstan made several attempts to develop a methodology for calculating transfers. The first one took place during the budgetary reform of 1999, when the calculation process started to be unofficially based on Resolution No. 529/99 (Wooster 2000). The second attempt happened in 2004 with Resolution No. 916 concerning the prognosis of official transfers and Law No. 602 concerning the volumes of official transfers 2005 to 2007. The new Budget Code for the first time established the volume of transfers for three years, thus providing a greater predictability of revenue at the local level, fewer grounds for corruption during the negotiation process, and better incentives for revenue raising at the local level. In fact, the legislation concerning the calculation is poorly enforced and can be said to have a mere declarative character. According to local *hokims* and governors, in practice, transfers are still just covering the budget gap.[18] Targeted transfers, however, are often used as a kind of flexible instrument for financing different funds and 'private' joint stock companies (like the JSC 'National Innovation Fund' or the JSC 'International Airport of Astana City') as quasi-budget institutions. The utilization of these funds is hard to trace.[19] However, the treasury regularly publishes cases that demonstrate how money declared as spent on a certain measure is, in fact, saved and stays with the local budgets (Schynbekov 2005).

In Uzbekistan, at the time of the 2000 budgetary reform, two kinds of grants were defined, namely positive transfers and subsidies. The first constitutes an equalization transfer. The second are targeted transfers, the objectives of which should be defined by higher levels of the government. Furthermore, there exists a non-transparent heading 'mutual settlement grant', which (as in Russia[20]) plays a non-transparent correction role during budget execution. The positive transfers of Uzbekistan are based on *ad hoc* coverage of the deficit. Subsidies, according to Uzbek authors (Nuriev 2003), have a 'subjective character' and lack concrete objectives, since regional programs are not elaborated. All transfers are still to be negotiated either during the budget process or unofficially during the fiscal year. In Turkmenistan, the same characteristics of intergovernmental transfers can be observed, albeit with a still higher amount of discretionary decisions taken at the central level.

In spite of certain improvements in budget legislation, the transfer systems of Kazakhstan, Turkmenistan and Uzbekistan poorly address the issues of vertical imbalances. Still not based on regional formulas and standards and norms for cost calculation at the local level, transfers do not ensure full funding of the local services to be provided to the population according to the national standards. This worsens the accountability of local administrations substantially. The main local tasks of education and healthcare are chronically underfunded and their functioning has significantly worsened over time.[21] State programs are simply not implemented at the local level because of underfunding.[22] Additionally, the transfer system is not transparent and thus does not create incentives for revenue mobilization at the local level. In Uzbekistan and Turkmenistan, the transparency is aggravated by the presence of discretionary mutual offset mechanisms. In both countries, the problem of underfunding is often solved with the 'voluntary' help of local state and even private enterprises (for example, Myradova *et al.* 2006) – a highly undesirable result in terms of creating a business-friendly environment.

Horizontal imbalances

The second important issue that should be addressed with intergovernmental grants are the horizontal imbalances between the same levels of the budget. They are usually caused by non-homogeneous distribution of natural resources, problems of certain regions with climate and topography, and other regional peculiarities that are responsible for differing regional fiscal capacities. The correction of horizontal fiscal imbalances faces a trade-off: on the one hand, equity is welcomed as a means of poverty-fighting; on the other hand, excessive equalizing reduces incentives for increasing local productivity and labor migration, and thus fosters poverty in the long term.

Table 6.20 shows that the variation of regional per capita revenue before transfers to Kazakhstan and Turkmenistan has been substantial. After accounting for transfers,[23] this indicator shows an excessive equalization. With the help of intergovernmental transfers, the coefficient of variation in Kazakhstan was reduced by half, from 1.06 to 0.56 in 2004. The latter became possible partially due to the system of withdrawals and subventions introduced in 1999. In Turkmenistan, the effect of intergovernmental transfers was less, cutting the coefficient of variation from 0.76 to 0.24. In Uzbekistan the variation of regional per capita revenue is less severe before transfers. Accordingly, equalization after transfers is most obvious: in 2003, intergovernmental transfers assignment resulted in a reduction of the coefficient of variation of revenue from 0.44 before to 0.12 after transfers.

The excessive equalization of regions observed in Uzbekistan and Turkmenistan may be considered as a heritage of Soviet times. In the early stages of transition this excessive equalization could be justified to alleviate the distributive effects resulting from the severe output decline. That may still be a feature for the three countries under consideration. From the incentive point of view however, the degree of equalization in Turkmenistan and Uzbekistan is disappointing and intensifies credibility problems of the centre concerning the withdrawal of local over-plan revenue.

Table 6.20 Coefficient of variation of regional per capita revenue by oblast

	1996	1997	1998	1999	2000	2001	2002	2003	2004	2005
Turkmenistan										
Revenues before transfers						0.77	0.58	0.76		
Revenues after transfers						0.26	0.15	0.24		
*Uzbekistan***										
Revenues before transfers	0.36	031	0.26	0.39	0.31	0.30	0.35	0.44	0.38	
Revenues after transfers	0.17	0.20	n/a	0.23	0.16	0.09	0.11	0.12	0.18	
*Kazakhstan**										
Revenues before transfers			0.45				1.14	1.09	1.06	1.02
Revenues after transfers			0.32				0.71	0.67	0.56	0.53

Source: Ministries of Finance of Kazakhstan, Turkmenistan and Uzbekistan; own calculations.

Notes: * Not taking into account Astana city. ** Not taking into account Tashkent city.

Conclusions

In Central Asia, we find high quantitative indicators of fiscal decentralization, but fiscal autonomy at the local level is close to zero, on the expenditure as well as on the revenue side. The transfer system lacks transparency and predictability. This is partly due to the legal transition status of the countries. Many new laws still lack supporting administrative rules, and thus enforcement is weak. However, the centralized state structure also plays a role. Administrative decentralization, which delegates competence to the local level is falling behind in all three countries. Most parameters of the budget are set centrally. Especially in Turkmenistan and Uzbekistan, information and control rights rest completely at the central level. From a comparative perspective, Kazakhstan is well ahead of the other two countries, which lag behind on any terms. Compared to other transition countries, however, Kazakhstan is also falling behind.

Clearly fiscal decentralization in Central Asia so far does not follow the Chinese model. Although as in China political parties would be strong enough to execute effective control at the local level, at the centre there seems to exist a deep mistrust of delegation of information and authority. But it is just this delegation that makes incentive mechanisms work. If fiscal decentralization in Central Asia is to render positive effects on growth, governance and corruption, the design of fiscal decentralization has to be changed carefully, together with administrative and political decentralization, without endangering control.

Notes

1 A longer version of this chapter is available as *Osteuropa Institut Working Paper 261* (April 2006). The authors gratefully acknowledge financial support from Volkswagen Foundation.
2 For instance, after the break-up in 1992, Uzbekistan lost 18% of its GDP due to transfers from Moscow. Transfers from the USSR budget to Kazakhstan constituted nearly 14% of GDP in 1990 (Economist Intelligence Unit (2003) *Kazakhstan: country profile,* Y 40251, p. 30, available at www.eiu.com).
3 Social spending obligations of local governments had to be increased due to release of state-owned enterprises (SOEs) from 'objects of social infrastructure' that provided local infrastructure services in Soviet times (for instance' roads, heating, electricity, sewerage, health services, etc.). The states also had to finance pension systems.
4 The registration principle implies that the tax is collected according to the place of the official registry of the enterprise.
5 For example, the right to dismiss *Akym* has never being executed by any *Maslikhat*. Source: RGP Institute for Economic Research (2005) 'Fiscal Decentralization in Kazakhstan', Almaty, mimeo.
6 There are six hiakims of velayats, 47 hiakims of etraps, seven hiakims of city subordination etraps, and 12 hiakims in the cities of velayat subordination.
7 Local representative assembly in Turkmenistan, Economist Intelligence Unit (2003) *Turkmenistan: Country profile*, Y 38183, p. 31, available at www.eiu.com.
8 These included The State Fund of Development of Agriculture (1996), The State Fund of Development of Ashgabad (1999), The State Fund of Development of Health Care in Turkmenistan (1998), and The State Fund of Golden Century Development of Turkmenistan (2000).

9   Peter Epstein and Matthew Winter (2004) *Assessment of Intergovernmental Relations and Local Governance in the Republic of Uzbekistan*, The Urban Institute, Washington, DC, February, p. 37.
10 Evidence suggests that elections at all levels are highly falsified and often manipulated.
11 A rather high negative correlation coefficient of expenditure per capita and population by oblast in each country is peculiar for Uzbekistan: it is close to –0.8. For Kazakhstan, it increased in magnitude after the reform and reached –0.79 in 2000, before declining in 2004 to –0.53. For Turkmenistan, it is still negative but less significant, for example, –0.39 for 2001 and –0.38 for 2003. At the same time, the variation of distribution of population among oblasts is the highest in Kazakhstan, and the lowest in Turkmenistan.
12 In Turkmenistan, only few enterprises were privatized. In mid-2000, 200 small-scale companies out of 4300 were privatized. For the medium-scale enterprises this ratio constituted six out of 280. Source Economist Intelligence Unit (2003) *Turkmenistan: Country profile,* Y 38183, p. 26, available at www.eiu.com.
13 The levels were set according to the minimum wage level after 1998. Prior to that, the levels were set in absolute terms.
14 IMF observance of standards and codes of Fiscal transparency in Kazakhstan 'The role and types of the transfers were not clearly specified by law. However, evidence suggests that some of the transfers were conditional (for instance, contingent on satisfactory tax collection standards being achieved), the others appeared to be block transfers, and the investment earmarked transfers'.
15 VAT collected from the gas sector in 2003 was 57% of total VAT collections. For 2004, the rate was 29%. In 2003, ENPT collections from the gas sector reached 61% of the total ENPT collections. For 2004 they reached 33%.
16 The size of Turkmenistan local budgets has increased unevenly during recent years. In comparison to 2001, the local budgets expenditure increased by 75.8% for Akhalskiy veloyat, by 36.6% for Ashgabad city, by 38.8% for Maryyskiy velayat, by 53.4% for Dashoguzskiy velayat, by 74.5% for Balkanskiy velayat, and by 94.1% for Lepabskiy velayat.
17 Vertical imbalance is measured as the share of local revenue without transfers to local expenditure. A vertical imbalance coefficient equal to one means perfect vertical balance However, we should mention biases in the vertical imbalance measure we use. First, the calculated coefficient of vertical imbalance might be underestimated due to local budget arrears and substantial quasi-fiscal activities, which were especially common in the early 1990s. Furthermore, the vertical imbalance might be larger taking into account the still limited possibilities of local governments to borrow from sources other than higher-level budgets and soft constraints that existed until recently. This issue was most acute for Uzbekistan and Turkmenistan.
18 Based on personal interviews in Almaty, Karaganda and Astana oblasts.
19 (2005) 'Budget Process in the Caspian Countries: Experience of Kazakhstan and Azerbaidjan', *Policy Studies*, 7(2), April (Public Policy Research Center, Almaty).
20 For Russia, Tabata (1998) states that 'the nature of transfers included in "mutual settlements" is not clear at all'.
21 Economist Intelligence Unit (2003) *Turkmenistan: Country profile*, Y 38183, pp. 16–24, available at www.eiu.com; Economist Intelligence Unit (2003) *Uzbekistan: country profile*, pp. 13–19, available at www.eiu.com; Economist Intelligence Unit (2003) *Kazakhstan: country profile*, pp. 21–8, available at www.eiu.com; CER (2004) *Major directions of reform of government bodies at the local level in Uzbekistan*, Report 2004/05, Tashkent, p. 34.
22 Surveys undertaken in 2002 among *hokims* in Kazakhstan showed that the number of settlements without medical care, which according to the Ministry of Health

should have been reduced to 112, in fact still stood at 1094 (Institut Ekonomiceskich Issledovanij 2003: 33).

23 Due to data limitations, we did not distinguish between equalizing non-targeted and targeted transfers here, although this is formally not correct. In the absence of a clear assignment of tasks and program financing, we found it hard to distinguish between targeted and non-targeted grants even if the data were available. Due to the inclusion of targeted transfers, equalization will be overestimated.

Part III

MICROECONOMIC ANALYSIS OF REDISTRIBUTION

7

REDISTRIBUTION OF OIL
REVENUE IN KAZAKHSTAN[1]

Boris Najman, Richard Pomfret,
Gaël Raballand and Patricia Sourdin

Kazakhstan's economy has been driven by an oil boom since the discovery of large new oilfields coincided with the upturn of world oil prices at the turn of the century. This chapter uses high-quality microeconomic data (the national survey of the expenditure of 12,000 households) to examine Kazakhstan's experience. We assess the extent to which the benefits from the oil boom are retained in the oil-producing regions, or spread evenly across the national economy, or are concentrated in the main metropolitan centre, Almaty, which is geographically far from any oilfields but home to the country's elite. We then analyse the data to determine the transmission mechanisms (higher wages, social transfers or informal income) from the oil boom to household expenditure.

The cross-country evidence suggests that there may be pitfalls to exploiting the abundance of natural resource for national benefit. Sachs and Warner (1995) found a negative relationship between resource abundance and economic growth in cross-country regressions. Subsequent contributions have refined the debate of oil as a curse, establishing that the relationship is conditional (on variables proxying for institutions or on democracy) and that the negative relationship is stronger for oil and minerals than for agriculture.[2] Papyrakis and Gerlagh (2004) obtain a negative coefficient on their natural resource variable (share of minerals in GDP) in a simple conditional convergence growth regression, but the coefficient becomes positive when measures of corruption, openness and schooling are added to the right-hand side. This fits with the observation that successful resource-rich countries like Norway, Australia or Malaysia have open economies and low levels of corruption, but does not address the issue of whether resource abundance has fuelled corruption in countries like Nigeria or Venezuela.

The Sachs–Warner results also beg the next questions. What transmission mechanisms make a resource boom a curse? How is oil revenue redistributed in an oil economy? How should redistribution mechanisms be designed to benefit the population as a whole? As oil exports increase, discontent in oil-producing regions and in the poorest regions of the country grow, as oil-producing regions wish to retain a higher share of oil revenue while the poorest regions want a larger redistribution of the revenue.[3]

The main innovation of Chapters 7 and 8 is the use of microeconomic (household survey) data to analyse the impact of an oil boom. Kazakhstan is an interesting case study because the oil boom has a clear starting point, the discovery of large new oilfields in the late 1990s coinciding with a sharp increase in the world price of oil, and its extent was unexpected. Comparable high quality household survey data for 1996, before the start of the oil boom, and since 2001 can be used to assess the extent to which the benefits from the oil boom were retained in the oil-producing regions, spread evenly across the national economy, or concentrated in the two metropolitan centres (Almaty, the former capital and current financial centre and home to the country's elite, and Astana, the capital since 1997).

The first section, extending the analysis in Chapter 2, briefly describes the oil sector in Kazakhstan, dating the oil boom and assessing its importance for the economy. The second section presents data on poverty and living standards figures before and after the oil boom, and uses the household survey data to identify regional differences in the impact of the oil boom on living standards. The third section defines three redistribution mechanisms, and gives a preliminary assessment of the importance of each of the mechanisms in Kazakhstan. The fourth section concludes the chapter.

Kazakhstan before and after the oil boom

Oil has had a strong positive impact on Kazakhstan's economic growth. After a miserable economic performance during the 1990s (Pomfret 2005), real GDP achieved double-digit growth in the early 2000s (Figure 7.1).

Oil production generates major revenue for Kazakhstan, especially since the tax code was amended in 2004.[4] Since 2000, current fiscal receipts from the oil sector, excluding one-off payments, have accounted for almost 20 per cent of

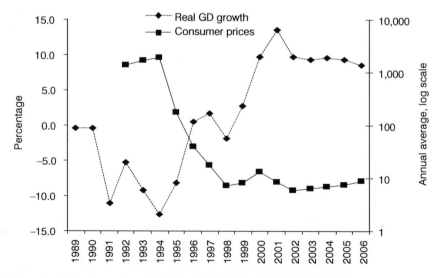

Figure 7.1 Output growth and inflation in Kazakhstan 1989–2006 (%)

Source: European Bank for Reconstruction and Development: *Transition Report*, 2006.

general government revenue (IMF 2004: 18). In 2003, oil exports brought almost $2 billion to the budget revenue. By 2010, revenue stemming from oil exports should reach more than $7 billion, and the IMF is forecasting undiscounted revenue of $270 billion over the next 45 years (IMF 2004: 27), equivalent to $99 billion discounted at 5 per cent or $6,600 per capita.

Oil production in Kazakhstan is geographically concentrated in two oblasts, Mangistau and Atyrau, on the shores of the Caspian Sea in the country's far west (see Map 2.1). After the start of extraction operations in Tengiz, Atyrau became the country's main oil centre. The huge offshore Caspian field of Kashagan, whose operational base is in Atyrau oblast, is often described as the largest new oilfield discovery for over 30 years, with an estimated 45 billion barrels of which 8 billion to 13 billion are recoverable with existing technologies. Unexplored areas of the north Caspian may also contain large reserves. In the last decade, Aksai in West Kazakhstan, with the Karachaganak oil and (primarily) gas field, Aktobe, and Kyzylorda with the Kumkol field in central Kazakhstan, have emerged as new (or relatively new) oil-producing regions, although oil production in these oblasts is expected to remain limited. In sum, although the oil-producing areas are not all isolated from pre-existing towns, they are far from the country's metropolitan centres of Almaty (in the extreme south-east) and Astana (in the centre-north). For a detailed map of oil-producing fields see Map 2.1.

Poverty and living standards in Kazakhstan before and during the oil boom

This section uses two sources of information, regional descriptive statistics and LSMS data, to provide preliminary assessments of the impact of oil revenue. Oil-producing regions seem not to have experienced any sustained employment growth, and poverty and inequality remain worse in oil-producing regions than in non-oil regions. The most surprising results from analysis of the LSMS data is that in 2002, in the midst of an oil boom, being located in the oil-producing western region is not associated with higher living standards, and indeed the relative position of households in those regions was worse than in 1996.

The direct employment impact of the oil boom is limited. In 2002 the unemployment rate in all the producing regions was above the national average; direct employment in the oil sector was estimated to be less than 50,000 people, including employees working in the refining sector, which is equivalent to less than 1 per cent of Kazakhstan's active population of 7.4 million (Abdiev 2003: 478).[5] Oil production expands construction activities, but only on a temporary basis, for example, construction of the CPC pipeline was positive for employment in western Kazakhstan between 1998 and 2000 but after the inauguration of the pipeline building activities decreased (see Map 2.2).

Except in Aktöbe oblast, the poverty headcount in all oil-producing regions remains above the national average (Table 7.1). The highest poverty rates among the five oil-producing oblasts are in the oldest, and largest, producers, Mangistau and Atyrau. Despite the importance of oil production in Mangistau, almost 40 per

Regional stub ⇒ regions with higher activity exports
B. NAJMAN, R. POMFRET, G. RABALLAND AND P. SOURDIN
are also poorer ⇒ so will safge

of the population of the oblast is poor, and Mangistau has a higher poverty count than even Jambyl, the oblast with the lowest regional product per ta. In contrast, in Astana and Almaty cities only 2.2 per cent and 4.1 per cent of the population lives below the poverty line (UNDP 2004: 58).

In all of Kazakhstan's oblasts the poverty headcount is higher in rural areas than in urban areas, but the rural–urban difference is especially pronounced in the oil-producing oblasts, where the poverty headcount is two to three times higher in rural compared to urban areas. In the oil-producing regions, cities may benefit from oil rents, for example, in Mangistau oblast the town of Aktau has a poverty headcount of 18 per cent which is well below the regional average of 40 per cent. At the narrower geographical level, producing oil in a rayon is not a guarantee of lower poverty. In the three oblasts mixing oil-producing and non-oil-producing rayons (Aktöbe, Kyzylorda and West Kazakhstan), only four out of 10 rural oil-producing rayons experience less poverty than the regional average poverty headcount (Ivashenko 2004).

Inequality has grown substantially in oil-producing regions. These regions lie above the national average (Table 7.2). The discrepancy between poor and rich is especially acute in Atyrau region, and to a lesser extent in Mangistau region

Table 7.1 Urban and rural poverty rates by oblast, Kazakhstan, 2002

	Total	Urban	Rural
Kazakhstan average	24.2	15,6	34.7
Aktöbe	22.6	6.9	43.8
Atyrau	34.1	27.5	44.4
Kyzylorda	32.3	22.1	48.0
Mangystau	39.8	28.8	84.6
West Kazakhstan	28.0	11.4	39.0
Astana city	2.2	2.2	–
Almaty city	4.1	4.1	–
Akmola	18.6	15.0	21.3
Almaty oblast	36.3	25.8	40.8
East Kazakhstan	20.0	13.9	27.9
Jambyl	35.8	31.3	39.1
Karagandy	19.3	16.0	33.1
Kostanay	22.3	12.9	33.4
North Kazakhstan	14.3	4.3	20.7
Pavlodar	21.6	12.2	34.9
South Kazakhstan	27.5	22.3	30.4

Source: UNDP (2004: 58, 62).

dot from exchng rate

Table 7.2 Gini coefficients, Kazakhstan, 2002

	Gini coefficient
Kazakhstan average	0.33
Aktöbe	0.34
Atyrau	0.43
Qyzylorda	0.32
Manghystau	0.36
West Kazakhstan	0.35
Astana city	0.31
Almaty city	0.29
Jambyl	0.29
South Kazakhstan	0.28

Source: Abdiev (2003: 147).

The remainder of this section reports the results of applying a human capital model to explain the determinants of per capita household expenditure in Kazakhstan during the 1990s transition era and during a year from the sustained growth period (2002).[6] Data availability in the 1990s was hampered by the poor quality of the inherited household budget surveys. External researchers have relied almost exclusively on the one-off 1996 LSMS survey, and the starting point for the present exercise is the analysis of that dataset by Anderson and Pomfret (2002a, 2003). In 2001 the National Statistical Agency revised the household budget survey using sampling techniques and questionnaires comparable to those of the LSMS, although the data are now collected continuously and reported quarterly and annually rather than for the two-week period of the 1996 survey. This chapter reports results using the 2002 data.

In all of the formerly centrally planned economies, the transition to more market-based systems was accompanied by changes in labour markets and in the determinants of household expenditure levels. Human capital variables, which are consistently significant determinants of earnings in established market economies, became more important. In Central Asia this pattern was accompanied during the 1990s by a large increase in the cost (in terms of lower per capita household expenditure) of large family size, especially the presence of children. Large regional differences in household expenditure, *ceteris paribus*, also indicated that national labour markets were not yet established in Central Asia.[7] In Anderson and Pomfret (2002a, 2003), these three sets of variables (education, family size and location) were consistently significant in various specifications, while other demographic characteristics such as the ethnicity, age, health or marital status of the head of the household were seldom statistically significant and had little explanatory power.

The dependent variable is household expenditure per capita, based on a headcount of household members[8] and the reported expenditure on goods (excluding vehicles), food, health, education and other services, housing, utilities, communication and transportation.[9] In the estimating equation, per capita household expenditure is determined by the level of human capital, the number of household members, and the household's location. The education level attained by the head or the highest-educated household member is assumed to be indicative of the household's human capital.[10] Household composition is measured by three variables describing the number of children under the age of 18, the number of elderly, and the number of non-elderly adults in the household.[11] Location of the household is measured by five region-specific dummy variables, with Almaty, the largest city, as the omitted category for regional location: the Central region is Akmola and Karaghandy oblasts and Astana City, the South is Jambyl, Kyzylorda and South Kazakhstan oblasts, the North is Kostanai, Pavlodar and North Kazakhstan oblasts, the East is East Kazakhstan and Almaty oblasts, but not Almaty city, and the West is Aqtöbe, Atyrau, West Kazakhstan and Mangistau oblasts, where most of the country's oil-production is located (see Figure 7.1).

Summary statistics for the two years are reported in Table 7.3. The main change in location is an increase in the proportion of households in the oil-producing western region and a decline in the proportion in the Centre and North. The number of people per household increased slightly from 3.59 to 3.69, due to an increase in working age adults per household and a smaller increase in the elderly, partially offset by a smaller number of children.[12] In the education categories the major change has been the fall in the portion reporting vocational-technical education.[13] The proportion of households without anyone who completed secondary education is higher in 2002 than in 1996, although there appear to be some anomalous entries in this category.[14]

Table 7.4 reports the regression results for 1996 and 2002. Although the datasets are not a panel, the sampling techniques were the same and the results for the two years should be comparable.[15] The three groups of variables, which dominated in 1996, remain statistically significant in 2002, but the magnitude of the coefficients changes considerably.

Family size continues to be negatively related to household living standards, but the magnitudes are much smaller in 2002 and there is little distinction between the age groups. Whereas in 1996 having an extra child was the largest cost in terms of lower per capita household expenditure and an elderly person brought the next highest cost, the impact of these two age groups in 2002 differs little from that of an additional working-age adult.

Education remains important. In 2002 having a university or Tecnikum educated person in the household is associated with 6 per cent to 7 per cent higher per capita household expenditure, *ceteris paribus*, than having no one educated beyond completed secondary education. The changes in the magnitudes of the effect of different levels of human capital between 1996 and 2002 are difficult to assess because there is a difference in definition (household head in 1996 versus highest-educated person in 2002) and in control group between the first and last columns of Table 7.4.[16] Nevertheless, it does appear that the returns to greater skill and education levels were lower in 2002, which is surprising.

Table 7.3 Kazakhstan household surveys 1996 and 2002: summary statistics

Variables	1996	2002
Per capita expenditure:	4,963.8 (3,515.3)	112,524 (75,999.7)
Education of most highly educated:		
University (%)	26.8	24.9
Technikum (%)	33.1	32.9
Vocational/technical (%)	26.6	12.9
Completed secondary (%)	7.8	19.9
Incomplete secondary (%)	5.7	9.4
Location of household:		
Central (%)	20.7	19.5
South (%)	18.1	18.8
West (%)	8.5	12.5
North (%)	22.3	19.5
East (%)	21.0	21.0
Almaty city (%)	9.4	8.8
Household composition:		
Number of children	1.3 (1.2)	1.2 (1.2)
Number of elderly	0.4 (0.7)	0.5 (0.7)
Number of non-elderly adults	1.9 (1.1)	2.1 (1.4)
Sample size (households)	1,890	12,000

Notes: Standard deviations of continuous variables are in parentheses. Expenditure is in national currency units (tenge); note that the two surveys' observation periods differ so that the nominal tenge values are not comparable even apart from problems of measuring inflation.

The location variable shows the most striking differences between 1996 and 2002. In 1996 a household located in the North had on average a 30 per cent higher living standard than a similar household in Almaty and a household located in the South had a 45 per cent lower living standard than one in Almaty *ceteris paribus*, while the other regions were not significantly different from Almaty. In 2002 households in all locations outside Almaty had significantly lower living standards than otherwise similar households in Almaty. The difference is still most pronounced, negatively, in the South, but the situation of households in the North and East is significantly worse than Almaty in 2002 whereas they were better off than Almaty households in 1996. The improved position of the Central region (relative to all other regions except Almaty) may have been due to moving the capital to Astana, located in the Centre, and the substantial public construction associated with that decision. The most striking aspect of the location results is that in 2002, in the midst of an oil boom, location in the oil-producing western region is not associated with higher living standards.

Table 7.4 Household expenditure model, Kazakhstan, 1996 and 2002

Variables	1996		2002	
	Coefficient	t-statistic	Coefficient	t-statistic
Intercept	8.54*	89.60	12.19*	488.62
Education:				
University	0 .27*	5.62	0.07*	4.53
Technikum	0.17*	3.63	0.06*	3.97
Vocational/technical training	0.11*	2.56	0.02*	1.13
Completed secondary	−0.001	−0.02	–	–
Location of household:				
Central	−0.04	−0.70	−0.53*	−23.43
South	−0.45*	−8.38	−0.97*	−42.16
West	0.09	1.43	−0.63*	−25.92
North	0.29*	5.67	−0.72*	−31.72
East (not Almaty city)	0.04	0.74	−0.74*	−33.02
Household composition:				
Number of children	−0.17*	−14.04	−0.02*	−5.02
Number of elderly	−0.12*	−3.82	−0.02*	−1.97
Number of non-elderly adults	−0.06*	−4.18	−0.01*	−2.87
R-square	0.30		0.17	
F-statistic	47.14*		223.44	
Sample size	1,890		10,716	

Note: * Significant at the 5% level.

A typology of redistribution oil revenue in an oil economy

In Kazakhstan (as in most oil-exporting countries), oil is produced in few regions of the country: oil is produced in five out of the 14 oblasts, and there are 21 oil-producing rayons out of the country's 158 rayons (cities excluded).[17] Concentration of oil production in a limited number of districts should enable us to assess the preliminary impact of the oil boom in Kazakhstan. Early revenue from the oil boom appears to have benefited cities in non-oil producing regions, whereas people living in rural areas or in oil-producing rayons do not seem to benefit from this rent. Consequently, oil revenue has strengthened the inequality gap between rich and poor people in the country. An assessment of the redistribution mechanisms could partially explain why cities benefit more from oil revenue than urban areas. A similar methodology is used for Azerbaijan in Chapter 8.

Why should oil revenue be redistributed in an oil economy?[18] As Isham *et al.* (2003: 3) point out, oil is a 'point-source' natural resource, which means that it is extracted from a narrow geographic and economic base. First of all, it is worth noting that oil revenue is not wholly redistributed in Kazakhstan. Indeed, a large share of oil revenue is allocated to the NFRK.[19] Second, commentaries on Kazakhstan emphasize the high levels of corruption, particularly associated with the appropriation of oil rents by the elite. Third, oil-producing regions may disproportionately benefit from additional revenue whereas poor regions could be left out of this revenue flow. Growing inequality between regions as a result of an oil boom justifies redirection of oil revenue to the centre, which may ensure efficient redistribution of oil revenue by producing economies of scale in the production of a public good and by insuring against region-specific shocks (Ahmad and Singh 2003: 2–3). However, balance between the oil-producing and the poorest regions of an oil-rich country is difficult to reach; as equalization and stabilization mechanisms performed by the centre start to operate, oil-producing regions express discontent because they wish to keep locally a larger share of oil revenue and poorer regions of the country express discontent because they wish to benefit more from redistribution schemes.

To analyse the redistribution mechanisms in Kazakhstan, we distinguish three categories based on two main questions: who redistributes oil revenue, and how is it organized?

First, *official public redistribution* encompasses taxes and revenue stemming from oil production shared locally as well as financial transfers from the centre. In oil-producing regions, revenue-sharing schemes generally replace financial transfers from the centre, unlike what happens in the poorest regions. Local governments may redistribute oil revenue through social transfers. Regional budgets in oil-producing oblasts have largely benefited from oil revenue. However, transfer mechanisms have been put in place and are increasingly important for lagging regions, especially in the South of the country. Between 1997 and 2002, budget revenue of the five oil-producing regions increased by 280 per cent whereas budget revenue of the other regions increased by 180 per cent (Table 7.5). Regional authorities in oil-producing regions have increasingly used fines and quasi-fiscal policy as a means to increase regional revenue. Previously, central authorities levied greenhouse gas emission rights, but this has become the mandate of regional authorities and, probably as a result, environmental fines increased by 400 per cent in 2004 compared to the previous year. Besides, some taxes are collected locally like social and income taxes, although oil-producing regions transfer a major share of revenue collected – more than 40 per cent of the total expenditure of Mangistau and Atyrau oblasts.

Several regions (oil-producing or not) have succeeded in benefiting from the oil boom revenue. Social expenditure per capita is, on average, higher in oil-producing regions than non-oil producing regions (Figure 7.2). However, Kazakhstan remains a centralized state and local fiscal autonomy in Kazakhstan appears limited (Dabla-Norris *et al.* 2000). Fiscal federalism with revenue-sharing arrangements was tentatively developed (McLure *et al.* 1999), but the implementation seems

Table 7.5 Regional budgets, Kazakhstan, 1997–2002

	1997		2000		2002	
	Balance	*Budget/ GDP*	*Balance*	*Budget/ GDP*	*Balance*	*Budget/ GDP*
Aktöbe	0.98	14.6	1.02	24.5	1.02	17.1
Atyrau	0.98	9.0	1.12	36.1	0.92	22.7
Kyzylorda	1.00	47.9	0.98	40.4	1.03	27.3
Mangistau	0.99	9.6	1.05	32.3	0.94	20.1
West Kazakhstan	0.96	26.3	1.05	18.7	1.00	24.0
Astana city	1.00	74.4	1.00	40.3	0.96	32.9
Almaty city	1.05	8.6	0.99	22.7	1.01	18.6
Akmola	1.02	48.7	1.02	29.8	1.01	31.3
Almaty region	1.00	23.3	1.02	25.2	1.00	30.9
East Kazakhstan	1.01	21.9	1.01	31.2	0.96	22.1
Jambyl	0.99	30.7	1.00	33.5	0.97	42.1
Karaghandy	0.90	15.2	1.13	20.6	0.96	16.9
Kostanaï	0.96	16.5	1.02	16.7	1.00	22.0
Pavlodar	0.92	18.7	1.03	17.0	0.96	20.8
North Kazakhstan	1.00	25.4	1.04	28.1	0.98	29.2
South Kazakhstan	1.00	25.1	0.99	27.6	1.00	30.8
Oil Regions Average	0.99	17.4	1.07	30.7	0.97	22.0
Kazakhstan average	0.99	19.8	1.04	26.6	0.98	23.6

Source: Smailov (2001) and Abdiev (2003).

to vary across regions and criteria to identify benefiting regions are obscure. On average, the share of official transfers in regional revenue is higher in most poor regions (Figure 7.3).[20] Thus, poor regions mainly depend on official transfers from the central authorities. As expected, official transfers do not reach oil-producing regions (except Kyzylorda region). Two facts remain disturbing about the equal redistribution of oil revenue: central and southern regions of the country mainly benefit from those transfers (Jambyl, South Kazakhstan, Almaty, Akmola and Kyzylorda) and not the northern regions, which are equally poor, and Astana also benefits from those transfers (almost one-fifth of regional revenue).

Second, *company redistribution* includes direct, indirect and induced revenue that oil companies invest or spend locally. In the case of the oil sector, there is no

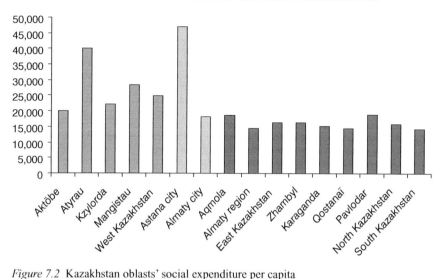

Figure 7.2 Kazakhstan oblasts' social expenditure per capita

Source: Data from Sarsenov (2005).

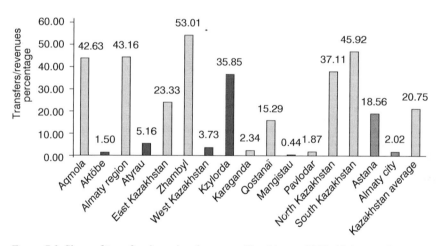

Figure 7.3 Share of transfers in regional revenue, Kazakhstan, 2000–03 (average)

Source: Calculated on average for the period 2000–03 from official data in Shokmanov (2004).

need for large employment or for social programs (or 'social assets'), so this type of redistribution may be geographically limited. Oil companies' headquarters, especially in the case of non-operating foreign companies, employ a limited number of staff. In terms of value added, oil production makes a difference. Since 1997 the growth of regional product per capita has been above the national average for all oil-producing regions, except for Kyzylorda oblast (Figure 7.4). The difference is especially great for the old oil-producing regions such as Mangistau and Atyrau

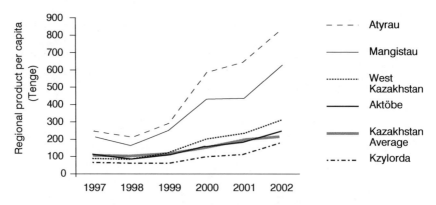

Figure 7.4 Regional product per capita, Kazakhstan, 1997–2002

Source: Smailov (2001) and Abdiev (2003).

regions (three and four times above the national average). However, the largest increases in regional product were recorded in Astana and Almaty cities.

Oil companies try to contribute to the development of communities where they operate (see Chapters 9 and 10). However, taking into account the immense needs, these projects only address a fraction of infrastructure needs. In the PSAs, consortia are requested to invest in social infrastructure projects. Regional authorities propose local development projects, which should reflect the real needs of local communities. Despite their possible local impact, AgipKCO's investments represent only 1.25 per cent of the revenue of Mangistau and Atyrau regions and Karachaganak Petroleum Operating 6.5 per cent of the revenue of West Kazakhstan region (Abdiev 2003: 426). Until now, AgipKCO has mainly financed the building of schools, hospitals, gas pipelines to villages and other infrastructure. Annually, this consortium spends $5 million (or 0.15 per cent of regional GDP) in Mangistau and Atyrau regions.[21] KPO invests annually $10 million in West Kazakhstan (or 0.8 per cent of regional GDP).

Third, *unofficial redistribution* results from two factors: unregistered household activities and informal 'leakage'. First, oil production generates money and people inflows. In order to fulfil the new demands, individuals or households may start small businesses. Self-employment can therefore result from oil production. Second, revenue may be used for political or individual purposes, i.e. by informal 'leakage' oil revenue is redistributed to the economy. This type of redistribution is the least easy to measure, but the 'oil curse' literature refers to such mechanisms, emphasizing their negative impact on institutions and consequently on growth.[22] An example of unofficial redistribution is the bargaining and negotiation processes between oil companies and local and central authorities. The local employee quotas, previously agreed in Astana (in the Ministry of Labour and Social Protection), have now become the mandate of *hakims* (regional governors), which is said to increase revenue redistribution in the circles around *hakims* in oil-producing regions.

122

Unofficial incomes are underestimated in surveys. When one compares a household's income and expenditure, a large share of expenditure is not covered by corresponding income. The size of this gap can be treated as a proxy for the unofficial income of the household. Specifically, we assume that if a household's total expenditure is more than double its total income, then the household participates in some kind of informal activities.

To analyze the three types of redistribution (official public, company and informal), the following mutually exclusive categorical variables are constructed for each household:[23]

1   Official public redistribution is the dominant mechanism if the income from wages is less than the income from social transfers, and total household expenditure is lower than twice the total income of the household. In a household that fulfils both conditions, we conclude that the household essentially benefits from official public redistribution (social transfers). This category represents 12.5 per cent of the sample.

2   Company redistribution is the dominant mechanism if the income from wages is greater than the income from social transfers and if total household expenditure is less than twice the total income. About 44 per cent of the sample is in this category, which is indicative of how little importance the formal sector has in Kazakhstan, and how difficult it is to tax wages.

3   Informal redistribution is the dominant mechanism if total household expenditure is more than twice the total income.[24] In this case we conclude that the household essentially benefits from informal redistribution, i.e. undeclared activities. The informal redistribution group represents 43.5 per cent of our sample.

Cross-tabulating the redistribution dummy on some of the main individual characteristics of the household head (see Appendix) yields some preliminary results.

As might be expected, social redistribution goes primarily to women, the elderly and the less educated. First, women benefit more (58.5 per cent) from social transfers. This is quite normal because women during the transition are usually a more vulnerable part of the society especially when they are single mothers. For both formal and informal redistribution, males more frequently (about 55 per cent) have access to a job and income. A second observation is that older household heads receive more social transfers than others. Third, less educated heads of household rely more on social redistribution. Company redistribution is relatively more prevalent in non-oil rayons, and informal redistribution is more prevalent in oil-producing rayons.

The results of a multinomial logistic regression to analyse the three different redistribution mechanisms are reported in Table 7.6. We also tried using a continuous variable for household income shares (official public, company and informal) and the results are the same. The three mechanisms (social, enterprise and informal redistribution) are mutually exclusive, and are assumed to be not

Table 7.6 Multinomial logistic regression results

Variables	Coefficient	Standard error	p–value
1. Official public redistribution			
Sex	−0.08	0.04	0.06
Age	0.05	0.00	0.00
Married	−0.32	0.04	0.00
Education	−0.26	0.01	0.00
Almaty	−1.49	0.12	0.00
Astana	−1.77	0.39	0.00
Medium city	0.24	0.08	0.00
Small town	0.34	0.07	0.00
Rural	0.99	0.05	0.00
Oil production	0.07	0.10	0.45
Size of the household	−0.19	0.01	0.00
Constant	−1.88	0.12	0.00
3. Informal redistribution			
Sex	0.12	0.03	0.00
Age	0.01	0.00	0.00
Married	−0.33	0.03	0.00
Education	−0.13	0.01	0.00
Almaty	0.11	0.05	0.03
Astana	1.30	0.09	0.00
Medium city	−0.05	0.06	0.42
Small town	0.44	0.04	0.00
Rural	1.30	0.03	0.00
Oil production	0.23	0.06	0.00
Size of the household	−0.13	0.01	0.00
Constant	−0.08	0.07	0.29
Number of observations	32,229		
LR chi2(22)	6,618.2		
Prob > chi2	0.0000		
Pseudo R2	0.104		

Notes: The dependent variable is the redistribution variable defined in the text. Category 2 (enterprise redistribution) is the control group.

correlated. We use a simple multinomial regression without any conditionality, assuming that individuals are free to choose the redistribution they want, which is of course a simplification.

Compared to the control category (enterprise redistribution), social redistribution is positively associated with residence in a small town or in a rural area and is negatively related to the household head's education level or residence in Almaty or Astana. Comparing the incidence of social redistribution to that of enterprise redistribution, the effect of residence in an oil-producing rayon is not statistically significant. Informal redistribution is positively related to residence in a small town or in a rural area and negatively related to the household head's education level, but, unlike social redistribution, it is positively related to residence in the capital city and to residence in an oil-producing rayon (see also Chapter 8 for a discussion of these results using Azerbaijan data).

In sum, the results of analysis of the 2002 household survey data to distinguish between channels for redistribution of the oil boom benefits suggest that little happens through higher wages in oil-producing districts or through social transfers, but that 'informal' earnings (captured by households having much higher expenditure than income) are more important in the oil districts than in the country as a whole. The informal redistribution may include small-scale agriculture, which could explain the rural area effect. Both social and informal redistribution are more prevalent for less educated household heads and small town inhabitants relative to company redistribution, and there is some evidence that low skilled people and rural area inhabitants are not benefiting from the oil sector development, which is consistent with reports from the Tengiz region of complaints by the local population that they are not employed in oil production. Households in the two large cities seem to benefit from the oil boom mainly through informal redistribution; informal earnings are even more prevalent for households in Astana, the new national capital, and to a lesser extent in Almaty, the financial capital, than they are in the oil-producing regions.[25]

Conclusions

Whether resource abundance is a curse or a blessing depends upon the nature of the resource and on variables reflecting institutions and governance. Of all resources, oil appears to produce the most extreme outcomes, from Nigeria to Norway. Kazakhstan is interesting because the scale of the future oil boom was scarcely anticipated during the 1990s and because key institutions remain in embryonic and malleable form. The evidence from this case study is preliminary, as the story is still unfolding; political and institutional developments during the decade after independence created a situation where political economy mechanisms could turn oil wealth into a curse.

The household survey analysis presented in this chapter gives a preliminary assessment of the impact of oil revenue expansion. The benefits have not been redistributed evenly across the country. The oil boom has not resulted in higher average living standards in the oil-producing regions, but has been associated with higher living standards in the metropolitan centres where the country's elite lives. As a Kazakh living in Sarykamys, a settlement near Tengiz oilfield, said: 'we have a lot of oil, but we're not the masters of this oil', expressing a feeling many people in Kazakhstan share. Unofficial redistribution seems to be the main transmission channel of redistribution of oil revenue.[26] A complementary analysis would be needed, especially in oil-producing regions, to distinguish if it results from unregistered household small activities or 'leakage' of oil revenue. Use of oil revenue remains an evolving process. In Kazakhstan, the early stage of the oil boom means that the jury still has a long wait before determining whether oil will be a blessing or a curse.

Appendix

Table A7.1 Descriptive statistics by type of redistribution

1 Type of redistribution

Redistribution type	Number of people	Percentage
1 – Official Public	4,039	12.5
2 – Company	14,166	44.0
3 – Informal	14,024	43.5
Total	32,229	

2 Gender of household head

Gender	Official public	Company	Informal	Total
Male (in %)	134 (41.5)	2,268 (55.7)	1,956 (54.1)	4,358 (54.4)
Female (in %)	189 (58.5)	1,801 (44.3)	1,659 (45.9)	3,649 (45.6)
Total	323	4,069	3,615	8,007

3 Age of household head

	Average age	Standard deviation	Number of households
Official public	48.5	9.0	323
Company	44.9	8.4	4,069
Informal	45.3	8.4	3,615
Total	45.2	8.5	8,007

4 Education of household head

Redistribution	Primary only	Secondary	University	Total
Official public	48 (14.9%)	239 (74.0%)	36 (11.2%)	323
Company	187 (4.6%)	2,922 (71.8%)	960 (23.6%)	4,069
Informal	297 (8.2%)	2,791 (77.2%)	527 (14.6%)	3,615
Total	532 (6.6%)	5,952 (74.39%)	1,523 (19.0%)	8,007

5 Cross table oil/non-oil rayons

Redistribution	Non-oil rayons	Oil-producing rayons	All households
Official public	303 (4.0%)	20 (5.6%)	323 (4.0%)
Company	3,924 (51.3%)	145 (40.9%)	4,069 (50.8%)
Informal	3,425 (44.8%)	190 (53.5%)	3,615 (45.2%)
Total	7,652	355	8,007

Source: Own calculations using LSMS Kazakh data for 2002.

Notes

1 Earlier versions of this research were presented at the American Economic Association annual meetings in Boston in January 2006, the British Association for Slavonic and East European Studies conference in Cambridge in April 2006, and at seminars at the Australian National University, the University of Adelaide, Universita di Trento and Université Paris-XII (Créteil), from all of which we received valuable comments.

2 See, for example, the literature review and regression analysis in the first two sections of Sala-i-Martin and Subramanian (2003), and Stevens (2003). Isham *et al.* (2003) distinguish between point-source resources (oil, natural fertilizers and cotton) and coffee/cocoa, which have been associated with poor growth performance, and other natural resources, which have not. This is the usual result, although Korhonen (2004) finds that the largest negative effects on growth come from non-fuel extractive raw materials.

3 Nigeria has experienced this conjunction of discontents for decades (Ikein and Briggs-Anigboh 1998). In Russia, approximately three-quarters of oil revenue flows to Moscow creating a struggle between the politicians in regions of oil extraction and the central authorities (Dienes 2002: 451).

4 The main sources of revenue are the state's share of export earnings, taxes on producers and other taxes. Under PSAs the share of crude oil exports by consortia attributed to Kazakhstan is determined after deduction of the cost recovery expenses, which may not exceed 75% of revenue prior to payback and 50% post-payback. The tax on oil producers depends upon the type of tax regime of the contract. PSA and EPT contracts entered into force after 1996 and before 1 January 2004 are unequivocally grandfathered (Ernst & Young 2005: 17). Under a PSA the foreign oil company, at its own risk, is expected to pay all initial exploration and development costs, while the government receives a share of the field's production, in cash or in kind, without making any investment. The key factors determining the foreign oil company's profits are the ratio of initial cost to revenue, procedures to determine profits, and the company's share of the profits. Under a PSA tax regime, foreign companies are exempted from excise, property tax, land tax and vehicle tax. In an EPT regime, the company is liable to pay bonuses, royalty, excess profits tax and a rent tax on export of crude oil, and 'top up tax'. Additionally, there are taxes on profits, indirect taxes such as VAT, excise and customs duties, and other taxes such as environmental fees, property tax, land tax, vehicle tax and other fees and licenses.

5 The 50 companies included in *Kompass Kazakhstan* (the largest company directory in Kazakhstan, in which all the major oil companies (foreign and national) are included) in the sector of oil production only have 41,500 employees. The largest employers in this sector are mainly branches in which Kazmunaigaz is a major shareholder such as Ozenmunaigaz (12,500 people), Embamunaigaz (12,000) or Mangghystaoumunaigaz (4,400). Kazmunaigaz has 400 employees at its headquarters in Astana. As far as joint foreign–Kazakh companies or foreign operators in Kazakhstan are concerned, Tengizchevroil has 2,800 employees, Karachaganak 500 and Petrokazakhstan 900. For the foreign companies, which do not operate oilfields (such as British Gas, Total or Lukoil), the presence on the ground is limited to a dozen or so people to represent the interests of the company.

6 Other examples of use of the dataset are Anderson and Pomfret (2002a, 2002b, 2003), Rama and Scott (1999), and Verme (2001).

7 All data are in nominal terms and hence ignore regional price differences. Although relative prices vary widely across Kazakshtan (Grafe *et al.* 2005), published oblast price indices do not indicate large differences in price levels. Beegle (2003: 37–8) reports food price indices for each oblast in 2001 which vary from Mangistau 135, Astana 117, Atyrau 116, Almaty 115, to South Kazakhstan 94 and Jambyl 86; the

national price level is set at 100. The survey data include home-produced items, which are recorded in quantity terms and then priced for inclusion in aggregate household expenditure.

8 Anderson and Pomfret (2002a) test the sensitivity of the results to this assumption (i.e. assigning equal expenditure weight to all children and adults in the household) by estimating the model with an alternative dependent variable in which children, women and the elderly are assigned lower expenditure weights than prime working age adult men. The results do not change in any significant way. The numerical results might also be sensitive to the implicit assumption of no scale economies in the provision of household services; adjusting for economies of size with a scaling such as $E^* = E/n^\theta$, where E is household expenditure and n is family size, would soften the conclusion about household size and perhaps affect other results. However, Jovanovic (2001) reports that varying θ within a plausible range did not alter his results for Russia in any significant way.

9 The aggregate level of household expenditure is not of interest in the present context because we are trying to understand the determinants of relative living standards. Expenditure is preferred to income because the arrears problem in former Soviet republics during the 1990s meant that income often came in lumps so that many households reported zero income during the two-week survey period. We also expect under-reporting to avoid tax or other impositions to be less prevalent for expenditure. Non-purchased items, such as food grown on household plots, are valued and included in expenditure. Because the log of expenditure more closely follows a normal distribution, the estimating equations are semi-logarithmic regressions of the log of per capita expenditure on household characteristics.

10 Education is characterized by five levels: higher education (university and postgraduate), Technikum education, vocational or other technical training, completed secondary education, and incomplete secondary schooling. In analysing the 1996 situation Anderson and Pomfret found no significant difference between using education variables based on the head of household's education and using the highest-educated person. For 2002, we use highest-educated person because, rather than following a consistent definition, the surveyors appear to have treated the person who answered the questionnaire as the head of household.

11 For 1996 Anderson and Pomfret (2002a) defined a person as elderly if he or she was eligible for a state pension, i.e. at age 60 for a man and age 55 for a woman. For 2002 'elderly' is defined as aged 60 or over.

12 This reflects the demographic patterns of the 1990s when the birth rate fell and the death rate rose. It also might be influenced by emigration patterns, as a disproportionate number of elderly were among the Germans and Slavs who left Kazakhstan during the 1990s.

13 This is consistent with other evidence from Central Asia and elsewhere that during the 1990s much of the specialized lower-level technical training from the Soviet era had no market value in the transition economy. People ceased taking such courses, and in some cases may no longer have claimed this type of training as an education. The drop in the vocational-technical category is largely matched by an increase in the number reporting completed secondary as their highest level of education.

14 In 2002 the average per capita expenditure level for households in the lowest education category is over 114,000 tenge, which is above the sample average and higher than for any other education category apart from those with university degrees. The reason for this anomaly appears to be the presence of a few households reporting no education but having high expenditure levels; 28 of the households reporting no one with completed secondary education had income levels around 600,000 tenge, i.e. over six standard deviations above the sample mean.

15 The only major difference is in the control group for human capital. In analysing the 1996 data, Anderson and Pomfret used the incomplete secondary schooling as the

B. NAJMAN, R. POMFRET, G. RABALLAND AND P. SOURDIN

omitted education category, but with the 2002 data this led to generally insignificant coefficients. The reported regression results for 2002 use completed secondary education as the control variable, and, because of the anomalies reported above, the lowest education group (with 9.4% of households) is omitted; the results for the other variables are almost identical to the results when the entire sample is used.

16 In regressions using the entire sample and having incomplete secondary education as the control, the coefficients on all education levels apart from university did not differ from zero at the 5% significance level.

17 Aqtöbe region: three (out of 17), Atyrau region: seven (all rayons of the oblast), West Kazakhstan: four (out of 12), Kyzylorda region: three (out of seven), Mangistau region: four (all rayons of the oblast). We identified oil-producing rayons combining detailed maps of oilfields and oblasts.

18 A trade-off exists between spending and saving oil revenue. Volatile oil revenue may lead to poor public investment decisions. Also, an oil boom might have deleterious effects via Dutch disease mechanisms (i.e. an appreciating exchange rate makes production of other traded goods unprofitable). In this chapter, these macroeconomic effects are ignored, and the focus is on redistribution mechanisms which can be analysed with household data.

19 The National Fund was established in 2001, with the main objectives of reducing the impact of volatile world market prices and smoothing the distribution of oil-wealth over generations. Initially, the authorities identified 12 major companies in the natural resources sector, but this figure was reduced to six in 2004 and the list limited to petroleum companies. Flows consist of a *savings* component equal to 10% of the budgeted baseline revenue invariant to price changes and a *stabilization* component that includes all revenue above the baseline price, fixed at $19 per barrel. The Fund's capital is supplied by shares of government income from the oil sector, royalties, bonuses and revenue from PSA. The Fund is invested in foreign equities. Thus, a large share of oil revenue is allocated to the NFRK, which had accumulated $5 billion by late 2004 (or approximately 17% of GDP). See Kalyuzhnova and Kaser (2005) and IMF (2004: 19).

20 The difference between the poorest and richest regions in terms of budget revenue is declining, whereas in terms of regional product per capita the difference is widening. Regarding regional budget revenue, in 1997, the ratio between the richest and the poorest regions was equal to 5.4 and, in 2002, it decreased to 3.6. Regarding regional product per capita, this ratio was equal to 5.6 and, in 2002, it increased to 10.3.

21 This amount will grow to $18 million per year when Kashagan is fully operational (or 1% of expenses to develop Kashagan oilfield).

22 Ross (2001) describes in detail the effects of oil on political economy. According to Ross, the 'rentier effects' may characterize the link between oil and a type of rule. In this case, 'governments use oil revenue to reduce social pressures that would otherwise result in demands for greater accountability' (IMF 2004: 12). Robinson and Torvik (2005) argue that governments may finance 'white elephants' because such projects produce political benefits.

23 Redistribution may combine several types of redistribution, but this chapter focuses on *the* main source of incomes, which means that the three types of redistribution are defined to be mutually exclusive.

24 We tried alternative definitions of informal redistribution, and hence of the other categories; setting the lower bound for informal expenditure at households whose expenditures exceeded 1.5 or 2.5 of their total income did not significantly change the share of households in the three redistribution categories.

25 The transmission mechanism may differ between the two cities. Troschke and Ufer (2007) show that budget transfers to Astana were largely for construction projects. Informal earnings in the new capital may have been associated with the huge and

130

rapidly disbursed expenditure on constructing a new national capital. Almaty remained the financial centre and home of the non-political elite.

26 In Azerbaijan, Luecke and Trofimenko (see Chapter 8) found different results, however the history of oil production is not similar in Kazakhstan.

8

WHITHER OIL MONEY?

Redistribution of oil revenue in Azerbaijan[1]

Matthias Luecke and Natalia Trofimenko

Introduction

According to forecasts from the Economist Intelligence Unit, the surging exports of oil and gas will help raise Azerbaijan's GDP by about 25 per cent in 2006 and make it the fastest growing country in the world.[2] The challenge imposed on the country will be to translate this temporary resource-driven stimulus to the economy into sustainable growth. Way too often resource-rich countries develop deficient political systems that descend into a spiral of embezzlement, cronyism and wasted government expenditure, with large income disparities fuelling radical political or religious movements. And way too often non-oil sectors become uncompetitive and shrink greatly because export revenue is spent quickly rather than saved to meet long-term expenditure commitments or provide a capital stock for future generations after reserves are exhausted (Gylfason 2001; Sachs and Warner 2001). This chapter contributes to a still scattered literature on the resource boom in Azerbaijan. Our aim is to elucidate the changing patterns of the use of oil revenue and to appraise the extent to which the benefits from the oil boom are retained in the oil-producing regions or transferred to the rest of the country.

It is no secret that the benefits from oil are uneven in their incidence and many regions, sectors and individuals will be net losers. Specifically, while the resource-endowed parts of the country benefit from the expanding economic activities in the oil sector and from the inflows of investments, resource-poor regions are most likely to be left out of this process. Similarly, if a resource boom is accompanied by a real appreciation, the manufacturing sector will shrink and the non-tradable sector will expand, creating very different prospects for the employment and wages of the workers employed by these sectors. While efficiency demands that such structural change should not be discouraged, equity demands that its consequences be made more tolerable for those adversely affected by the boom in the oil sector (Forsyth and Kay 1980). In this chapter we concentrate on the regional redistribution of oil revenue and present empirical findings suggesting that the flows of resources to disadvantaged regions were evident in Azerbaijan even before the government officially engaged in the fight against regional inequality in 2004.

Numerous studies consider the driving force of interregional redistributive policies and the implications of interregional transfers on interregional and interpersonal inequality and social welfare in both developed and developing countries (Bergman 2003; Rossello 2003; Garcia-Mila and McGuire 1996). Less well investigated are the resource transfers in the context of oil-rich countries and, specifically, the role of oil revenue in reducing interregional inequality (Kawagoe 1998; Najman *et al.* in Chapter 7). This in large part reflects the difficulty of identifying the pattern of government expenditure in the absence of oil money. We contribute to the small literature by employing a quasi-natural experiment framework, whereby we take advantage of the variation in the oil-based revenue generated by an increase in oil production following the cease-fire with Armenia in 1994.

Although oil production in Azerbaijan dates back to the 1870s, the 10-year conflict between Azerbaijan and Armenia, as well as the overall economic collapse following the independence from the former Soviet Union, brought it down to less than 200 b/d by 1995 – barely enough to cover domestic consumption. In September 1994, however, Azerbaijan and 11 international companies signed a contract to develop Azeri, Chirag and Gunashi fields with estimated reserves of 5.4 billion barrels of oil and the oil production has been growing at an average of 10.2 per cent since 1997. Using the exogenous shock to oil production as a plausibly exogenous variation in revenue of the resource-rich regions, we compare the changes in the composition of the recipients of the state benefits between 1995 and 2002.

The empirical analysis uses household surveys, supplemented by government budget data and suggests significant changes in redistributive public expenditure policies. While over three-quarters of government revenue in both years has been generated by oil-producing regions, in 1995 most of the revenue stayed within the producing regions and urban areas. The amount of state benefits received by the household was proportional to the resource-endowment of the region in which it was located, with highest benefits received by households in Baku and other oil-rich regions. There was also a strong pro-urban bias with the amount of benefits higher in urban areas. In 2002 the level of state support was lowest for the residents of Baku and one can see a strong pro-rural bias even in the resource-rich areas of the country. Overall, the dependency on government, measured as the share of state benefits in total income, has decreased over the period from 30 per cent to 8 per cent.

The study is organized as follows. The following section provides an overview of the current economic developments in Azerbaijan and a brief history of oil production in the country. The third section describes the sources of oil revenue and the mechanisms put in place for their management. The fourth section uses economic geography to identify potential beneficiaries and losers from the current economic boom. The fifth section introduces the data, the identification strategy and the estimation procedure employed in the analysis. The estimation results are discussed in the sixth section, followed by a brief conclusion and suggestions for future research. Throughout the chapter we provide the reader with the most current data available, even if at the expense of slightly deviating from the primary emphasis on the 1995 to 2002 period. Since some of these current data come from media sources, we have identified those in the text so that the reader could make his or her own judgement regarding their accuracy.

Oil-propelled growth

'Unprecedented economic growth' is what describes best Azerbaijan's performance over the last decade. The GDP growth rate, negative in 1995 and merely 1 per cent in 1996 soared to 26.4 per cent in 2005 and it is forecasted to grow further over the next few years.[3] Its GDP per capita in terms of the purchasing power parity increased from $1800 in 1995 to $4700 in 2006.[4] The trade account has been in positive since 2000 and registered a surplus of $2701 million in 2005, driven by burgeoning exports of oil and a slow down in imports of machinery and equipment for the oil and gas sector. Government spending increased significantly (24.4 per cent in 2005 and is expected to increase by up to 65 per cent in 2006) with the increase going primarily into public sector wages, pensions, consumer subsidies for energy products and social services. Through these channels private consumption benefited from the additional oil income. This, together with the limited ability of the National Bank to sterilize the inflow of petrodollars, resulted in the deterioration of the consumer price inflation (from 1.8 per cent in 2000 to 6.7 per cent in 2004 and 9.5 per cent in 2005).

Since it is oil and gas that are powering both the double-digit growth[5] and the deterioration in such macroeconomic indicators as consumer prices, it is important to take a look at the history of oil production in the country. Azerbaijan is the oldest known oil producing region in the world. Since the first oil field exploitation in the environs of its capital city in 1848 the country experienced several oil booms and descents: stalled after joining the emerging Soviet Union in 1920, its oil production peaked during the Second World War and relapsed in the post-war years when Russia shifted attention to the Volga-Ural oil fields. The leading oil producer during the war (Azerbaijan accounted for approximately 70 per cent of the USSR's petroleum output), Azerbaijan was producing 60 per cent of Soviet oil extraction machinery and spare parts, but less than 2 per cent of the oil when the USSR disintegrated.

The 10-year long conflict between Azerbaijan and Armenia, 'the bloodiest and most intractable disputes to emerge from the break-up of the Soviet Union', and the overall economic collapse following the independence from the former Soviet Union (the country's GDP contracted by almost 60 per cent from 1990 to 1995) stalled the oil production. Following the cease-fire with Armenia in May 1994, in September of the same year Azerbaijan signed a $7.8 billion 30-year contract with 11 international companies to develop Azeri, Chirag and Gunashi (ACG) fields with estimated reserves of 5.4 billion barrels of oil.

This consortium originally featured oil companies from Azerbaijan (SOCAR), the USA (Amoco, Unocal and Pennzoil), the UK (British Petroleum and Ramco), Norway (Statoil), Russia (LUKoil), Turkey (Turkish Petroleum-TPAO) and Saudi Arabia (Delta Nimir). Since then, Exxon (USA) and Itochu (Japan) have also joined the club (see Map 8.1). The oil production under this agreement started in

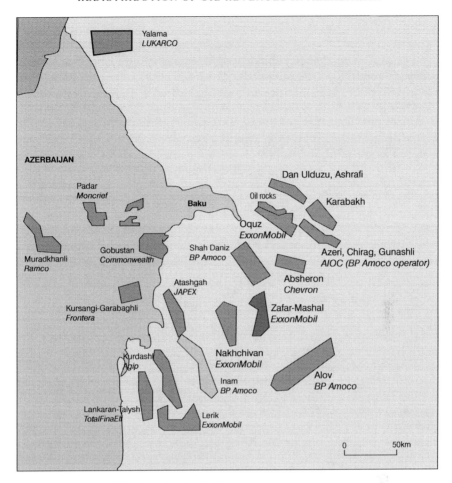

Map 8.1 Location of Azeri production fields

1997 and has been growing at an average of 10.2 per cent since 1997. The ACG contract has paved the way for a dozen more PSAs (see Appendix A8.1) – by the year 2002, the country has signed 20 PSAs with a total investment of more than $60 billion in Azerbaijan's oil development. These investments have paid off: oil production reached 22.21 million tons in 2005, a 42.9 per cent increase relative to the previous year, 28.6 million tons in 2006 and is projected to increase threefold over the next three years.

In the past, oil was transported through Baku–Novorossiysk pipeline (northern direction) and, since April 1999, through Baku–Supsa pipeline (western direction). The Baku–Tbilisi–Ceyhan (BTC) and Baku–Tbilisi–Erzerum (BTE) pipelines that will be used for the exports of oil and natural gas to the Turkish and, potentially, European markets were completed in 2006.[6] Both pipelines are expected to increase greatly fiscal revenue and, just as important, to reduce the Azerbaijan's dependence on Russia.

The completion of the BTC oil and BTE gas pipelines of course implies a major slow down in foreign direct investment flows. Some of this slow down will be offset by an increased inflow of concessional funds and grants estimated at around $3 billion.[7] Whether or not the rest can be offset by an increased domestic investment in the non-oil sector remains to be seen. However, the lost investment flows are small relative to the anticipated revenue. Both pipelines are expected to generate approximately $140 billion in revenue over the next 20 years, a staggering amount considering that the state brought in about $2 billion in revenue in 2005. Actual revenue will prove much higher since the forecasted $140 billion was based on an oil price of $40 per barrel. The next section outlines the mechanism put in place to manage this revenue.

The regulatory framework for the management of oil revenue

All natural resources of the subsoil in Azerbaijan are in the state ownership and may not be owned by individuals. Individuals may, however, acquire exploration or production rights from the state pursuant to tenders, licences and/or other arrangements (such as PSAs). The ownership and exploitation rights to resources and energy-related activities are governed primarily by the Law on Subsoil Reserves adopted in February 1998 and the Law on Energy adopted in November 1998. These laws establish a system of permits, licenses and energy contracts granted to successful applicants wishing to engage in oil and gas exploration and/ or production.

Oil revenue stems from two sources: Soviet-era oil and gas fields with very weak prospects for a further expansion of production and operated by the state oil company (SOCAR) and from the development of new oil fields under PSAs with international companies (Wakeman-Linn *et al.* 2004). Each PSA creates a specific regulation regime for the exploration/production activities for the relevant oil fields. After being signed, a PSA is submitted to the Parliament and adopted into a law that takes precedence over existing and future laws and regulations of Azerbaijan. This provides the foreign investors additional guarantees against possible adverse changes in the legislature. Moreover, the PSAs usually envisage fewer requirements for foreign investors, compared to the general regulatory scheme of Azeri laws. For example, most foreign PSA participants are exempt from paying the majority of otherwise applicable taxes (such as VAT, excise, etc.) and are only required to pay the profits tax. This illustrates the government's commitment to provide additional incentives to the investors in the oil and gas sector.

Two government bodies (the state budget and the State Oil Fund) are involved in the management of oil revenue. The government receives profit oil and income tax from the development of new fields, as spelled out in the PSAs with the foreign contractors. The profit oil component of these flows accrues to the State Oil Fund while the income tax components go to the state budget. The oilfields operated by SOCAR generate income tax revenue that also goes to the state budget.

Since 1999, the State Oil Fund (SOFAZ) has been the main institution for the management of oil wealth in Azerbaijan (see Appendix A8.2). According to the UNDP Azerbaijan Development Bulletin, the Fund's assets reached $1.5 billion by 30 July 2006 and are expected to exceed $50 billion within the next 18 years.[8] Its main purpose is to save funds for the future, but assets are also used for investment and social projects. For example, of the $357.3 million spent by SOFAZ in the first half of 2006, almost $40 million went to the construction of housing for refugees and internally displaced persons. Over $200 million was transferred to the state budget in the first half of 2006 and this amount was expected to surpass $600 million by the end of the year. Additional oil revenue accrues to the state budget from the tax payments of the state oil company SOCAR.[9] In 2002, for example, they amounted to $340 million.

A subject of contention on today's political agenda is how the central government will absorb this additional revenue and which policy choices will maximize the welfare of the country. With transfers to individuals as one of the options for absorbing windfall gains (Gelb *et al.* 1988), it is important to know to what extent the beneficiaries of the oil bonanza share their affluence with the rest of the economy through central government transfers. In the next section we use descriptive statistics to illustrate the differential effect of the oil boom on various population segments.

Economic geography of Azerbaijan

There are several reasons to look at the economic developments in Azerbaijan through the spatial prism. This country expands over several climatic zones and this affects strongly the regional production structure, with well-defined agricultural and manufacturing areas. It had a border conflict with Armenia and parts of the territory are still under the Armenian occupation. The effects of this, of course, spill beyond the occupied territories, through the pressures placed on the labour markets in the rest of the country by the migration of the displaced persons, to name one such channel. The most important reason is, however, the spotty distribution of natural resources – while some regions are randomly endowed with many, others are left with none.

Azerbaijan consists of over 50 districts and 11 metropolitan areas that are aggregated into eight economic zones: Baku, Absheron–Guba, Mugan–Salyan, Ganja–Gazakh, Sheki–Zagatala, Lankaran–Astara, Shirvan and Karabagh–Mil. The variation of the indices of industrial production portrayed in Table 8.1 may be best viewed in the context of the economic activities prevalent in the regions:

- Baku is the home to most of the country's industry, including oil refineries.
- The economy of Absheron–Guba is dominated by oil and gas production, petrochemical and chemical industries, ferrous and non-ferrous metals and power production.

Table 8.1 Indices of industrial production, Azerbaijan, 1996–2004 (constant prices, as a percentage of the 1995 level)

	1996	1997	1998	1999	2000	2001	2002	2003	2004
Baku	101	102	106	110	117	126	130	136	142
Absheron–Guba	84	53	45	47	39	40	54	62	64
Mugan–Salyan	77	59	57	49	44	45	46	65	56
Ganja–Gazakh	62	36	26	35	58	59	81	118	130
Sheki–Zagatala	58	83	43	55	46	73	63	73	60
Lankaran–Astara	60	56	75	176	160	310	220	260	320
Shirvan	56	52	28	20	35	38	27	33	47
Karabagh–Mil	74	79	44	27	16	19	35	35	26

Note: * Values for the economic zones are medians based on the regional indices of industrial production.

- Mugan–Salyan is known for its chemicals and construction materials, as well as machinery production, textiles and food industry. The region also produces negligible amounts of oil.
- Ganja–Gazakh is home to the extraction and processing industries for ferrous and non-ferrous metals.
- Sheki–Zagatala is an agricultural region. It contributes only around 3 per cent to the industrial production of the country, mostly textiles and food industry.
- Lankaran–Astara economic region shows the fastest and highest recovery rates. Its industrial production in 1996 was only 60 per cent of the 1995 level and it more than tripled by 2004. The core of the economy is the processing of locally supplied agricultural products (90 per cent of the industrial output is contributed by the food industry).
- Shirvan is a mountainous region specializing in agriculture, primarily livestock husbandry.
- Karahbakh-Mill's industry has been traditionally based on processing of local farming products and, hence, shows the most dramatic rates of the economic downfall in the country – as the region under the Armenian occupation, it felt the most direct effects of the military conflict.

In the light of the distribution of the economic activity presented above and the figures in Table 8.1, it is fair to say that it is the remote areas relying on agricultural production with no local processing industry that have been affected adversely by the current developments in the country. The common characteristic of the regions showing steady economic improvements is the region's endowment with natural resources, both energy and minerals, and a more or less diversified industrial structure.

As indicated in Table 8.2, oil production is dominated by very few regions. Of more than 60 districts, only six report positive values of oil production. Since 80 per cent of Azeri oil is produced offshore (Map 8.1) and processed at the refineries of the Baku area, Baku is clearly the oil centre of the country. It is also

Table 8.2 Oil production (thousand tons) by region and aggregated by economic zone, Azerbaijan, 1996–2004

	1995	1996	1997	1998	1999	2000	2001	2002	2003	2004
Baku	8416.8	8389.4	8366.2	10711.2	13132.3	13564.5	14429.4	14538	14497.3	14613.8
Ali Bayramli	386.7			216.7	214.7	352.1	364.3	360.7	398.3	443.2
Salyan	199.6	202	200.5	205	184.8			306.2	359.2	369.7
Siyazan		74.6	70.6	72	61.7	58.2	61.8	50.2	48.9	48.9
Imishly	37.9	35.9	39.8	38.4	30.0		8.5	33.4	30.5	30.5
Neftchala	34.3	37.3	38.6	41.8	43.0	42.2	45.1	45.0	44.5	42.7

Source: Regions of Azerbaijan 2004–5, the State Statistical Committee of Azerbaijan Republic.

the only district covering its own expenses (Table 8.3) – its local revenue accounts for approximately 70 per cent of the total revenue collected by the districts. Other districts depend heavily on transfers from the central government to cover their local expenditure.[10]

In spite of the very heterogeneous economic performance across economic zones during 1995 to 2004 that we observed in Table 8.1, one is more struck by the similarities than the differences in the spread of development across the country. The dynamics of the regional real wages show strong signs of convergence – in each region the wages increased five-fold. Some of the highest increases (6–6.1 times) were actually observed in the peripheral areas (Shirvan, Karabagh-Mill), which pulled their wages closer to the country's average. Another factor worth mentioning is that Baku continues to offer the highest wages (2.5–3 times the country's average), even though inward migration and the abundance of labour from the internally displaced persons have put pressures on the local labour market (Table 8.4).

The numbers portrayed in Tables 8.5 and 8.6 provide evidence of significant structural changes in the economy of Azerbaijan. While real wages increased across all industries, they increased at very differing rates relative to the country's average. In particular, relative to the country's average, real wages tripled in the mining, construction and hotel and restaurant industries, but decreased in virtually all other sectors (with the exception of trade, where they marginally increased).[11] If the workers in agriculture received more than a half of the average wage in 1995, by 2002 their wages were barely a third of the country's average. A similar pattern follows the wages in public administration and defence – while low historically (60 per cent of the average wage in 1995), they have not been keeping up with the developments in other sectors and by 2002 were only a quarter of the country's average. In January 2006, the government doubled the wages in the defence sector. Whether it should be interpreted as an attempt to reduce the corruption prevalent among the Azeri military and police or as an attempt to use part of the oil wealth to buy off those whose assistance may be required in settling social unrest remain two competing and equally plausible hypotheses, each one with very different consequences for the country's future.[12]

Table 8.3 Local budget data, Azerbaijan, 2004–06 (economic zone's percentage in total)

	2004			2005			2006		
	Revenues	Expenditures	Funds allocated from the centralized expenditures in order to regulate local revenues and expenditures	Revenues	Expenditures	Funds allocated from the centralized expenditures in order to regulate local revenues and expenditures	Revenues	Expenditures	Funds allocated from the centralized expenditures in order to regulate local revenues and expenditures
Total local budgets (thsd manat)	714,142,823	1,832,902,994	1,118,760,171	839,830,217	2,222,415,908	1,382,585,691	216,728,495	572,092,527	355,364,032
Baku	74.10	28.87	0.00	70.50	26.64	0.00	69.58	26.36	0.00
Absheron–Guba	5.69	10.80	14.06	6.90	11.18	13.78	8.06	11.19	13.10
Mugan–Salyan	3.77	8.24	11.09	3.76	8.56	11.47	3.70	8.53	11.47
Ganja–Gazakh	4.95	10.69	14.35	5.68	11.02	14.26	5.46	10.89	14.20
Sheki–Zagatala	2.76	6.52	8.92	2.93	6.71	9.00	2.92	6.81	9.18
Lankaran–Astara	2.77	8.59	12.31	3.24	8.95	12.42	3.25	9.09	12.65
Shirvan	2.45	7.74	11.12	2.69	8.02	11.25	2.74	8.09	11.36
Karabagh–Mil	3.44	18.36	27.88	4.23	18.74	27.55	4.22	18.68	27.78

Table 8.4 Real monthly wages (in local currency) by economic zone and in oil-producing regions, Azerbaijan, 1995–2004*

	1995	1996	1997	1998	1999	2000	2001	2002	2003	2004	2004/1995
Baku	101,952	140,096	135,544	168,557	188,368	257,683	282,434	364,118	425,952	576,124	5.65
Absheron–Guba	40,633	49,064	66,890	83,576	98,099	137,184	139,588	148,240	169,017	232,285	5.72
Mugan–Salyan	57,665	73,424	87,543	93,989	117,638	130,717	160,100	145,309	201,908	255,294	4.43
Ganja–Gazakh	31,744	42,070	55,780	74,013	100,332	115,231	120,160	122,724	143,743	193,570	6.10
Sheki-Zagatala	39,303	37,620	62,485	79,539	78,344	104,960	115,697	116,221	134,964	204,776	5.21
Lankaran–Astara	31,545	40,080	64,661	79,154	98,297	108,719	116,532	116,843	133,000	199,698	6.33
Shirvan	42,540	39,015	51,919	72,419	93,398	111,318	125,411	114,957	134,178	198,679	4.67
Karabagh–Mil	40,549	37,660	54,287	64,808	91,745	110,631	118,906	129,613	152,117	213,571	5.27
Ali;Bayramii**	89,900	100,657	108,605	94,097	124,953	183,069	385,792	268,643	408,865	450,802	5.01
Salyan	79,720	111,610	121,372	123,039	134,330	135,478	134,447	131,966	328,425	301,994	3.79
Siyazan	78,226	98,923	132,036	155,784	185,238	240,664	238,156	237,133	273,199	321,281	4.11
Imishly	57,426	83,864	73,034	102,423	114,520	118,718	127,059	126,377	154,905	225,272	3.92
Neftchala	61,683	84,309	99,125	104,257	183,514	180,210	177,738	173,539	180,966	225,058	3.65

Notes: * Nominal wages have been deflated by regional price indices. The construction of regional price indices started only in 2005 and we use the pattern of regional inflation relative to the country's average to approximate the price indices for years 1996–2004. This of course hinges on the assumption that there are no abrupt changes in 'within region' inflation level during the period in question. A look at the variation in inflation levels in 2005 (regional inflation ranges from 1% to 15%) suggests that this approximation, while imperfect, is still preferable to using the country's average. ** There are several plausible explanations for a sporadic pattern of wages for some regions. Since the values in the table refer to the region's average, any structural change affecting regional unemployment and/or the mix of skilled and unskilled labour (for example, a closure of a major plant) may have a large impact on the measured average. Data entry errors are equally possible.

Table 8.5 Real wages by sector, Azerbaijan, 1995–2002

	1995	*1996*	*1997*	*1998*	*1999*	*2000*	*2001*	*2002*	*Increase 1995– 2002*
Country average	54384	93249	153272	180848	181086	221606	263995	329158	274775
Agriculture	29208	39413	53645	47201	63963	69081	80152	93851	64643
Construction	86079	174441	324477	474185	420846	416663	443652	568899	482820
Electricity, gas and water supply	83192	152519	250294	297496	218552	267932	328345	338765	255573
Fishing	29208	39413	53645	47201	52332	52103	54493	63137	33929
Health and social services	22900	48919	73417	75233	69833	73395	81871	93934	71034
Hotels and restaurants	42839	78396	122924	129849	337239	314858	425906	505046	462207
Financial intermediation	147187	176673	258417	357356	580442	632626	734749	1064572	917385
Manufacturing	83192	152519	250294	297496	239742	284272	307832	364024	280832
Mining	83192	152519	250294	297496	618908	814540	1107543	1346722	1263530
Public administration and defence	50073	72288	118414	17719	178511	1945528	226862	331415	281342
Real estate	147187	176673	258417	357356	270033	334051	548391	690354	543166
Trade	32664	52798	72957	81382	115844	119284	151953	480260	447596
Transportation, storage and communication	85529	156982	245389	312506	245422	292421	335367	384344	298815

In the context of our study, these structural changes in the economy between 1995 and 2002 imply a changing segment of the population requiring government assistance. In particular, the workers in the non-tradable sectors should become less reliant on state benefits, while marginalized workers in agriculture or fishing may now qualify for assistance from the state. The most dramatic shift in living standards, according to Table 8.5, may have been experienced by the workers in the transportation and communication sector. Their wages were nearly three times the average level in 1995 and fell to below the average by 2002. While this drop may not necessarily qualify the workers for state benefits, it is nevertheless important to identify this group as potential losers from the oil boom.

To conclude, the unequal distribution of natural resources and the staggering size of the oil boom have generated regional and sectoral changes that are unusually well suited for identifying and empirically isolating the effects of the oil boom and the government's response to the influx of oil revenue.

Table 8.6 Real wages relative to the country average

	1995	1996	1997	1998	1999	2000	2001	2002	*Increase 1995–2002*
Agriculture	0.54	0.42	0.35	0.26	0.35	0.31	0.30	0.29	−0.25
Construction	2.95	4.43	6.05	10.05	6.58	6.03	5.54	6.06	3.11
Electricity, gas and water supply	0.97	0.87	0.77	0.63	0.52	0.64	0.74	0.60	−0.37
Fishing	0.35	0.26	0.21	0.16	0.24	0.19	0.17	0.19	−0.16
Health and social services	0.78	1.24	1.37	1.59	1.33	1.41	1.50	1.49	0.70
Hotels and restaurants	1.87	1.60	1.67	1.73	4.83	4.29	5.20	5.38	3.51
Financial intermediation	3.44	2.25	2.10	2.75	1.72	2.01	1.73	2.11	−1.33
Manufacturing	0.57	0.86	0.97	0.83	0.41	0.45	0.42	0.34	−0.22
Mining	1.00	1.00	1.00	1.00	2.58	2.87	3.60	3.70	2.70
Public administration and defence	0.60	0.47	0.47	0.06	0.29	2.39	0.20	0.25	−0.36
Real estate	2.94	2.44	2.18	20.17	1.51	0.17	2.42	2.08	−0.86
Trade	0.22	0.30	0.28	0.23	0.43	0.36	0.28	0.70	0.47
Transportation, storage and communication	2.62	2.97	3.36	3.84	2.12	2.45	2.21	0.80	−1.82

Data, identification strategy and estimation method

We strive to shed light on the government's response to this influx of the oil revenue, by comparing the pre- and post-boom amounts of state benefits to the households in oil-poor and oil-rich regions.[13] Our study combines data from regional statistics, the state budget, the 1995 Azerbaijan survey of living conditions (LSMS 1995) collected under the aegis of the World Bank and the most recent available Azerbaijan household budget survey (AHBS 2002) collected by the State Statistical Committee of Azerbaijan Republic. The LSMS 1995 data capture the pattern of government support in the period before the oil boom. The AHBS 2002 data are chosen to capture the changes in the pattern of government support after the first oil production under the PSAs has started and the country has received its first windfalls from the oil boom.

The LSMS 1995 survey covers 2,016 households and 10,012 individuals. The AHBS 2002 survey covers 8,157 households and 33,000 individuals. Both surveys provide detailed information on a wide range of topics, including food consumption, non-food consumption, labour activities, etc.; it suffers, however, from several limitations. For instance, most of the data on the sector of employment is missing and this makes it impossible (at least for now) to investigate whether the government's attention has shifted towards people employed in traditional sectors at the expense of those employed by the expanding mining sector. In addition, some variables in the two surveys have somewhat different definitions. We used our best judgement to overcome these differences by adjusting, censoring and aggregating respondents to comparable categories. All results presented in this chapter are weighted using the household-analysis weights that adjust for differential sampling.

In earlier sections we illustrated how the shock to the oil production translated into a jump in the government's revenue and altered the income levels and living conditions of oil-rich regions and workers employed in the petroleum sector and supporting industries. Given the data limitations, we choose to sidestep the issue of the inter-sectoral redistribution of oil revenue through wages or employment possibilities, and concentrate instead on the inter-regional redistribution through government transfers to individuals.

Our strategy is to document the mechanism driving government transfers in oil-rich and oil-poor regions in 1995, when the limited oil production should have made the differential treatment of the regions unnecessary or less pronounced, and to compare our findings with those for 2002. By tracing the changes between the two periods, we draw inferences about the uses of the additional oil revenue.

Our main variable of interest is the state benefits to the households. The transition period has placed particular demands on Azerbaijan's social protection system. First, because the state had to relieve the economic hardship and disruption faced by most of its population in the initial transition period and, secondly, because the previous system was designed during the Soviet period and had to go through a series of reforms. Our measure of the state benefits includes a series of pensions (old age pensions, disability pensions, pensions for loss of the breadwinner and social pensions to those with serious birth defects), social allowances (allowances for child birth, for children under 16 and for guardianship[14]), and unemployment benefits. In this study we concentrate on monetary transfers through the state budget and abstract from a range of privileges such as the exemption from education fees, food, rent and utilities payments, vouchers of resort services, free medication, etc. The decision to abstract from these types of assistance is driven purely by the data availability concerns and is not a reflection on their importance in the household's budget.

We use two statistical methods in out analysis: a probit, which is an appropriate statistical procedure when the dependent variable (whether of not a household is a recipient of state benefits) is dichotomous, and a tobit, which is appropriate when the dependent variable (the share of state benefits[15]) is zero for some households which do not, for example, qualify for state support or choose not to apply for it for whatever reason. We connect each of the aforementioned variables to the oil endowment of the region in which the household is located.

As we discussed earlier, the oil-poor areas of the country are far from homogenous and consist of the regions with manufacturing production, a strong agricultural sector with or without local processing and remote, poorly developed regions. Rather than bulking them into one category, we choose to group them according to the economic activity prevalent in the region.

In both specifications we net out the effects of the following household characteristics: an indicator for displaced persons, an indicator for rural location, household size, number of children, an indicator for married couples, an indicator for male headed households, real wage earnings of the household head, household head's age and his or her years of schooling.

All of these control variables affect the probability of receiving government support and/or the generosity of the benefits. Common sense suggests that in a war-torn country, internally displaced persons would be the first to receive government assistance, irrespective of the oil endowment of the region and the size of the oil windfall. Hence, we expect the coefficient on the indicator for internally displaced persons to be positive and highly significant in all specifications.

Rural families are already among the poorest segments of the population even in resource-poor economies. In an oil rich country they are even more vulnerable as they derive most of their income from agriculture, a sector adversely affected by the expansion in the extractive industries, and the government may want to alleviate their losses by additional transfers.

A larger family needs more resources, is more likely to be poor at any level of income and, hence, is more likely to receive government support. The number of adults affects the family's earnings potential, while children may establish eligibility for benefits that are not available to adult-only families. Similarly, single-headed households may be eligible for benefits that are not available to families with both parents. Single mothers have lower earning potential, are more likely to be poor and to receive government support. We also control for age since elderly people qualify for old age pensions.[16]

Oil boom results in serious structural changes in the economy putting at disadvantage the households whose incomes stem from the activities in the contracting sectors. The government may react to such changes by transferring some of the oil rents to the displaced workers. Unfortunately, missing data on the sector of employment prevents us from classifying the households according to the occupation of their members. Some papers (Kawagoe 1998) handle the lack of reliable data by aggregating the sectors based on an artificial dichotomy of rural vs urban on the presumption that the households in the rural areas derive their income from indigenous agricultural activities, while those in urban areas derive theirs from manufacturing. We go a step further and use the education level of the household's head as a proxy for the skill intensity of his or her sector of employment. Assuming that the workers in extracting and processing industries, as well as those in non-tradable sectors (in particular, banking and financial intermediation), are high-skilled, the negative coefficient on this variable would indicate the government's attempt to soften the detrimental effect of the oil boom on low-skilled workers. The variable 'real wage earnings' of the household's head serves simultaneously as a variable directly affecting the household's eligibility for government support and, potentially, as another proxy for the skill intensity of the employment sector.

145

Targeting to the oil-poor? Evidence on reallocation of oil revenue

The summary statistics presented in Table 8.7 provide us with a snapshot of the government's redistributive policies in pre- and post-boom periods and can be read as cautiously supporting the view that the oil revenue has been redistributed throughout the country. The proportion of households receiving benefits in 1995 was highest in Baku and Absheron-Guba, another region dominated by oil and gas production. In 2002 the benefits went primarily to oil-poor regions, both in terms of the proportion of the recipients and in terms of the generosity of the benefits – while the benefit amounts increased in all regions, the most dramatic changes are observed in oil-poor areas. This is consistent with the story of the flourishing economic activity in the post-boom period in oil-rich regions and a reduced need for the government support. Overall dependence on benefits, measured as their share in total income, has decreased across all regions, with the change proportional to the region's endowment with oil (largest decrease in Baku, somewhat smaller in Absheron-Guba, yet smaller in the rest of the country).

The effect of the region's endowment with oil on the distribution of state benefits is presented in Table 8.8. Having defined a dichotomous variable which equals one for the households with non-zero values of state benefits and zero otherwise, we first estimate the effect of the region's endowment with oil on the probability of obtaining state benefits. The coefficients have been restated as marginal probabilities at the mean for continuous variables, and the marginal probability effect of changing from zero to one in the case of indicator variables.

Table 8.7 Regional distribution of the recipients of government benefits and the amount of government support among households not eligible for old age pensions, Azerbaijan, 1995 and 2002

		Proportion receiving benefits		State benefits in constant 1995 prices		Share in total income	
		1995	2002	1995	2002	1995	2002
Oil-rich	Baku	0.82	0.41	26,032	28,186	0.46	0.04
Some oil	Absheron–Guba	0.78	0.56	17,360	40,529	0.47	0.06
Oil-poor Non-agricultural	Mugan–Salyan	0.63	0.70	19,857	73,612	0.29	0.11
	Ganja–Gazakh	0.67	0.66	14,398	33,963	0.31	0.06
Agricultural	Sheki–Zagatala	0.59	0.62	14,489	37,700	0.16	0.07
	Lankaran–Astara	0.55	0.61	11,687	39,013	0.11	0.06
Other	Shirvan	0.69	0.65	11,999	39,991	0.27	0.07
	Karabagh–Mil	0.70	0.65	22,191	79,865	0.27	0.13

Table 8.8 The effect of the region's endowment with oil on the probability of receiving state benefits and on the household's dependency on government support

	Recipient of benefits		Share of benefits in total income	
	1995	2002	1995	2002
Absheron–Guba relative to Baku	0.004	0.080***	0.051	0.014***
	[0.058]	[0.025]	[0.045]	[0.005]
Non-agricultural relative to Baku	−0.137***	0.131***	−0.105***	0.016***
	[0.052]	[0.022]	[0.039]	[0.004]
Agricultural relative to Baku	−0.184***	0.079***	−0.270***	0.019***
	[0.058]	[0.025]	[0.044]	[0.005]
Other relative to Baku	−0.145**	0.087***	−0.135***	0.034***
	[0.061]	[0.022]	[0.043]	[0.004]
Rural	−0.074**	0.035*	−0.055*	0.005
	[0.037]	[0.019]	[0.032]	[0.003]
Indicator for displaced persons	0.251***	0.350***	0.069**	0.182***
	[0.027]	[0.016]	[0.029]	[0.005]
Household size	−0.005	0.086***	−0.011	0.002
	[0.011]	[0.009]	[0.010]	[0.001]
Number of children	0.071***	0.091***	0.043***	0.014***
	[0.016]	[0.009]	[0.013]	[0.002]
Dummy for married households	−0.017	−0.035	0.081	−0.031***
	[0.061]	[0.031]	[0.052]	[0.005]
Dummy for male headed households	0.025	−0.120***	0.022	−0.018***
	[0.064]	[0.027]	[0.052]	[0.005]
Log (real earnings of household head)	0.008***	−0.013***	0.004***	−0.004***
	[0.002]	[0.001]	[0.001]	[0.000]
Age of household head	−0,001	−0.001	−0.002	0.001***
	[0.002]	[0.001]	[0.001]	[0.000]
Years of schooling of the household head	0.001	−0.013***	0.006	−0.001***
	[0.005]	[0.002]	[0.004]	[0.000]
Constant			0.348***	0.043***
			[0.091]	[0.010]
N. Obs	1003	5126	967	5104
R-Squared	0.13	0.17	0.16	0.34

Notes: Standard errors in brackets. * Significant at 10%. ** Significant at 5%. *** Significant at 1%.

All the findings are presented with Baku as the comparison base. While somewhat arbitrary, this choice is motivated by several considerations. First, our interest in how the outcomes are affected by the region's endowment with oil makes either the region with no oil reserves or the region with the largest oil reserves a natural candidate for a comparison group. We opt for the region richest in oil. One may argue that reporting a mean outcome for Baku, other oil-rich and oil-poor regions may be a more convenient presentation of our findings. Unfortunately, neither probit nor tobit procedure allows us to fit a model that would be equivalent to an ordinary least squares regression without an intercept term, i.e. a model that would allow us to include all region variables in the estimating equation without running into perfect collinearity problems. Finally, we are interested in how the magnitude of the effect changes with the size of the oil endowment. As indicated in Table 8.2, Azerbaijan provides a perfect setting for such analysis – several regions of the country are endowed with oil, however, the amounts of oil in other regions are almost negligible when compared to Baku. Reporting the findings relative to Baku has the advantage of allowing the reader immediately to assess the significance of the relationship between the magnitude of the effect and the size of the oil endowment.

In 1995, a household locating in an oil-poor region, irrespective of that region's economic activity, was 13.7 per cent to 18.4 per cent less likely to obtain state benefits as a household with similar characteristics locating in oil-rich Baku. In 2002 the situation was dramatically different as indicated by positive and, for the most part, significant coefficients on the regional dummies – the government shifted focus to the oil-poor regions and it is households in those regions which are more likely to obtain state benefits. Thus, the patterns described in Table 8.8 hold even when we net out the household characteristics.

The fact that the coefficient on the indicator for Absheron–Guba is insignificant suggests that the scale of oil production (much higher in Baku as illustrated in Table 8.2) did not matter in 1995. This is not the case in 2002 – as the production of oil in Baku became nearly 20 times the size of the production of oil in other regions (increasing from 12 times), the scale started to matter. A household in the less oil-rich Absheron–Guba was 8 per cent more likely to obtain state benefits than a household in Baku. A very similar picture arises when we look at the share of state benefits in total income: in 1995 state benefits made up a higher share of the total income for a household in Baku than for a household in other parts of the country and the situation reversed in 2002.

The role of the economic activity prevalent in the oil-poor region is not very clear. The differences in the coefficients on the non-agricultural, agricultural and other regions are negligible and inconsistent in most cases. One strong finding is that the benefits make up a smaller share of the total income in the agricultural than in other oil-poor regions. You will recall from Table 8.1 that Lankaran–Astara showed some of the highest growth rates, driven by the flourishing food industry processing locally produced agricultural goods. This, combined with the fact that agriculture is strongly subsidized in Azerbaijan, may be the reason behind our finding – the households simply have other sources of income and do not rely so heavily on government support. Somewhat more difficult to explain is the fact that a household located in an agricultural region has a different probability of obtaining benefits than an identical household in other oil-poor regions.

The coefficients on the household characteristics provide interesting insights into the benefit of the distribution policy. The switch of the coefficient on the indicator for a rural household from negative to positive indicates a much stronger emphasis on the rural households in 2002. As expected, the households with internally displaced persons are much more likely to receive state support irrespective of whether these transfers are sponsored through oil money or not (the coefficients are positive and significant in both pre- and post-boom periods). The size of the coefficients increased in 2002. This change is consistent with the story of the improved coverage of the internally displaced persons and inconsistent with the story of the state benefits being crowded out by an increasing support of the internally displaced people from the non-government sources (NGOs, international organisations, private firms' social activities). Similarly, adding a child or being a single parent also increases the probability of receiving benefits.

An eye-catching observation from Table 8.9 is a much stronger emphasis on low-skilled workers (as indicated by negative and highly significant coefficients on the household head's years of schooling variable). It is also clear that in 2002 the government shifted its attention to the households with low wage earnings – surprisingly, in 1995 having higher wage earnings increased the probability of receiving state benefits. In 2002, it is the households with low wage earnings that are more likely to benefit from the government support.

Turning to the results for the share of state benefits in total income (columns 3 and 4 of Table 8.8), we see that rural location, household size, number of children, the household head's education and wage earnings affect not only the eligibility for benefits, but also their share in total income. In 1995, the highest benefits were received in Baku (as evidenced by negative and highly significant coefficients on other variables) or other urban areas (as indicated by negative and significant on the indicator for rural location), by families with many children, relatively high wage earnings and high-skilled household heads. In 2002, holding other factors constant, the highest benefits were received by oil-poor areas. Also, the effect of an additional child decreased in magnitude, while the effects of rural location, wage earnings and household head's education switched their signs and have become highly significant.

To summarize, the findings presented in Table 8.8 indicate a changing emphasis of government support. State benefits have a much stronger 'pro-poor' element, whereby it is rural, unskilled households in low wage occupations and residing in oil-poor regions who are receiving more assistance.

Finally, in Table 8.9 we introduce an interaction term between the region and the urban/rural location of the household. Note that introduction of this term has not affected the significance of the coefficients on the regional variables, our main variables of interest (the changes in magnitudes are negligible). The insignificant results in 1995 column are most likely due to the lost degrees of freedom. The negative and for the most part highly significant coefficients on the interaction

Table 8.9 The effect of the region's endowment with oil on the probability of receiving state benefits and on the household's dependency on government support

	Recipient of benefits		Share of benefits in total income	
	1995	*2002*	*1995*	*2002*
Absheron–Guba relative to Baku	−0,012	0.052*	0,033	0.015***
	[0.067]	[0.028]	[0.050]	[0.005]
Non-agricultural relative to Baku	−0.136**	0.144***	−0.089*	0.017***
	[0.062]	[0.025]	[0.046]	[0.005]
Agricultural relative to Baku	−0.170**	0.063*	−0.278***	0.016**
	[0.070]	[0.034]	[0.057]	[0.007]
Other relative to Baku	−0.145*	0.106***	−0.125**	0.033***
	[0.084]	[0.025]	[0.063]	[0.005]
Rural	−0.029	0.140***	0.006	0.001
	[0.099]	[0.048]	[0.080]	[0.009]
Rural* non-agricultural	−0.047	−0.138**	−0.086	0.001
	[0.122]	[0.062]	[0.095]	[0.011]
Rural* agricultural	−0.066	−0.083	−0.048	0.007
	[0.127]	[0.066]	[0.101]	[0.011]
Rural* other	−0.047	−0.146**	−0.075	0.004
	[0.136]	[0.060]	[0.105]	[0.010]
Indicator for displaced persons	0.252***	0.352***	0.074**	0.182***
	[0.027]	[0.016]	[0.030]	[0.005]
Household size	−0.005	0.086***	−0.01	0.002
	[0.011]	[0.009]	[0.010]	[0.002]
Number of children	0.070***	0.091***	0.043***	0.014***
	[0.016]	[0.009]	[0.013]	[0.002]
Dummy for married households	−0.018	−0.036	0.08	−0.032***
	[0.061]	[0.031]	[0.052]	[0.005]
Dummy for male headed households	0.026	−0.120***	0.024	−0.018***
	[0.064]	[0.028]	[0.052]	[0.005]
Log (real earnings of household head)	0.008***	−0.014***	0.004***	−0.004***
	[0.002]	[0.001]	[0.001]	[0.000]
Age of household head	−0.001	−0.002	−0.002	0.001***
	[0.002]	[0.001]	[0.001]	[0.000]
Years of schooling of the household head	0.001	−0.013***	0.006	−0.001***
	[0.005]	[0.002]	[0.004]	[0.000]
Constant			0.345***	0.043***
			[0.092]	[0.010]
N. Obs	1003	5126	967	5104
R-Squared	0.08	0.17	0.16	0.34

Notes: Standard errors in brackets. * Significant at 10%. ** Significant at 5%. *** Significant at 1%.

of rural with oil-poor regions indicates that rural households in oil-poor regions are less likely to obtain government support than a rural household in oil-rich Absheron–Guba (you will recall that the region with most oil is also the capital city of the country). The results for the share of state benefits are insignificant.

Before concluding this section, we would like to put our findings in perspective by comparing them with the findings of the previous chapter on the impact of oil revenue expansion in Kazakhstan. Najman *et al.* find that the oil benefits have not been redistributed evenly across the country. Using household survey data, they show that the expansion of the oil sector has benefited only the capital city and other metropolitan areas where the country's elite lives, the finding that bolsters the conjecture that the oil revenue is often used to sponsor grand projects and to reinforce the riches of the already wealthy elite. An analysis of the underlying factors for the divergence of our results with those described above may be an interesting avenue for future research.

Conclusions and directions for further research

Our analysis supports the view that the Azeri government is using part of its rents to mitigate the losses of the vulnerable population segments in order to avoid ethnic, social and other tensions. Using quasi-experiment setting, we find that the Azeri government has used its expanding oil revenue to increase both the amount of state benefits and the number of its recipients. We document the altered preference of the government for truly poor segments of the population – unskilled, rural, female-headed and single parent households, with a particular partiality for the residents of the oil-poor regions. Our evidence is consistent with the findings of the Progress Report of the State Program on Poverty Reduction and Economic Development, which commends the extent to which the existing funds for social protection are reaching those in most need.

The above conclusions are preliminary in several respects. First, the cautiously optimistic outlook for the Azeri poor presented in this chapter hinges upon the quality of the household data. Second, we concentrate on direct monetary transfers from the government and abstract from forms of assistance such as low-cost energy prices. Although under-priced energy creates a host of macroeconomic problems such as delayed enterprise restructuring, undermined economy-wide productivity growth, reduced incentives to save energy and distorted resource allocation whereby resources are locked in energy- and capital-intensive production, it also represents a transfer to the household (Saavalainen and ten Berge 2006). Since the emphasis of this chapter is on fiscal redistribution, we also abstract from two other important channels for the redistribution of oil revenue – market-based transfers in terms of increased relative wages in extracting activities and supporting industries and oil companies' transfers through social projects. Finally, the findings of this chapter may only be read as proving the existence of income redistribution in Azerbaijan. To what extent this redistribution is compensating the population groups displaced by the developments in the oil sector cannot be deduced from this study. Further research is needed to examine these issues and to substantiate or expand some of the tentative conclusions outlined in this chapter.

It is important to note that apart from the obvious economic consequences for income inequality across and within regions, 'fair' redistribution of oil revenue has important political implications. The surging exports of oil can simultaneously increase the discontent in oil-producing regions and the rest of the country, as oil-producing regions wish to keep a higher share of oil revenue whereas the rest of the country insists on a higher redistribution share (Nigeria: Ikein and Briggs-Anigboh 1998). Alternatively, the struggle can occur between the oil-producing regions and the central government, as the bulk of the resource rents leaks to the capital city, leaving oil-producing regions in poverty (Russia: Dienes 2002; Kazakhstan: Najman *et al.* in Chapter 7). Our study complements the existing literature by providing a case in which the capital city and surrounding areas are also home to the majority of oil-extracting and oil-processing businesses. Hence, the benefits of the burgeoning extracting sectors go directly to the already prosperous region, potentially magnifying income inequality even further and creating fertile grounds for social unrest. We have documented the attempt of the government to prevent such developments and we hope that the findings of this chapter can serve as a starting point for political scientists to evaluate to what extent the government's redistributive policies have succeeded in ensuring relative political stability in the country.

Appendix

The State Oil Fund of the Republic of Azerbaijan

On 29 December 1999, Azeri President Heidar Aliyev issued a decree creating a State Oil Fund designed to use money obtained from oil-related foreign investment on education, reducing poverty and raising the living standards of the rural population in Azerbaijan. As of January 2002, the State Oil Fund held $499 million, and by the end of 2006 this had risen to between $1.3 billion and $1.4 billion. The State Oil Fund of the Republic of Azerbaijan (SOFAZ) was established in December 1999. The cornerstone of the philosophy behind the Oil Fund is to ensure intergenerational equality of benefit with regard to the country's wealth while improving the economic wellbeing of the population today and safeguarding economic security for future generations. It is a mechanism whereby energy-related windfalls will be accumulated and efficiently managed. In so doing, the government is demonstrating its over-riding desire and determination to avoid the inherent risks for any nation in the midst of an oil and gas boom to spend excessively and create macroeconomic distortions.

SOFAZ is a state extra-budgetary fund, functioning as a separate legal entity, with its own specialist management team and government supervisory hierarchy. SOFAZ is headed by the Executive Director, who is appointed and dismissed by the President of the Republic of Azerbaijan. SOFAZ's activities in the field of asset accumulation and spending are overseen by a Supervisory Board, which consists

Table A8.1 Production sharing agreements in Azerbaijan

	Estimated reserves	*Details*	*SOCAR*
1 Offshore PSA			
Azeri, Chirag, and Deepwater Gunashi	5.4 billion barrels of oil	Exports began late 1997. Producing 144,000 bbl/d at Chirag field as of July 2004. First exploration well drilled at Azen field.	10%
Shah Deniz	2.5 billion barrels of oil; 14 Tcf of natural gas	First phase of development approved in February 2003. Production to begin in Autumn 2006.	10%!
Lankaran–Talysh	700 million barrels of oil	First test well (2001) came up dry.	25%
Yalama/D-222	750 million barrels at Yalama field	Drilling to 4,400 meters failed to find commercial reserves. Lukoil announce it may abandon well but must drill at least one more well.	20%
Absheron	858 million barrels of oil; up to 100 Tcf of natural gas	Project closed. Chevron abandoned first exploratory well in 2001. In November 2003, Chevron and Total paid $40 million in compensation rather than drill a second well as required under contract	50%
Oguz	290 million barrels of oil and 685 bcf of gas	Dry well drilled in April 2001. ExxonMobil announced plans to quit the project in April 2002.	50%
Nakhchivan	750 million barrels of oil	ExxonMobil drilled one successful well, will drill a second well.	50%
Kurdashi–Araz–Kirgan Daniz	730 million barrels of oil	First test wells drilled, with poor results.	50%
Inam	2.2 billion barrels of oil	BP suspended drilling of its first appraisal well in Aug.2001 due to high pressure. New well planned to be completed by 2005	50%
Araz, Alov, and Sharg	4 billion barrels of oil	In exploring phase in 2004. Confrontation with Iranian gunboat in July2001; exploration suspended, pending resolution of Caspian Sea borders between Azerbaijan and Iran.	40%
Atashgah	600 million barrels of oil in Atashgah, Mugandeniz, and Yanan Tava fields	Seismic work being undertaken. Second well at the Yanan–Tava field, part of a concession that also includes Ateshgah and Mugan–Deniz, struck gas, but not enough to be commercial. In June 2003, JAOC announced it would leave Azerbaijan.	50%
Lerik, Jenab, Savalan, Dalga	1 billion barrels of oil	Exploration D-43, D-44, and D-73 blocks	50%

continued…

153

	Estimated reserves	Details	SOCAR
Zafar–Mashal	1–2 billion barrels of oil, 1.8 tcf gas	Exploration D-9 and D-38 blocks. Reached final drilling point in September 2004, well likely to be shut down due to abnormally high pressure, and Exxon-Mobil failed to reveal commercial hydrocarbon reserves.	50%
2 Onshore PSA			
Kalamaddin–Mishovdagh	200 million barrels of oil	Production averaged 2,700 bpd of oil in 2004. Plans exist to raise level to 3,200 bpd	15%
Anshad Petrol	219 million barrels at Neftchala, Khilly, Babazanan	Drilled 4 wells 1998–9. Oil production averaged 77,000 bpd in 2004. Gas production averaged 1.1 mcf/day for 2004.	51%
AzOeroil	140 million barrels at Ramany, Balkhany, and Sabunchi fields	Production averaged 1,000 bbl/d in 1999.	51%
Southwest Gobustan	147 million barrels of oil; up to 7 trillion cf of natural gas	Gas found at onshore East Duvanny field, well tested at a flow rate of 8.6 million cubic feet/day. Azeri government estimates oil should be found in offshore portion of block.	20%
Zykh–Govsany	66–150 million barrels of oil	Rehabilitating fields; produced 1,830 bbl/d in 2000. Contract start date pushed back due to environmental issues.	50%
Kursangt–Garabagli	730 million barrels of oil	10 additional wells drilled in 2003 to increase production; fields producing 6,600 bbl/d in June 2004.	50%
Muradkhanli–Jafarli– Zardab	730 million barrels of oil	1st test well at Muradkhanli shut down in April 2001. CNPC won a tender to develop the block, although no new PSA has been signed yet.	50%
Padar–Kharami	580–750 million barrels of oil	Seismic work being undertaken.	15%
Shirvanoil	650 million barrels of oil at Kyurovdag field	Rehabilitating existing wells since 1997. Oil production averaged 57,000 bpd in 2004. Gas production was 1.5 mcf/d.	49%
West Absheron (Karadag–Kergez–Umbaki fields)	200 million barrels of oil	SOCAR moved to take over the concession in December 1999 following BMB's request to suspend operations.	

of both representatives of executive and legislative powers including government ministers and members of the Parliament. The board reviews the Fund's draft annual budget and annual report and financial statements, prepared by the Executive Director, along with the auditor's opinion and provides its comments. Execution of the SOFAZ budget has to be approved by the President.

The major sources of income for SOFAZ are:

1 Proceeds from sales of the Azerbaijan's share of hydrocarbons (exclusive of hydrocarbons' transportation costs, banking expenses, customs costs, independent surveyors, marketing and insurance costs, and also exclusive of the revenue from the share in those projects in which the State Oil Company is an investor, shareholder or partner).
2 Oil and gas agreement signature and/or performance bonuses paid by investors to the State Oil Company or an authorized state body.
3 Acreage fees paid by foreign investors for use of the contract areas in connection with the development of hydrocarbon resources.
4 Dividends and profit participation revenue falling on the share of Azerbaijan in connection with implementation of oil and gas agreements.
5 Revenue generated from oil and gas passing through the territory of the country.
6 Revenue from the management of SOFAZ's assets.
7 Revenue generated from the transfer of assets from investors to the State Oil Company and/or an authorized state body, within the framework of oil and gas agreements.

One important expenditure category funded by SOFAZ during the period covered by this study is assistance to internally displaced persons.

Notes

1 We thank the participants of the Workshop on the Impact of Oil Boom in the Caspian Basin in Paris (June, 2006) for their comments.
2 The growth rate is from the European Bank for Reconstruction and Development *Transition Report 2006*; see also the article on Azerbaijan in *The Economist*, 25 February 2006.
3 *Asian Development Outlook 2006*, Asian Development Bank (ADB), Manila.
4 Comparable 2006 numbers for Uzbekistan and Kyrgyzstan, for example, are $2,000 and $1,800. The success is slightly less impressive when compared with that of other resource rich countries in the region – Kazakhstan and Turkmenistan, report values of $8,800 and $6,100. However, these countries also had a better start – $3,618 and $2,996 in 1995 (Data sources: World Development Indicators and 2006 CIA World Fact Book).
5 In 2005 the share of oil sector was 42% in GDP, 84% in exports, 87% in foreign direct investment, 64% in total investment and 40% in state budget revenue.
6 The completion dates are July 2006 for the BTC oil pipeline and the end of 2006 (scheduled) for the BTE gas pipeline.
7 The World Bank, for example, is expected to allocate $1.2 billion to the country, of which $850 million will be used for the roads and other infrastructural projects. The World Bank is also ready to give $50 million for cleaning more than a century's worth of environmental damage caused by oil production (*Asian Development Outlook 2006*, ADB).
8 *Azerbaijan Issues and Options Associated with Energy Sector Reform*, World Bank Report No. 32371, March 2005

9 SOCAR was established in September 1992 with the merger of Azerbaijan's two state oil compnies, Azerineft and Azneftkimiza. SOCAR and its many subsidiaries are responsible for the production of oil and natural gas in Azerbaijan, for the operation of the country's two refineries, for running the country's pipeline system and for managing the country's oil and gas imports and exports. While government ministries handle exploration and production agreements with foreign companies, SOCAR is party to all of the international consortia developing new oil and gas projects in Azerbaijan. The company (excluding subsidiaries) employs 75,000 people. Most of SOCAR's production (approximately 65% in 2002) is derived from the field 'shallow-water Guneshi', 60 miles off Azerbaijan's Absheron Peninsula. SOCAR also operates 40 other older fields, many of which are in disrepair.

10 Each district has its own sources of revenue which consist mostly of taxes, fees and interest payments on overdue fine payments. The district defines, independently from the State Budget, the level and structure of its local expenditure. The deficit is covered by the subsidies from the State Budget. In theory, the level of the subsidies is determined by the district's population and its share in the generation of the country's financial resources. Other factors may be taken into account – the areas under the Armenian occupation, Karabagh–Mil, receive twice the amount of subsidies to other regions. More details on the interrelationships between the State and the Local Budgets can be obtained from 'The Law of Azerbaijan Republic on Budget System', available at the website of the Ministry of Finance (www.malizze.gov.az).

11 It would be wrong, of course, to describe the workers of the oil industry as winners. That oil boom is a poor vehicle of job creation is already felt in Azerbaijan – by the end of 2006, almost half of the 17,000 jobs originally created will be phased out as the oil-related infrastructure is put in place and the locally provided blue collar labour is no longer needed (Eurasianet.org). The number of people directly engaged in mining, if anything, decreased – from 44,000 workers in 1995 to slightly over 40,000 in 2005, even though the number of acting enterprises quadrupled during the same period (State Statistical Committee).

12 Azeri military and police have proved themselves to be ardent supporters of the current regime and have been willing to use force to suppress riots and demonstrations organized by the opposition (EurasiaNet Human Rights reports and periodicals).

13 We use the term 'post-boom' loosely to conform to the terminology used in the project evaluation studies (as in pre- and post-treatment stages). It is meant to identify the period of the first influx of petrodollars and not the wrap-up or slow down of oil production.

14 There are, in fact, over 30 distinct types of benefits and one of the goals of the social assistance reform is gradually to reduce their number.

15 One may be interested in the generosity of state benefits across various regions. Since this measure depends on the accuracy of the regional price indices (see footnote to Table 8.4 for details), we choose the share of state benefits in total income as the preferred measure. The findings for the logarithm of the real state benefits are available from the authors upon request.

16 Ideally, we would like to exclude old age pensions from state benefits, however this is not possible due to data deficiencies. To mitigate the problem, we restrict our analysis to the households with members under 60 years of age.

Part IV

GOVERNANCE AND LOCAL IMPACT
Alternative viewpoints

9

IMPROVING THE BENEFICIAL SOCIO-ECONOMIC IMPACT OF HYDROCARBON EXTRACTION ON LOCAL/ REGIONAL DEVELOPMENT IN CASPIAN ECONOMIES

Richard Auty

The literature suggests that large capital-intensive mining investments create inflated expectations of local benefits mainly because an unusually high share of the mining revenue flows abroad to service foreign capital. In addition, fiscal linkage (taxation) dominates domestic linkages and tends to accrue to the national government, so that local mining communities may be inadequately compensated for the environmental, social and economic costs of production. Inadequate compensation is evident in the Caspian hydrocarbon fields. However, mining companies increasingly see enhanced local welfare as a condition for project viability. This chapter identifies three ways to maximise local welfare and argues that multinational corporations (MNCs) should: (i) establish a stakeholder committee prior to investment to identify realistic expectations for local benefits and to coordinate their realization; (ii) promote local business formation to sustain the economy when mineral extraction ceases; and (iii) underpin business formation by strengthening social capital at both the local level and at the national level. The adaptation of PSAs to promote enterprise formation within early reform zones (ERZs) can help large mining projects not only to boost local welfare but also to function as catalysts for *national* economic reform.

Large hydrocarbon projects and local welfare: literature review

Large mining investments tend to over-inflate expectations about the size of their beneficial local impacts in developing countries. The literature identifies the exceptionally capital-intensive production function of most mining projects as the principal reason for this, because foreign investment is usually required and a large share of the mineral revenue leaks abroad to service capital. This reduces the share of backward, forward and final demand linkages to the domestic economy compared with, for example, most manufacturing. The share of purchased inputs (backward linkage) in the gross value of mining is 40 per cent or lower compared with 70 per cent for manufacturing (Di Boscio 2004). In addition, scope for local production of mine inputs (backward linkage) is restricted by the absence in developing countries of localization economies on which the efficient production of such specialised inputs often depends (Eggert 2002). Moreover, final processing of minerals (forward linkage) tends to be more competitive at the market than at the mine. Finally, since mining is often foreign-owned and employs a small albeit highly trained workforce, the second round domestic expenditure from miners' wages is small. Although the local mining employment multiplier is typically 2.0 to 3.0 and the output multiplier from local expenditure is 1.5 to 2.4 (Aroca 2001; Mulkey and Hodges 2004; Wheeler 2003), the small mine workforce renders the aggregate impact modest.

These constraints on local economic linkage arising out of mining's capital intensity are stronger: (i) the remoter the mine location (which shrinks local agglomeration economies); (ii) the earlier the stage in the mining cycle (which further cuts agglomeration economies); (iii) the shorter the expected life of the mine (because short-lived mines discourage linked local investment); (iv) the lower the per capita output of the host economy (due to skill gaps); and (v) the less socially responsive the mining corporation. The type of mineral also has an effect: ore mining's generally shorter perceived life expectancy compared with hydrocarbon extraction further discourages local linkages. However, in the case of hydrocarbon extraction, the typically very high share of rent in gross output means that sound government policies can capture rent via taxation, although the taxes mainly accrue to the central government and not to the mining region. The net effect of these features of hydrocarbon's unusually capital-intensive production is to render fiscal linkage by far the strongest domestic economic contribution.

The size of the *local* fiscal linkage is sensitive to the scale of the rent, the negotiating strength of the central government and the relative strength of central and local administrations. Weak national governments may forfeit fiscal linkage (EBRD 2001; see Table 9.1) to mining firms (by conceding over-generous contract terms), workers (through high wages extracted by exploiting the vulnerability of capital-intensive activity to production stoppages), and consumers (through subsidised energy supplies). In turn, weak regional governments and/or local communities may concede fiscal linkage to a more powerful central government. The typical hydrocarbon project may have a much larger turnover than the local economy, so that it can transmit strong shocks that can inflict sizeable costs that arise out of mineral price swings, culture clashes, under-regulated pollution and/or Dutch disease effects. These considerations regarding the local linkages of capital-intensive mining projects increase the risk that local and regional communities will bear high social and environmental costs as a consequence of mining activity, with little compensation.

Table 9.1 Estimated energy rents, selected Caspian Basin countries 2000 (% GDP)

	Export rent	*Domestic producer rent*	*Total rent*	*Domestic consumer subsidies*
Azerbaijan	31.2	16.8	61.4	13.4
Kazakhstan	20.2	9.8	33.6	3.6
Turkmenistan	43.0	-5.2	65.3	27.5
Uzbekistan	6.3	26.2	36.4	3.9

Source: Esanov *et al.* 2006: 43.
Notes:
Export rents = actual export revenue – transport costs – production costs.
Total rents = total output x export price – transport cost – production cost.
Domestic consumer subsidies = domestic consumption x (domestic price – import price).
Domestic producer rent = total rent – export rent – domestic consumer subsidies.

The literature provides numerous examples of the negative impacts of mismanaged mining revenue on both the national and local economies (Auty and Mikesell 1998; Eggert 2002). The local economy may experience unbalanced growth if the revenue received by the local administration fails to match expanding infrastructure requirements or to provide enabling institutions for linked economic activity. In addition, the typically high wages within the oil sector tend to bid factors of production away from non-oil activity and to inflate their costs. High wages in the hydrocarbon sector also skew local income distribution, which contributes to local social tensions, not least in communities with a memory of greater wage parity.

In recent years, the rise of self-appointed groups to lobby on behalf of developing countries has promoted a strong critique of the developmental impact of capital-intensive oil, gas and mineral ore projects. Many such groups recently coalesced around the report of an internal review, the Extractive Industries Review, which evaluated World Bank policy on lending to mining projects (World Bank 2003). In response to such pressure, mining companies have increasingly made improved regional welfare a prerequisite for proceeding with such investment (Humphreys 2000). This chapter argues that although development economists may prefer more labour-intensive activity like farming to propel low-income economies compared with large capital-intensive finite mining projects, large mines can enhance local, national and global welfare if soundly managed. The outcome is sensitive to the quality of governance and of policy, which is a sobering fact for both former Soviet Union and developing market economies that lag in terms of progress with economic and political reform.

This chapter argues that recent efforts by mineral MNCs to promote sustainable local development are becoming over-extended and that they should instead focus upon three core objectives, namely to: (i) neutralise the potential negative local impacts of mining; (ii) foster competitive enterprises to diversify the local economy and generate revenue to sustain the region's stock of produced, human and social capital; and (iii) encourage resilient social capital, which moulds the efficiency of local capital accumulation and wealth creation. We measure social capital here in terms of the effectiveness with which local civic associations identify and pursue legitimate means of raising social welfare and the capacity of institutions to facilitate efficient investment in wealth generating assets. Finally, it is argued that all three core objectives can be most expeditiously pursued, not through top–down reforms at the national level, which are all too easily blocked by vested interests, but at the local level within ERZs, under conditions similar to those negotiated in the mining companies' PSAs. In this way, local mineral projects can become catalysts for beneficial national economic reform.

Potential and actual local impacts

Before exploring the constraints on sustainable linkages from mining (in section three) and on complementary policy improvements (in section four), we first need to establish the nature of the potential and actual local linkages in the Caspian hydrocarbon fields. Northeast Scotland provides a useful template for evaluating the potential local impacts of a large hydrocarbon investment in a peripheral region (Table 9.2, line one). It suggests that within a well-managed economy, large mineral projects can strongly and positively impact the local economy even in an extremely peripheral region that faces strong centrifugal forces from the national core region. Oil expansion not only abruptly reversed the previous rapid decline of Northeast Scotland's economy, but the region's new dynamism continued unabated more than 15 years after investment into offshore oil activity had began to wind down (Kemp 2005). A second lesson from Northeast Scotland is that the rate of growth in oil-linked activity is lagged and it is initially characterised by low technology. Even in a mature economy, oil-linked local firms initially supplied technically simple products and services. This early response fed demands by critics for government intervention to force localization, demands that UK governments heeded when oil prices were high during 1974 to 1985 (Hallwood 1988) by strengthening local-content policy. However, Kashani (2005) estimates that the policy boosted local supply costs by 5 per cent to 8 per cent, in effect leaking rent to local firms.

During the expansion phase of UK oil production some researchers berated the preference of the oil companies for working with established foreign input suppliers at the expense of local firms. Yet linked local firms eventually emerged and followed a learning curve during the first decade of oil investment that upgraded their products. When fears about low local content and simple technology proved overblown, some critics forecast that the oil supply firms would be unable to adjust to the decline in oil production. Once again, they were wrong. Local supply firms adjusted when the oil majors embarked on cost cutting in the mid-1980s, even though the UK government intensified that adjustment by simultaneously scaling down its local content policy when EU competition directives hardened. Local firms successfully adapted by a mix of geographical diversification, sector diversification and investment in research and development (Chapman et al. 2004). This experience strongly suggests that an active local content policy

Table 9.2 Estimated domestic local economic impact for hydrocarbon extraction projects

Project	Total investment ($million)	Direct jobs (000)	Investment/job ($000)	Indirect + induced multiplier	National expenditure/yr on O + M ($ million)	Local expenditure/yr on O + M ($ million)
NE Scotland	359,000.0[a]	51.30	7,039.0	1.78	5,250.0[b]	1,578.0
ACG1	3200.0	0.34	9,412.0	1.43	38.0	7.6
BTC (Azeri)	850.0 [bc]	0.25	3,400.0	n.a.	35.0	35.0
Sumgait Petro	n.a.	12.00	n.a.	3.00?	115.0[c]	115.0
Tengiz1	8,000.0	8.00	1,000.0	1.52	564.0[cd]	n.a.
Karachaganak	3,800.0	n.a.	n.a.	n.a.	n.a.	n.a.
Kashagan1	10,000.0	n.a.	n.a.	n.a.	n.a.	n.a.
CPC	2,600.0	n.a.	n.a.	n.a.	n.a.	n.a.

Source: See text and tables.

Notes:

a Kemp's (2005) £205 billion in constant 2002 pounds with an average exchange rate of $1.75/£1.00.
b Total BTC investment in all three countries is $3.2 billion and operating employment is 850.
c Annual petrochemical revenue.
d Annual domestic supply expenditure.

may be redundant. In summary, UK experience shows that the market works. It should be permitted to work in the Caspian Basin, not least because government intervention in these countries is vulnerable to policy capture, which saps the competitiveness of linked activity and dissipates the rents.

The projected greater scale and longevity of hydrocarbon production in Kazakhstan compared with Azerbaijan offsets West Kazakhstan's greater remoteness to confer on it considerable potential for regional industrialization. Forward linkages are already developing apace along with backward linkages as Atyrau emerges as an important petrochemical producer within the Central Asian and Caucasus region. The MNCs promote linked economic activity either through direct downstream investment, like LDPE plants (which link back to the construction phase of the hydrocarbon investment by supplying plastic pipes), or by working through PSA local content requirements to encourage small- and medium-sized enterprise (SME) formation to supply inputs at adequate standards of quality and cost. But much linked activity is capital-intensive and employs relatively few workers, heightening income inequality within Atyrau oblast.

Oil has given West Kazakhstan one of the highest mean incomes in the country (Table 9.3). Yet only a minority work in the oil sector and the majority of the local population must put up with low wages and relatively high local prices, including those of basic commodities. They must also endure the legacy of under-investment in education, healthcare and economic infrastructure together with severe air pollution (despite investment in state-of-the-art production technology). The pollution is partly due to the continued operation of an oil refinery that was established during Soviet times. But it also reflects the difficulties that the MNCs have encountered in disposing of the very high levels of sulphur (15 per cent content) extracted from the region's oil. Atyrau has unusually high levels of respiratory and other illnesses, which most individuals, and also the state, lack the resources to mitigate. In the early-2000s the Atyrau government struggled

Table 9.3 Potential multipliers for ACG Phase 1

	Construction	*Operating*
Period	2002–2005	2005–2025
Direct employment	4,000	300
Total investment ($ billion)	1.955	
Direct impact ($ billion)	0.888	0.770
Indirect + induced impact ($ billion)	0.382	0.331
Total impact ($ billion)	1.270	1.101

Source: BP (2002).
Note:
AGC2 will entail an extra $1.3 billion, BTC $87 million, Shah Deniz $0.8 billion and SCP $67 million (BP 2003: 104).

to expand infrastructure, while transferring revenue in excess of 3 per cent of GDP per annum to the central government (Granovsky 2003). The PSAs provide inadequate tax revenue to the local community, which the government in Astana does insufficient to mitigate.

The MNCs seek to offset this neglect by allocating a fraction of their annual capital expenditure to social and economic infrastructure, but this still falls considerably short of requirements. Successful efforts to cushion adverse local impacts include siting transient labour camps away from small settlements and where possible in cities; mandatory local recruitment ratios for sub-contractors and oil firms alike (including worker recruitment and retraining every 50 km along the BTC pipeline) and preference for local supply firms (BP 2003, 2004). In addition, development of the hydrocarbon fields is staged, which spreads construction activity over time. Nevertheless, there have been large fluctuations in local construction activity and outlays, and the switch to the operating stage sharply reduces direct employment and input purchases, albeit to more stable levels (Table 9.4). Both the Atyrau and Sangachal regions, along with the linking pipeline tracts, experienced several years of large-scale construction activity, involving 8,000 to 15,000 workers at times.

In Azerbaijan, Sumgait might aspire to a similar role to that of Atyrau as a petrochemical and metals producer. In 1989 Sumgait had a population of 300,000 when its petrochemical industry alone employed 30,000 workers (Auty 1999). However, the loss of markets in the former Soviet Union severely slashed capacity use and rehabilitation efforts are crippled by obsolete industrial plant and the dominance of Sumgait production by largely unreformed state corporations. The state firms are unable to attract MNC partners to invest in the regeneration of the local economy, rehabilitate the decrepit infrastructure and clean up a 60-year legacy of environmental pollution (Smailes 2001).

Sumgait and the new oil terminal of Sangachal both illustrate how deficient social capital may constrain *local* socio-economic benefits if the settlements lie close to a relatively large economic centre like Baku. The expenditure of high levels

Table 9.4 Population and per capita income, principal economic regions of Kazakhstan, 1999

	Population (millions)	Share ethnic Kazakh (%)	Per capita income (US$ PPP)	Economic activity
Almaty	1.13	38.5	11,935	Financial and commercial capital
West	2.06	74.0	8,076	Oil and gas production
North	6.72	38.3	5,532	Mining, heavy industry and wheat
South	5.11	67.8	2,253	Cotton and intermediate industry

Source: Anderson and Pomfret 2003: 40 and 54, except column 2 from Olcott 2002: 247–8.

of oil rent in Baku is in marked contrast to lower amounts expended in either of the settlements where production installations are located. The case of Sangachal is less bleak than that of Sumgait, however, mainly because as a greenfield site its environmental legacy is less onerous. Sangachal also benefits from the presence of a progressive MNC (BP) that exhibits concern for local jobs, public services and environmental impacts (Table 9.5). Yet within a population of 4,500, only 200 workers from Sangachal had secured employment in oil sector construction and operations by early 2005, albeit at relatively high wages. Consequently, as with Atyrau, the mean income of Sangachal remains relatively low. The local authority has secured some increase in revenue through higher taxation of the improved housing purchased by oil sector workers. However, government revenue falls well short of the level needed to upgrade Sangachal's rudimentary infrastructure, which stands in stark contrast with that of Baku. It is necessary to strengthen social capital in order to boost local benefits from mining projects.

Constraints on policies to promote sustainable linked economic activity

In addition to deficient social capital, two other basic constraints on sustainable local development in countries of the CIS are government failure and market failure. By providing sound macro management an enabling government can substantially boost the benefits from new mining investment in terms of expanding sustainable employment and the social expenditure that it allows. The basic risk faced by oil-rich economies is the over-rapid domestic absorption of the rent due to government acquiescence to pressure from powerful rent-seeking interests. A heavy reliance on commodity revenue, as opposed to the income, sales and profits taxes that resource-poor economies must rely upon, is associated with reduced pressure for effective scrutiny of public finances. Improved revenue transparency can help tighten policy and both Azerbaijan and Kazakhstan have made progress here by establishing national oil funds and, in Azerbaijan, by embracing the EITI. Unfortunately, the oil funds lack checks against capricious political expenditure because the rules regarding revenue accumulation and allocation are flexible, while a president can override most obligations (Bagirov et al. 2003).

In addition, the market failure manifested in weak financial markets and uncontrolled rent seeking pushes a sizeable fraction of economic activity into the grey economy where it incurs lower predation but is less productive. Table 9.6 suggests that levels of corruption are high in both Azerbaijan and Kazakhstan compared with countries of a similar per capita income, which is a feature of oil-driven economies. The oil companies have limited their exposure to corruption by negotiating PSAs, backed by sanctions imposed by the international financial institutions, to achieve the investment security and efficiency that they require to justify their large sunk investments (Table 9.2). Field data for Azerbaijan indicate that BP can achieve its targeted risk-related 17 per cent return on investment, but manufacturing firms outside the PSA may target a 70 per cent return to cover the costs of an adequate profit and illicit imposts. This implies that illicit imposts

Table 9.5 Goldman Sachs Energy Environmental and Social Index 2004, selected MNCs

Company	Climate change	Pollution	Human rights	Management incentives	Investment for future	Workforce	Safety	Transparency and vision	GSEES Index Score
BP	23	3	11	20	6	22	21	14	120
RD/Shell	22	3	9	21	8	19	21	14	117
Statoil	18	7	11	18	5	19	18	13	109
Exxon-Mobil	13	3	8	18	8	23	23	12	108
Norsk Hydro	18	8	10	13	7	16	17	10	99
TOTAL	19	4	9	18	10	19	9	9	97
Chevron-Texaco	14	3	10	20	8	19	13	8	95
BG	17	8	10	15	5	13	16	10	94
ENI	15	8	10	16	6	13	12	10	90
Petro-China	5	5	7	17	4	10	7	8	63
Lukoil	5	4	6	12	2	8	5	4	46
Average[a]	11.9	4.7	8.2	15.7	5.0	13.6	12.1	9.3	80.5
Maximum[a]	25	8	12	23	10	25	25	14	142

Source: Goldman Sachs 2005: 39.

Note:

a Includes 12 additional 'regional' and 'emerging market' hydrocarbon companies from the original GEES Index list.

and associated market imperfections may reduce the economy-wide efficiency of capital to one quarter of the efficiency that can be achieved within the PSAs (Auty 1999). The high interest rates that arise out of inadequate financial markets also repress investment. An important reason for flawed financial markets is the inability of the banks to recover their capital, given the inadequacies in the judicial system. As a result, Azeri industry relies largely on oil investment because outside of the PSA protocol private firms face high risks if they lack political connections.

Rent seeking is a much greater deterrent to the indigenisation of linked economic activity than any inherent reluctance by the foreign mining corporations to work with local firms. If the deadweight cost of rent seeking can be reduced, then the oil companies have every incentive to take advantage of the relatively cheap and skilled labour and employ local suppliers, always provided that basic standards of cost and quality are met. However, local oil sector managers understandably resist pressure from their head offices to accelerate the use of local suppliers if the dependability of such supplies is compromised by rent-seeking activity.

The final constraint on policies to promote sustainable local economic activity is weak social capital, which manifests itself at the local level in a combination of petty rent seeking activity by public officials such as the police, and the inability of local governments to raise revenue and coordinate infrastructure and service provision in line with a realistic scenario for local economic development. The dominance of the hydrocarbon revenue stream by fiscal linkage fossilises the dependent social capital that is a legacy of central planning. Both firms and individuals look to the government to provide benefits and locals harbour deep cynicism over the likelihood of success, a scepticism that the domestic populace extends to the MNCs. There is an urgent need to strengthen civic voice and to build self-help civic associations so that local governments, firms and society can cohere to identify and achieve legitimate community interests within mining regions.

Policies to improve local impacts of hydrocarbon extraction

Concern for the risks that environmental damage poses to the successful construction, operation and decommissioning of a large-scale mineral project has been at the heart of the expansion of corporate social responsibility over the past two decades (Warner 2005). In consequence, best practice environmental standards are well established and most large companies strive to ensure that they comply with international standards, a stance that is more easily incorporated into greenfield investments like Sangachal than into the rehabilitation of brown field enterprises such as Sumgait. The international financial institutions play a critical role by making the espousal of best practice environmental management a condition for securing their financial participation. Nevertheless, as experience in Atyrau attests there is sometimes a gap between aspirations and practice (Nietalieva et al. 2005). The Caspian provides examples of both lax and over-

Table 9.6 Index of institutional quality 2005: Azerbaijan, Kazakhstan and comparator countries

Country	PCGDP (US$PPP 2005)	Voice and account- ability	Political stability	Effective governance	Regulation burden	Rule of law	Graft	Overall index
Nigeria	1,183	-0.69	-1.77	-0.92	-1.01	-1.38	-1.22	-6.99
Mozambique	1,364	-C.06	+0.04	-0.34	-0.60	-0.72	-0.68	-2.36
Benin	1,118	+0.34	+0.31	-0.69	-0.55	-0.59	-1.00	-2.18
Angola	2,425	-1.15	-0.82	-0.96	-1.24	-1.28	-1.09	-6.54
Azerbaijan	5,607	-1.16	-1.21	-0.73	-0.52	-0.84	-1.01	-5.47
Venezuela	6,531	-0.50	-1.22	-0.83	-1.15	-1.22	-1.00	-5.92
Kazakhstan	8,515	-1.19	+0.03	-0.71	-0.47	-0.79	-0.94	-4.07
Botswana	10.790	+0.68	+0.94	+0.79	+0.76	+0.70	+1.10	+4.97
Malaysia	10,843	-0.41	+0.49	+1.01	+0.50	+0.58	+0.27	+2.26
Trinidad + Tobago	13,758	+0.44	-0.05	+0.29	+0.65	-0.07	+0.01	+1.27
Saudi Arabia	14,729	-1.72	-0.70	-0.38	-0.01	+0.20	+0.23	-2.36
UK	32,005	+ 1.30	+0.34	+1.70	+1.53	+1.69	+1.94	+8.50

Source: World Bank (2005).

zealous enforcement of environmental standards. Local environmental officials have been reluctant at times to enforce compliance for fear of discomforting an important local industry that lays the proverbial golden egg. At the national level, the government of Kazakhstan has abused environmental enforcement by using it as a negotiating ploy.

Until recently, corporate policies have also been defensive towards social issues and focused upon limiting the adverse impacts of mining projects. In addition to adopting international standards for environmental protection and health and safety, companies have met gaps in basic social obligations by donating capital to local infrastructure projects, but seldom with provision for project maintenance costs. The oil majors allocate social spending in proportion to capital expenditure, with Total and Chevron allocating 0.8 per cent on this basis, Exxon and Shell around 0.7 per cent and BP trailing with 0.6 per cent (Goldman Sachs 2005). However, such social funding carries the twin moral risks of accommodating negligence by the various tiers of government that should provide the social facilities and of boosting dependence on mine revenue, which is transient.

This chapter argues that large mineral projects should, instead, rein in their social activity and focus their interventions on the potential of such projects to be a catalyst to accelerate the process of transition to a market economy. Ironically, their capacity to do so arises from the very same capital intensity that appears to diminish the potential local economic benefits of mining. This is because the risks associated with very large fixed capital investment motivate the mining companies to negotiate for, and achieve, what is in effect a geographical enclave, an ERZ, that immediately secures transition reform conditions. The oil and gas PSAs, backed by international financial institutions' sanctions against government intimidation, can facilitate early market reform to stimulate not only local economic activity but also to provide a strong demonstration effect to the national economy.

The extension of PSA conditions to embrace local linked and unlinked SMEs and micro-enterprises can maximise positive and sustainable local economic linkages and also demonstrate the capacity of efficient markets to generate wealth and promote social welfare within the national economy. Such ERZs can function as one track in a dual track economic strategy for market reform that builds as rapidly as possible a dynamic market economy alongside the second track, which is the distorted rent-driven economy bequeathed by central planning. Expansion of the dynamic market economy will increasingly absorb labour from the distorted economy while expanding taxes, skills and foreign exchange. It will also build a strong political constituency for economic reform of the distorted sector. This is in effect the successful politically sensitive reform strategy pursued not only by oil-rich Malaysia, Indonesia (Auty 2007a) and the United Arab Emirates (where Dubai spearheads the dynamic market track), but also by resource-poor China and Mauritius.

Within this context, this chapter proposes three measures to maximise the beneficial local impacts from mining. First, MNCs should help to establish local stakeholder committees in the mining region, preferably prior to the investment, to screen projects for their local contribution and maximise best practice. The

International Finance Corporation (2000) stresses consultation to build trust and establish realistic expectations for contributions to regional welfare among the community, government and corporation. A stakeholder committee can achieve these goals. Its first role is to screen projects to ensure there are likely to be net local benefits. The stakeholder committee can also help to reduce coordination failure, which is a frequently voiced concern among all groups involved in mineral-driven development. It also provides a tangible mechanism for the accumulation of local social capital, which is a vital but neglected ingredient in the transition. In addition, the stakeholder committee can establish practical goals for sustainable local development, determine how to achieve them, assign responsibility for their execution and thereafter monitor progress and make necessary adjustments. The resulting expanded Social Impact Assessment will help establish realistic expectations of what the mineral project can be expected to deliver. It can also ventilate and allay any concerns that local inhabitants may have. To reach an agreement, the stakeholder committee in effect screens the mining project for its social sustainability.

Second, PSA conditions should be extended to embrace businesses linked to the mineral project so that they too become part of the demonstration effect of what the efficient market-driven deployment of capital (including natural capital) and labour can achieve (Auty 2007b). The replication of PSA conditions within ERZs extends the PSA concept to include the economic and social outputs of the economic activity that is linked to mining. The *social* outputs take the form of contributions from oil-linked firms to local revenue and the resulting public expenditure. ERZs confer three basic conditions: (i) world-class infrastructure to link the mine to global markets; (ii) enabling public services (or, at the very least, strong constraints on the grabbing hand of rent-seeking); and (iii) efficiency incentives for competitive production. The ERZ can be more effective than corporate social donations as the principal vehicle for promoting social sustainability. Moreover, placing ERZs at the heart of the local development strategy will improve the coherence of the efforts made by the various private and public agency policies, which is often deficient.

There is considerable scope for local supply firms to develop from hydrocarbon extraction. For example, BP identifies a strong local comparative advantage for Azerbaijan in logistics, maintenance, engineering design, digital business, telecommunications, waste management, scaffolding, fabrication, laboratory analysis, inspection services and general supplies. In many cases, some initial assistance is required in attaining international quality standards for the product, in training workers, honing business skills and securing finance in the face of interest rates that may exceed 25 per cent. The SMEs linked to mineral projects have more to gain than the micro-enterprises from working within a PSA environment, since their greater size enhances the likelihood that they will become magnets for illicit imposts by rent seeking agents.

In addition, encouragement of micro-enterprises offers a route to sustainable poverty alleviation within the vicinity of mineral projects, and one that appears to give a high return to the resources invested. A BP-sponsored initiative as

Sangachal refugee camp shows that micro-enterprises can swiftly impact poverty alleviation. Within less than 18 months, a pilot programme had established more than 12 cottage businesses that fabricate gloves to international standards for BP. These businesses are triggering backward linkage to domestic raw material suppliers and diversifying production into industrial garments other than gloves. Pilot programmes include cottage chicken rearing, which does not entail battery production (because that is shortly expected to be banned within the EU), and the development of market garden produce to take advantage of the region's high solar insolation rate.

Such micro-enterprises function within the formal economy and consequently pay taxes, and their initial modest scale of operation appears to keep them below the radar of the rent-seekers. The purchase of additional sewing machines provides evidence of capital accumulation by the new enterprises. However, the advantage of the 'stealth' micro-enterprise may not last in the case of the most successful and dynamic firms, so there may be a case for setting up the micro-enterprises as well as SMEs within an ERZ area that offers protection from rent seeking.

Although the participation of international financial institutions, and perhaps donor governments, in the ERZs will strengthen their defence against rent-seeking, it would be prudent to build the capacity of both micro-enterprises and SMEs to defend themselves. This may be achieved initially by providing legal and other assistance, as is currently offered by BP, but increasingly by forming local civic associations to defend legitimate wealth creation against illicit imposts. In this case, functioning within a discrete local economy, the ERZ has an advantage over a more diffuse association such as that between an individual plant and the national economy, in as much as the community within a contiguous geographical area can more easily cohere to politically defend the creation of a prosperous local economy.

Third, instead of funding local social and economic infrastructure, corporate social policy should aim to boost the lobbying capacity of local groups so that mining localities can capture an adequate share of mining's fiscal linkage to permit local governments to meet their new obligations. Given the political sensitivity arising from the promotion of social capital (not least the accusation of engaging in social engineering), MNCs might strengthen local governance at arm's length by using NGOs as intermediaries. A responsible NGO coordinator is required because a minority of NGOs function as rent-extracting systems while others have political agendas that are likely to hamper the effective creation of wealth. For example, the Azerbaijan International Operating Company (AIOC) has commissioned the Open Society Institute to encourage NGOs to set practical development priorities and to select as representatives those among them who can cohere around an effective strategy to maximise local economic development. Such a strategy should centre upon creating an enabling environment for diversified local enterprise formation, as a means of generating the revenue to improve public service provision, especially services for those least able to fend for themselves.

However, the experience of local administrations in the oil-producing districts of Colombia identifies risks of over-rapid *regional* absorption causing local (and even national) Dutch disease effects and also of accumulating maintenance costs on newly expanded infrastructure that are too high for the community to service (Auty and Mikesell 1998: 237–53). Consequently, the scale of revenue allocated to local governments should be set to ensure a manageable rate of local investment in social infrastructure. This requirement reinforces the wisdom of building local social capital and administrative capacity as well as diversifying the local revenue base by promoting new business formation.

Summary

The literature suggests that large capital-intensive mining investments create inflated expectations of local benefits. This is mainly because an unusually high share of mining revenue flows abroad to service foreign capital but in addition, fiscal linkage (taxation) dominates domestic socio-economic linkages from hydrocarbon projects and it tends to accrue to the centre. Consequently, mining communities may be inadequately compensated for the environmental, social and economic costs of production. Inadequate compensation is evident in the Caspian hydrocarbon fields. However, mining companies increasingly regard enhanced local welfare as a condition for viable investment.

This chapter identifies three principal ways to maximise the positive local contribution of large mining projects. Table 9.7 provides a detailed summary. It proposes that the mining MNCs should: (i) establish a stakeholder committee prior to investment to identify realistic expectations for local benefits and to coordinate their realization; (ii) promote local enterprise formation to sustain the economy when mineral extraction ceases (PSAs establish best practice ERZs within which new entrants can limit onerous rent seeking imposts); and (iii) underpin new enterprise formation by strengthening social capital at the local level (by helping NGOs to strengthen community and local government voice and by upgrading administrative capability) and at the national level (by pushing for greater transparency). In this way, large oil projects can not only boost local welfare but also function as catalysts for *national* economic reform of distorted economies as part of a dual track development strategy, as set out elsewhere (Auty 2007b).

Table 9.7 Local impacts of mining together with polices to limit adverse effects/enhance benefits

Impact	Corporate policy	IFI policy
Economic		
Investment ($ b)	Full disclosure + transparency	Enable best practice projects to proceed
Direct local employment	Local content rules, if acceptable efficiency	Facilitate technical skill transfer to locals
Employment multiplier	Local training + promotion of micro-firms + SMEs	Skill + loans to sustainable micro + SMEs
Local goods + services inputs ($ m)	Local content from micro-firms +SMEs within ERZ	Facilitate business skill transfer + firm entry
Local further processing ($ m)	Within ERZ for efficiency enhancement	Back ERZ to maximise efficient investment
Local taxation ($ m)	Profit-related share of mine tax to local authority	Back profit-related share to local authority
Environmental		
Air quality (μg/ m³)	Particulates 50; NO_x 150; SO_2 50	Guarantor of EU best practice
Water quality	Ph 6-9; BOD 50 mg/l; TSS 50 mg/l;	Guarantor of EU best practice
Solid waste	Abate to EU levels	Guarantor of EU best practice
Noise	55 dB(A) except 45 22.00-07.00	Guarantor of EU best practice
Decommissioning	Accumulate protected fund for decommissioning	Protected fund a condition of loan
Social		
Pre-construction stage		
Feasibility analysis	ESIA + public consultation + physical plan	Monitor consultation + local physical plan
Construction stage		
Boom/bust Dutch disease	Facilitate temporary in-migration of labour	Assist establishment of local stakeholder committee
Large transient male workforce	Site labour camps in larger settlements/ at distance	Uphold basic human rights
Natural resource annexation	Satisfactory livelihood compensation	Guarantee adequate compensation
Resettlement	Satisfactory compensation	Guarantee adequate compensation
Operation stage		
Population increase via migration	Strengthen voice + local governance	Upgrade government capacity + promote stakeholder role
Rising mean income	Train local people to maximise local participation	Support skill transfer, credit, credit + SME formation

Heightened income inequality	Promote micro enterprises + female workforce participation	Finance/train micro enterprises + female opportunities
Expand social + economic SOC	Mutually beneficial joint SOC investment with government	Loans to government to boost administrative capacity
Closure		
Environmental rehabilitation	Restore sites to safe, stable and most productive uses	Monitor compliance
Employment loss	Redeploy redundant labour in diversifying local enterprises	Use physical plan to make incremental adjustment
Tapering regional expenditure	Local contingency fund for adjustment	Monitor adequacy of decommissioning fund

10

TENGIZ CRUDE

A view from below

Saulesh Yessenova

The Republic of Kazakhstan is a major gateway for renewed global ambitions in the energy-rich Caspian Basin. In the early-1990s, the government endorsed a plan to privatize its energy sector, and, in the following years, Kazakhstan's hydrocarbon reserves, altogether much smaller and entailing more costly recovery than many of those in the Persian Gulf, Sub-Saharan Africa and Latin America, attracted a respectful amount of foreign capital investment of approximately $18 billion. From 1999, crude production grew in Kazakhstan by about 15 per cent every year, reaching a net export of 1 mb/d in 2004. The oil output is likely to expand significantly in the future – by 2010 the country is forecasted to become one of the 10 largest crude oil exporters in the world.[1] This transformation from a designated 'bread basket' within the Soviet division of labour into an important player on the world's hydrocarbon market, impressive in its own terms, at the same time presents serious challenges to the country.[2]

Earlier in the twentieth century, Nigeria, Angola, Mexico and Venezuela embarked on ambitious petroleum projects with similar fervour. It has been observed, however, that despite much success in oil development, almost no resource-abundant state has prospered as anticipated, and, for many of them, the opposite is the case. The *Caspian Revenue Watch*, a timely project designed to raise awareness of the 'hazards of petroleum wealth', begins with a cautious note, reminding the emerging Caspian oil states that 'countries blessed with resource wealth have consistently underperformed resource-poor countries on almost every indicator of progress ranging from human development, economic growth, democracy and good governance, and preserving peace' (Tsalik 2003: 1).[3]

The literature on resource curse is a guiding means for the present discussion, but I intend to step back from its analytical framework and focus instead on the ways crude projects are entangled with social, economic and political matters on the ground by examining critical issues of business and labour organization at the forefront of oil production. The focus is on TengizChevroil (TCO), the enterprise that exploits Tengiz, the largest hydrocarbon reserve on the northeastern Caspian Sea coast (see the Kazakhstan oil fields in Map 2.1). Discovered in 1979, the field had been developed by Soviet companies until the withdrawal of the Soviet regime in 1991, which opened the way for multinational oil corporations. In 1993, Chevron consummated a deal with the government of Kazakhstan on the establishment of a joint venture (Table 10.1), which put Tengiz, containing 9 billion barrels of recoverable oil, on the global map.

Industry sources declare TCO to be one of the most dynamic hydrocarbon enterprises in the world. Over 10 years, its output has significantly increased, from 3 million tons in 1993 to 13 million tons in 2004. In the same year, TCO launched the Second Generation Project (SGP), including the installation of the fifth train in an oil plant complex and sour gas injection technology that would enable the increase of supply to 25 million tons in 2007.[4] The steady expansion of the enterprise and especially the latest project with an estimated cost of $4 billion boosted business activities around Tengiz. In 2005–06, TCO development projects and routine activities sustained the operations of nearly 100 companies concentrating around Tengiz.

Oddly enough, the economic boom, which significantly increased the local business market and labour demand at Tengiz, has been accompanied by recurrent labour conflicts. Grown out of poor labour arrangements, these conflicts progressed from the rise of a bottom–up labour movement at TCO in 1996 to its dissolution in 2001 to 2003 that was followed by spontaneous and violent labour disputes in 2004 and 2005 involving TCO subcontractors and their workers. The latter events, revealing the absence of conventional mechanisms of labour regulation and conflict resolution, led to the installation of a state-run office at Tengiz in charge of labour-management relations and workplace regulation, the surrogate public oversight.

This study retraces the hardening of the situation by focusing on the social engineering aggressively pursued by the oil corporation determined to insulate

Table 10.1 Ownership structure of TengizChevroil Ltd

Shareholders	Percentage
ChevronTexaco*	50
ExxonMobil**	25
KazMunaiGaz***	20
LUKArco****	5
	100

Notes:
* Chevron's initial stake (45%) expanded through a purchase of additional 5% from RK in 2000. Texaco entered through the merger with Chevron in 2001.
** Joined the joint venture in 1997–2000 through the acquisition of interest from the Government of Kazakhstan.
*** Kazakhstan's national company, 100% owned by the state.
**** LUKArco is a joint venture between ARCO (46%) and the Russian oil company LUKoil (54%) which acquired shares in 1997 – LUKoil (2.7%) and ARCO (5%). Through the acquisition of ARCO in 2000, BP has interest in TCO.

the enterprise from its surroundings and exercise maximum control over its assets, workforce, support businesses and broader forces, including local communities and the state.[5] One outcome of the corporate effort is a walled-off industrial colony, 'over-adapted' to the needs of the oil company, the implications of which have extended far beyond oil project's goals.[6] I examine the Tengiz colony by tracing its functions to: (i) the decline of organized labour, the only available organized force at Tengiz outside corporate bodies; (ii) subsequent business strategies and labour arrangements among subcontractors; and (iii) massive worker protests that ensued from them. I furthermore explain the failure of the state to transform Tengiz in a more just and transparent space in the aftermath of the latest protests. Towards the end of discussion, I locate the tensions and contradictions between business, labour and the state shaped by the oil capital and exposed in this study within broader developments in Kazakhstan and the debate on resource curse.

Situating the field

This study is based on the fieldwork conducted in the Atyrau oblast over several years.[7] Ideally, I would have stayed at Tengiz and interviewed as many business owners and their respective employees as possible. Under the conditions of a guarded industrial colony, which I discuss in more detail in the following section, such a systematic approach along with a direct observation of labour relations was entirely impractical. During my trips in 1997 and 2004, I interviewed local activists and state officials and had a chance to observe the everyday life at the TCO village from within the camp. When I came back in 2006 my relations with local residents from Kulsary (an administrative centre 80 km north of the colony), Kosshagil and Karaton (villages situated in the vicinity of Tengiz) helped me to gain access to local entrepreneurs, non-resident businessmen doing business in Tengiz, and labourers who work for them and other companies. In addition, I interviewed a number of individuals in Almaty (the former capital of Kazakhstan) who participated in the Tengiz project at various times from the mid-1980s to the present, whose discrepant views were helpful for capturing historical dynamics.

The information on the Tengiz labour movement comes from the local mass media, trade union's publicity and interviews with TCO employees and the former leader of the TengizChevroil Trade Union, Ms Tokzhan Kizatova. A native of Atyrau, she arrived in Tengiz in 1996 as a freelance journalist for the *Russian Petroleum Investor*. Her original plans to cover labour conflicts changed on 5 May 1998, when she was voted to the Chair at a union conference. Involving nearly 500 members, the conference was debarred from the company premises and held in the open steppe outside the Tengiz village.[8] In 2003, the union ceased to exist. At the time of my last visit, there was no sign of a public organization that could serve the interests of nearly 24,000 employees, many of whom reside at Tengiz for 10–11 months during the year. In June 2007 (the anticipated date of SGP completion) the Tengiz worksite was due to downsize, leaving thousands of unemployed workers behind the company gates without any mechanism that would help to mediate their work situation.

While I am hesitant to define Tengiz as typical, given its origins in the Soviet period and the rapid expansion in the past decade, I believe its case is particularly instructive with regard to spatial and political strategies of the corporation and the way they have shaped local social and economic situations, which I discuss in this chapter. Recent years have marked the serious expansion of global oil capital across the world, especially in the developing world, having a direct impact on local physical and social landscapes and environments. Anthropologists in particular have drawn attention to the increasingly walled-off design of industrial bases that have been established by oil multinationals in different countries in Sub-Saharan Africa and Latin America. This distinct industrial set up is a material expression of the corporate concern with unstable political situations, real or potential, among developing countries and post-colonial nations. It has been argued, however, that the corporate strategies to 'protect' their assets by insulating them from the immediate realities of the outside world correlate with an increasingly poor societal footprint of the industry, marginalization of indigenes, and tense labour relations that, in effect, foster inequalities and political instability.[9] This reverse relationship calls for a critical assessment of how industrial bases function and to what ends. This study examines the costs and consequences the Tengiz colony has carried for business and labour as well as a broader spectrum of regional economic and social development. Other hydrocarbon projects in Kazakhstan, for example, those in Aktobe and Uralsk, have been recently rationalized as industrial colonies in a fashion similar to Tengiz. The issues that the present study addresses therefore are not limited to a single project site; instead, they have direct relevance to other oil enterprises across the Caspian Basin and, perhaps, elsewhere in the world.

The Tengiz colony

I can tell that the establishment of a large enterprise makes the development of regional infrastructure inevitable. Roads, communication networks, housing, schools, hospitals are built. Secondary enterprises, service companies, cultural institutions, and entertainment industry emerge. What exactly would take place [around Tengiz] – we will decide together.

(M. Dupree, a Chevron Overseas executive, responding to questions at a press conference in Atyrau, 1992.[10])

The city of Atyrau (formerly Guryev) is a gateway to Tengiz situated 280 km southeast of this major urban centre at the Ural River Delta. A road and a railway track, connecting Atyrau with the Mankishlak Peninsula, form a main route to the field that spreads over 100 hectares under the earth's surface at the verge of the Caspian Sea. The landscape between Atyrau and Tengiz, frequently punctuated with aged and more recently installed oil collectors, pumping stations and other industrial outlets, is the evidence that crude production has been underway there for decades. The hydrocarbon industry has maintained a strong presence in this area since the 1940s, forever altering the local environment that had been previously shaped to serve the needs of pastoral nomadism.[11] It also transformed old herding communities in which it was aggregated into culturally mixed populations with the introduction of a wide range of oil-related projects. As invasive as it was, by the late-1970s, the early Soviet industry became an integral part of local social realities so that major communities in the area, such as Dossor, Makat, Kosshagil, Prorva, Emba and Kulsary, came to identify themselves with respective oil projects. When Tengiz, the most expensive and complex project, was launched in the early 1980s, it broke the existing tradition, giving rise to a new pattern of industrial infrastructure set up at a distance from local communities.[12] This proto-colony, governed by a distinct set of labour norms and expectations, formed a springboard for Chevron and its partners when TCO arrived in 1993.

Taking shape in the mid-1980s, the Tengiz colony included various support structures among which were two worker camps designed to accommodate rotation crews. One was used by Hungarian contractors who built the processing complex, while the other hosted thousands of shift workers arriving in Tengiz from different parts of the former Soviet Union. Since then the colony has expanded and became more isolated from local residential areas through the relocation of neighbouring settlements (Karaton, Kenaral and Sarakamis) further inland and away from the growing oil-production site. TCO upgraded the existing facilities so that they now include several camps lined up along the road 20 km to 30 km from the plant.[13] The oldest of these camps, comprising unadorned rows of long barracks, is the TCO village that was built by Hungarian contractors. TCO designed a new camp, giving it a more creative shape by arranging barracks radiating from a circular base that houses canteens and recreational amenities. The camp was given a Kazakh name, 'Shanrak', denoting a wooden frame that supports the roof of the yurt, a symbol of peace and home featured on Kazakhstan's national flag. But like the older camp, it is surrounded with a barbed-wire fence along its perimeter reinforcing its overall resemblance to a correctional facility with an interesting name. Identity regime is strictly enforced at both camps, which are populated exclusively by TCO employees and those of authorized subcontractors. At the end of their 14- or 28-day shifts, all employees are transported to the train station in Kulsary or other destinations in the area, and are not allowed to enter the camp grounds until replacement personnel are ready to leave. This well-orchestrated system of security and crew rotation functions to minimize a spontaneous flow of people around the camps, keeping unauthorized visitors and potential intruders away from TCO's major property, the Tengiz field and the associated processing complex.

Within a shift, labour is optimized through a non-standard work day, including 11–12 hour shifts from the early morning to late night. This practice of extended shifts and overtime work, introduced in the Soviet period, served the needs of thousands of Russian workers and engineers who dominated Tengiz during the Soviet period. TCO and its foreign partners pledged to reverse this situation with employment hurting labour development in the republic. However, they failed to enlist a local workforce, continuously relying on workers from outside the area and from abroad for whom they preserved the system of crew rotation despite the

Kulsary and Tengiz
Kazakhstan

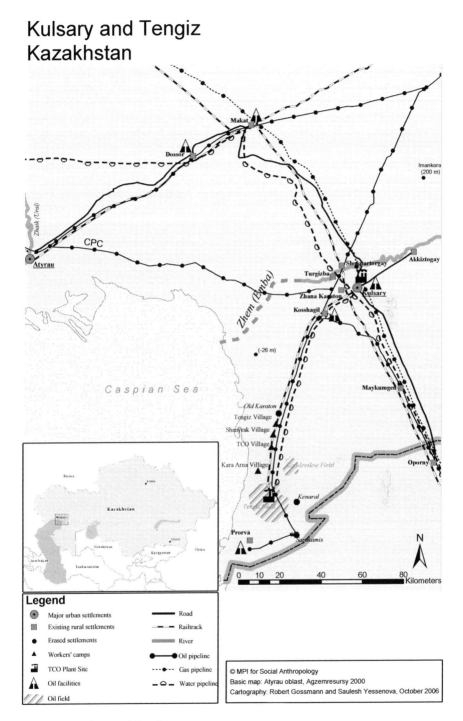

Legend

◉	Major urban settlements	——	Road
▦	Existing rural settlements	—·—·—	Railtrack
●	Erased settlements	▨▨▨	River
▲	Workers' camps	●—●—	Oil pipeline
⌂	TCO Plant Site	---●---	Gas pipeline
⚑	Oil facilities	—⌒—	Water pipeline
▨	Oil field		

© MPI for Social Anthropology
Basic map: Atyrau oblast, Agzemresursy 2000
Cartography: Robert Gossmann and Saulesh Yessenova, October 2006

Map 10.1 Kulsary and Tengiz

181

Figure 10.1 The Tengiz oilfield from above (Saulesh Yessenova © 1997)

heavy burden it imposes on the company (one employee in camp residence costs TCO $12,000 per month).[14] In addition, foreign employers have come to appreciate the situation when all employees engaged in work process, from supervisors and lead operators to kitchen and cleaning staff, are required to stay at the company premises day and night since it provides the administration with the most direct means of controlling their routine. At present, nearly 2,000 out of a total of 2,569 TCO employees work on extended shifts, so even local residents are requested to carry out rotations despite their homes' physical proximity to the worksite.[15]

Within the local context, the colony has grown into a secure industrial space, free of social distractions. By physically detaching the workforce from their homes, families and communities, the colony facilitates a focused production process, which, in effect, feeds corporate insensibilities to the local context. At the time of bargaining for resource access, Chevron executives, quoted at the outset, argued in front of a curious Atyrau audience that the expansion of oil extraction would 'inevitably' stimulate development by drawing in capital and labour.[16] The projected development of the area, however, has taken a peculiar form. The anticipated multiplier effect of the oil capital, i.e. when one thing leads to another, from 'housing' and 'service companies' to 'cultural institutions', has centred on the industrial colony itself, helping it to expand and become more complex in appearance and functions. Its major function is the isolation from outside influences, including those of the public and the state, the outcome of which is dramatic labour inequalities and pervasive business practices around the oil patch. The politics of the oil company did not go unchallenged, however, provoking a critical reaction from within the colony. On the following pages, I discuss a significant episode in the history of TCO centring on a labour movement, which I locate within a matrix of pre-existing social divisions and more recent relations.

Labour movement

We felt infinitely happy when our President signed the contract with Chevron, an internationally acclaimed oil company. Chevron has arrived not in an empty space; it now does what we began earlier. ... Allah endowed our nation with oil wealth and we would not tolerate the abuse of workers taking place today [at TCO]. We will fight till the end because there is no other way.

(A worker comment at a TCO general meeting in 1997.[17])

In June 1992, the Prime Minister of Kazakhstan arrived in Atyrau for an up-close and personal discussion of a progress report with the directors of Tengizneftegaz, a company that operated the field at that time. In 1990, Moscow had abandoned the ambitious project half-way through, including contractual obligations towards foreign construction firms and equipment suppliers as well as the oil company itself. About the same time, Kazakhstan's government engaged in negotiations with Chevron, which would determine its fate in the years to come. By 1992, they came to a preliminary agreement, according to which Tengiz was supposed to have the second block of trains fully installed by the time of ownership transfer. The construction, however, was falling behind schedule: the company needed $100 million to pay external debts and finish construction works. The Prime Minister pressured the directors to complete the construction as scheduled, insisting on a self-financing scheme (Nikolaev 1992). That was not good news for the company's employees whose representatives attended the meeting. The project masterminds reserved Tengiz for a highly skilled, experienced and dedicated workforce that was expected to endure all hazards of crude production. Totalling 6,000 people, they benefited from the highest rewards across the industry, causing significant resentment among local residents who had been sidelined by the project. Unexpected financial problems brought delayed payments and cuts, taking their toll on Tengiz workers, many of whom headed home for Russia (Kagirov 1992). Those who stayed were looking forward to the arrival of Chevron and the prospect of renewed stability and prosperity.

During the inspection of their future facilities in 1992, Chevron representatives reported that they were 'pleasantly surprised by the level of qualification of local employees' (Monastyrskya 1992). Once Tengiz changed ownership in 1993, the expectations of some workers were met and even exceeded. However, 3,000 employees were laid off, and many others were dissatisfied with the new labour arrangements. Frustrated by the disparities between corporate investment and foreign employee earnings, and their rewards at the lower end, TCO workers mobilized for a series of organized actions, shaping a labour movement by 1996. The movement revolved around workplace demands, a conventional agenda of business unionism that was infused with political claims. At that time, the TCO union numbered 3,300 members, accounting for over 50 per cent of domestic employees, who came up with a collective bargaining agreement, requesting union representation in labour-related corporate venues, such as safety, wages and reorganization procedures. The administration did not meet any of the union demands in any shape or form, except the collective bargaining agreement that it signed with a captive labour organization installed at TCO as part of a forthcoming corporate attack on grassroots unionism.[18] Wages were increased, however, to an average of $200 per month in 1997, which was interpreted among union members as a lousy enticement on the part of the company, and did not help to ease the tension.

Corporate measures to curtail organized labour actions subsequently blocked labour demands, which meant the end of wage expansion at TCO that started due to union pressure, and the beginning of a downward spiral of wages among TCO subcontractors. Between 1998 and 2005, the TCO workforce shrunk from 6,000 to a total of 2,569 employees. Within the same time-frame, the number of people at Tengiz working for subcontractors increased from 9,000 to nearly 24,000. All firms have lagged behind TCO in every aspect of work conditions, from safety standards to pay cheques and employment practices. This disparity, putting TCO workers in a relatively privileged position, shifted their expectations about representation and necessary compensation, driving the labour movement in recent years. An assessment of the labour situation by a TCO welder conveys this rather subdued attitude among TCO workers in 2006:

> They pay very little – 700–800 dollars a month – and we work around the oil patch and the plant, inhaling all gases and everything else that comes with it [i.e. crude production]. I'll probably die before I retire … There is not much we can do about it …; they've decided it that way, and if you don't like the rules, that's your problem. [On the other hand] It's not too bad around here … look what's happening among subcontractors! We're the lucky ones.

Back in the period 1996 to 1998, however, TCO workers pledged that they 'will use the most extreme measures', i.e. they would shut down the oil complex, if their demands of more equitable work arrangements were not met.[19] The security at the Tengiz village was put on high alert on several occasions during that period. The protest gained momentum after a mass layoff of transport department workers in December 1997. By then, most TCO non-core services, from drilling to catering, which were previously performed by oil company's own employees, were switched to contract labour. In the process, carried out to create a more streamlined and efficient structure, some lost jobs and many others ended up with lower pay and greater employment vulnerability at contracted firms. Anticipating the same problems, the transport department, including 500 employees, announced a boycott that escalated to include other union members who voted for a general strike.[20]

Trying to mediate the labour conflict, the union leadership reached out to Kazakhstan's Trade Union Federation, the government and the President of the country who, during his visit to Atyrau in January 1998, lent his 'moral support' to the workers.[21] Trapped in negotiations with the government and Kazakhoil, the national oil company that requested the administration to re-evaluate its labour policies, TCO reinstated the workers temporarily. Simultaneously, it launched a large-scale attack on the union as the source of trouble. The administration got rid of the union leadership with ties to the Union Federation and the government, while those officials who crossed the line were offered high-ranking managerial positions. They also brought white-collar workers on board to defend corporate interests. A new union and an employee association formed within the enterprise siphoned some members from the labour movement; however, neither of these employer-sponsored organizations became popular among blue-collar workers. Their presence, however, conveniently masked the assault on the labour movement allowing the administration to cease interaction with the old trade union whose activities were de-legalized and its leaders were denied access to the company premises. Under the conditions of the industrial colony and crew rotation, the company erected major communication constraints for the union, leading to its dissolution.

Still, the union remained active for another several years, carrying out a number of projects. In 2000, when the TCO payroll included 3,000 employees, the union enjoyed 900–1000 rank-and-file members. In response to corporate pressures, they began publishing a newspaper, the *Tengiz Trade Union*, in which they discussed their projects, seeking transparency of labour-related corporate practices and providing legal support to workers. They also tried to reduce a cultural gap within the enterprise by reprinting articles translated into English for the administration and offering English lessons to workers. In 2001, the union filed a complaint with the UN International Labor Organization that requested the government of Kazakhstan to address the case in 2002 (Sutyagin 2000). Facing a major bribery scandal related to Exxon/Mobil, a new TCO shareholder, and preparing to contest a TCO-proposed plan to self-finance SGP, the government was inimical to the company's labour affairs, blocking the appeal.[22] The lack of action on the part of the state, conveniently siding with one or the other side, discouraged the labour movement that then ran out of steam by 2003.

In retrospect, the defeat of business unionism at TCO was predictable. Studies of labour movements have demonstrated that the organizations narrowly focused on labour conditions are more isolated and therefore more vulnerable to corporate pressures than those whose agendas have been framed within the ideas of a social movement advocating democracy, social justice, human rights and environment protection (Turner and Hurd 2001). An agenda seeking a broad-based change potentially increases the outreach possibilities of the labour movement, of which powerful labour movements among oil workers in Mexico and Iran that mobilized the masses for regime change are particularly instructive.[23] Those events, however, took place under different historical conditions, including, among other factors (such as the elite's desire to alter the contractual terms with oil companies), the fact that oil workers were rooted in local societies that formed solid ground bases of their movements. The collective identity of TCO workers, however, as an elite group recruited among the outsiders during the Soviet period did not help the union to establish a dialogue with local communities. Even though a number of locals had joined the Tengiz workforce by then, they treated the labour situation at Tengiz as a matter distant from their long-standing local concerns with environmental damage, unemployment and poor infrastructural provisions. In fact, neither party, acting in isolation from one another and the rest of the society, has been able to develop a sound public agenda that would sustain organized activities in the long term.

Likewise, the TCO union failed to stretch the appeal and mobilize subcontractors' workers. Former union leaders comment that despite major disagreements between the union and TCO its very presence enabled negotiations with the administration and helped to mediate labour conflicts. The decline of unionism was followed by spontaneous strikes and violent clashes around the Tengiz village, which became home to 20,000 people working for various subcontractors, indicating the increased pressure of unresolved labour issues. The absence of a visible organized force has become a major factor that encouraged corrupted business practices, legal abuse and labour discrimination, which is discussed below, that downplayed the possibilities of gain at the time of the economic boom at Tengiz.

Business and labour

Most TCO subcontractors are located at the Tengiz Rotation (crew) Village, the colony's third camp, which is also a former base of the oil workers' union. Having no fixed territory or formal boundaries other than those of industrial grounds and piles of waste that surround it, the Tengiz village offered some opportunities for free movement and organized public action. In 2000–02, however, all TCO employees were moved to more secure and better organized camps (Shanrak and the TCO village), which helped to dissolve the labour movement. Centred on uniform Soviet apartment blocks, a local skyline originating in Soviet times, the Tengiz village has greatly outgrown its original plan. It now boasts a collection of disparate construction designs engrained in pre-fabricated buildings, barracks, camping wagons and bunkhouses separated from each other by concrete walls or wire fences that dominate the landscape on the ground. This camp is located outside the TCO territory, including 400,000 hectares of land around Tengiz.[24] The oil company, however, has laid claim to the buildings and the camp itself as essential to its economic activities, keeping local authorities, unrelated businesses and potential settlers away, which effectively blocked the camp from possibilities to diversify its profile and integrate into the local economy. Visualized as an industrial base, the camp has formed a field of intense transactions centring on a single patron, the oil company that protects it from the exposure to public oversight and open competition. This economic model has created the right environment for low standards of business and employment.

A principle strategy that has shaped the structure of business at Tengiz is extensive reliance on contract labour among TCO lead contractors and the sponsor company itself. One of the key players around Tengiz is PFD UK, a joint venture between Parsons E&C and Fluor Daniel Corporation, which is a prime

Figure 10.2 An old Soviet sign board saying 'Tengiz Rotation Village'. In the background are the silhouettes of Soviet apartment blocks (Saulesh Yessenova © 2004)

contractor for the SGP that holds most subcontracts and purchase orders.[25] PFD has created an outsourcing network consisting of 60 independent contractors, including equipment suppliers, engineering and construction firms (for example, Arctic Construction Intl, Able Instrument Co. and Chemimontazh), as well as various support services. In addition to development projects, both TCO and PFD have outsourced the entire packages of their non-core activities, from drilling and equipment maintenance to transport and facilities management to Parker Drilling Co., MI Drilling, and the Eurest Raytheon Support Services (ERSS) amongst others. Hired for the duration of TCO or PFD projects, these large international businesses have made similar outsourcing arrangements, helping them to manage costs and maintain organizational flexibility. For example, the PFD lead outsourcer – SK (Senimdi Kurylis/Reliable Construction) – a Turkish dominated company with a Kazakh name, regularly hires about the same number of independent contractors as its sponsor company. In effect, the company has retained only

187

Table 10.2 Companies at Tengiz rated among 100 largest businesses in Kazakhstan (sales volume, 2005)

Rating	Company	Company profile
1	TCO	Oil and gas
19	PFD International	Construction and services for oil and gas
27	Imstalkon*	Equipment and construction
42	Shlumberzhe Lodzhelko Inc.	Services for oil and gas
50	Halliburton International Inc.	Services for oil and gas
60	SK	Civil construction
80	Eurest Raytheon Support Services**	Services for oil and gas
86	Parker Drilling	Services for oil and gas

Source: *National Business* 2005/6:20, pp. 30–8.
Notes:
 * Imstalkon is the only domestic company in this list. It is also the largest domestic equipment supplier contracted by TCO.
** ERSS provides integrated facilities management, catering, and maintenance services.

a fraction of the contract volume centring on managerial and administrative functions for execution by its own employees; the rest is done by independent contractors that might hire others.

The outsourcing has helped to increase the share of domestic firms at the Tengiz business market. The largest among those are 'holding' companies such as Kazcomservice, Nefrestroyservice and Tengizneftestroy, each consisting of an amalgam of small firms with unrelated profiles, from engineering and civil construction to housing and trade (see Chapter 7). Their diversified structures correlate with a highly fragmented state of the Tengiz business market dominated by low-cost construction firms and vendors supplying labourers to perform specific tasks. Subcontracts at Tengiz vary greatly, depending on the nature of the work involved, seasonal demand, and other factors. However, a general tendency is that they become less complex and smaller in volume when they are passed down from TCO to PFD and then to other subcontractors and their hires. Sponsor companies keep confidential lists of potential outsourcers whom they invite to participate in closed biddings. The winner is expected to provide an obligatory kickback upon the contract signature (cash payment, amounting to 10 per cent of the project's total cost), which controls the subcontract's volume. The created atmosphere of secrecy surrounding biddings and contracts whose volumes are purposively set small enough to ensure a constant supply of illegal payments has hindered the maturity and expansion of individual businesses.

The Tengiz village offers competitive advantages to potential subcontractors. The companies based at the camp make their assets visible to sponsor companies. By keeping their equipment and workforces in the camp, they can quickly move from one worksite to another and are able to follow the pace of work schedule

Table 10.3 Tengiz' largest employers, summer 2006

1	TengizChevroil (TCO)	2,569
2	Senimdi Kurylis (SK)	2,500
3	Tengizneftestroy (NSS)	1,000
4	Parsons E&C and Fluor Daniel Corp. (PFD UK)	971
	Other companies	16,215
	Total Tengiz	23,255
	Foreign employees	2,294
	Kazakhstan's employees	20,861

Source: The Tengiz Department of Relations with Enterprises, July 2006.

at the sponsor company based on long workdays and extended shifts. Keeping the workforce within the camp, however, potentially increases operational costs of subcontracted firms. Some subcontractors hold million-dollar contracts while others barely survive; at the same time, neither category enjoys profits comparable to those of the oil company; nor are they entitled to tariff and tax privileges granted to foreign investors as part of the oil deal. This deal, in fact, allows TCO to recuperate the costs associated with the organization of workplace burden by the camp overhead expenses. Other companies are not part of the oil deal, the material evidence of which is the poor condition of the Tengiz village itself. In general, it makes sense for subcontractors to adopt a standard work pattern open to variations; however, no subcontractor has done so.

The workforce engaged by subcontracted firms has been drawn from all around the oblast and the nation. While both resident and non-resident populations have participated in all venues and occupations, those from outside the area prevail, especially in the lowest paid sectors. One explanation behind this overrepresentation is that non-resident workers do not enjoy moral, political and economic support of near-by communities allowing local workers to be more selective about jobs. In fact, local observers have blamed the rapid proliferation of what is called 'bad' jobs (with low wages, no benefits and limited in duration) on a wave of job-seekers from southern oblasts of Kazakhstan, where jobs are few and wages are even lower.[26] Cheap labour indeed provides employers with an incentive to pay less, downplaying the labour market. It is not strange that welders, fitters, metal workers, vehicle operators and entry-level workers, the occupations that can be found in almost every company at Tengiz, get higher pay for the same jobs at TCO than among subcontractors. A disturbing fact here is the way subcontractors have exploited workers' vulnerabilities under the conditions of the industrial colony, producing a situation in which competition and market forces have little value.

SK, the largest employer after TCO, has been positioned to control work patterns and employment practices among subcontractors. The company has cut its operational costs by transferring the burden of the non-standard work pattern to their employees: it has stripped domestic workers of the usual benefits, such as paid time off, accident insurance, room and board, and transportation to the

189

Table 10.4 SK: worker average earnings and amounts retained by the employer in 2005*

	Calculations in tenge	*Dollar equivalent*
Annual earnings:	300,000**	2,308
Per hour rate	83	
Annual input:		
Hours of straight time	2,400	
Hours of overtime	1,200	
Annual amounts retained:		
Overtime hours	49,200	
Paid time off	329,880	
Minimal transport allowance, accident insurance, room and board	100,000	
Total retained by employer:	579,080	4,454

Notes:
* Calculations are based on Kazakhstan's Labour Law, specifying regular employment as 40 hour/ week and 8 hour/day; overtime to be paid as 1.5 of straight time; duration of extended shift is defined as no longer than 15 days followed by an equal number of days off and 45 days annual holiday. Exchange rate is based on $1 = 130 tenge.
** After taxes and pension fund deductions, if they were applied.

worksite, retaining those amounts within the company (see Table 10.3). This practice has diminished labour compensation and increased economic inequalities between foreign and domestic workforces as well as between those who work for TCO and for subcontractors. It also eroded the schedule itself by forcing workers to stay at the camp as long as they have jobs.

In addition to no compensation for non-standard work schedules, companies have disregarded professional qualification, past experience, and assigned task complexity as the basis for calculating wages. Flat occupational rates have boosted corruption: human resource officers routinely retain first- and even second-month salaries earned by those whose paperwork they process. In 2005, the average wage, based on a 28-day shift, including 11–12 hours per day, which SK or its numerous hires paid to their blue-collar workers ranged from 20,000 to 30,000 tenge (approximately $150 to $230), i.e. less than $1 per hour. In terms of a regular work schedule, based on 40 hours of labour per week, this pay is below the legally enforced minimal wage in Kazakhstan.[27]

Worker protests and the state

In 2004–05, the Tengiz village witnessed a series of localized labour protests that centred on individual companies. The first wave of heated disputes, including the exchange of verbal and physical assaults between the management and small groups of workers, contesting labour norms practiced within the firms that hired them, was contained by means of company security followed by blacklisting and

Figure 10.3 SK (Senimdi Kurylis) checkpoint, Tengiz Rotation Village (Saulesh Yessenova © 2006)

firing of discontented employees. The labour dispute at SK in April 2005 began in a similar way; however, it spread out igniting a massive strike, involving nearly 3,000 domestic labourers from SK and other subcontractors who demanded fair compensation and respectful treatment. The protest also spilled over into a gender divide. Thousands of women serve the needs of the Tengiz colony, preparing food, cleaning rooms, doing laundry, counting heads and supervising those activities. Revolving around 'traditional' female roles, those occupations have been defined as unskilled labour. As a result, companies with a high concentration of female workers, those that run canteens or maintain facilities, have the lowest standards of pay and the poorest living conditions across Tengiz. Hundreds of female workers, the employees of canteens and maintenance companies, joined the male-driven protest, embarking on a strike against labour discrimination as well. An aggressive attempt by the SK administration to suppress the strike turned it into a violent clash between domestic employees and foreign managers who were reinforced by their fellow workers, which generated significant suffering on both sides. Alarmed by the disturbances, local authorities, arriving in Tengiz, tried to rescue the situation. To calm down and stop the strike, the authorities promised the domestic workers, both men and women, that they would address their case and deal with the labour situation around Tengiz in general. In response, managers and administrators locked themselves up with other foreign workers, a total of 1,500 people, in an attempt to make a statement to show who the real victim was, which paralyzed the entire construction process.

That was not what the central government expected to happen at Tengiz. A core crude producer in the country, TCO generates $200 million of annual revenue for the national budget, and the completion of SGP construction would almost double the share of the state. Since the inception of the project, the central government has requested that local authorities facilitate the construction process and 'support business' at Tengiz. Following the mandate, local authorities have retreated from the Tengiz colony leaving the area to its own devices, which worked for the state and the business until the crisis situation that forced the former to take a more proactive position. Workers' testimonies and a sample investigation indicated that companies excessively relied on foreign labour, violated the Labour Law, practiced double accounting, evaded retirement plans, disregarded safety measures and underpaid domestic workers.[28] Those findings were communicated to the upper levels of the state administration in Atyrau and Astana who approved the state involvement and recommended soliciting foreign investors' help to address the problem.

Within days, local authorities held an extraordinary meeting with TCO, PFD, SK and other major business players at Tengiz. They produced a Memorandum of Understanding concerning the salary structure and labour conditions among subcontractors. The memorandum determined the minimum wage for Tengiz workers – 42,500 tenge per month (approximately $300), suggesting the introduction of basic benefits and requesting employers to meet monthly with their workers to discuss their concerns. The head of administration addressed broader issues at that meeting, expressing his unease with the Tengiz village, an overcrowded place with poor sanitary conditions and significant crime rates. TCO has claimed no responsibility for these conditions or anything else that might happen at the camp, pointing out that it is located outside the corporate property. At the same time, the oil company has declined any proposal to improve the situation through interference from the outside, explaining that it would violate the autonomy and integrity of its economic activities, which are protected by the TCO contract with the state. In the end, however, TCO approved the establishment of a state office at the Tengiz village to deal exclusively with labour-management relations and workplace regulation among subcontractors.[29]

The Tengiz Department of Relations with Enterprises opened its doors to workers and their workplace-related grievances shortly after. From May 2005 to July 2006, the office, consisting of three employees, addressed 700 individual cases, the most frequent of which were cases of missing contracts and cheating on pay. Workers' personal testimonies attest the degree to which legal abuse of labour has been a pervasive phenomenon around Tengiz:

Well, they say, we're busy now, come back next week, we'll prepare your contract by then. Another week goes by … you still work for them, waiting until the next week … Once I worked for several months before I saw my contract. And when I finally got it, it was not what I had been promised! I got very little money for the work I've done for them. However, those who stopped coming to work, trying to pressure them to pay and sign contract … did not get any money at all, and had to look for new jobs.[30]

The office has helped to solve some individual cases; however, its work has been slow and inefficient due to the volume of complaints. Labour committees that could otherwise help workers to frame collective appeals have taken shape as extensions of company administrations; as such they are of little use either to the office or to the workers, many of whom remain unaware of both. The office serves predominantly male workers who constitute the overwhelming majority of plaintiffs, indicating that its procedures are an incentive to female workers, especially their concerns with sexual abuse as a means of and in addition to labour discrimination.[31] The memorandum remains a goodwill document since there is no mechanism that would help to enforce the minimum wage and the benefits related to the non-standard work pattern it has entailed. 'We do what we can', one of the officers commented, 'however, those are private companies, and, as the representatives of the state, we can only suggest the course of actions'.

The role of this state office is indeed awkward: its major responsibilities revolve around the issues defining traditional agendas of trades union and other NGOs, which are better positioned to address labour issues and have better approaches to handle them than the state.[32] Why has the state chosen such a weak strategy to reinforce its authority and stop pervasive business and labour practices? Local authorities have been misguided by the bold 'top–down' policy of promoting business within their jurisdiction, the effect of which is prioritization of commercial interests over law and social issues, including labour development. As a result, they have taken up a passive approach incapable of contributing to the creation of a more just and transparent environment. Local authorities came to think in the aftermath of the crisis that should they realign their objectives, it would 'hurt' business and push many subcontractors out of the Tengiz market, creating major inconveniences for sponsor companies, and might even provoke highly undesirable work delays. Based on this reasoning, SK (a major player in SGP construction) has never been charged or even properly inspected.

Conclusion

To sum up the discussion on a broader note, the economic growth trend observed around Tengiz in the past few years has brought no sensible advantages to domestic workers or business that can be translated into a long-term gain. The situation around Tengiz has demonstrated strong corporation, weak state and non-existent civil society, allowing the colony to harbour corrupt practices and systematic labour discrimination and abuse that stirred violent worker protests. While the state was appalled when learning about legal violations at Tengiz, its subsequent actions were inconsequential and contradictory. On the one hand, the state sought to reassert its power by placing business and employment at Tengiz under control; on the other, it produced inept initiatives, severely circumscribing its authority and serving the interests of the oil corporation. This left other companies ill-adjusted to the conditions of the single-sponsor market, hurting business and labour. As a form of excessive adaptation to the oil extraction, the colony has been imposed over an already existing territorial and social template, the heritage of the earlier industrial effort, which insulated the enterprise from its surroundings, helping the corporation to manage the workforce and dissolve the organized labour force. The latter contributed to a dysfunctional relationship between business, labour and the state, which placed the oil project at odds with the ideas of economic and human development and free market.

Tengiz is situated in the Atyrau oblast, which generates 95 per cent of the total oil revenue of Kazakhstan, which has provided the basis for fairly successful rates of economic growth at the national level. The oblast itself, however, occupies one of the most desperate places among other regions in terms of economic development and human development. It displays one of the lowest rates of living standards and the highest rate of earning discrepancy (between rich and poor as well as between men and women), and suffers from unemployment, poverty and poor-quality local infrastructures. Following the resource-politics scholarship, the answer to this situation would have to do with the absence of 'good governance' (a notion denoting uncorrupted government and democratic practices open to public involvement), weak state institutions and, perhaps, the ensuing poorly linked oil projects (Luong, 2000). While such an assumption is plausible, questions remain: how open are multinational oil projects to good governance and whether their goals and strategies are adequate, in terms of promoting sustainable development and fostering a market economy?

Research on resource politics has long recognized the consequences that the state's enthusiasm about the oil industry and its windfall revenue has on the society.[33] An interesting aspect of this literature, centring on the state as the resource proprietor, is the absence of MNCs that escaped from the academic equation on resource curse.[34] The *Caspian Revenue Watch*, for example, barely acknowledges the relationship between the state and the oil industry as something that has to be placed under public scrutiny. Among Western democracies, this relationship has been regarded as crucial to developmental processes; at the same time, it appeared to be one of the most problematic areas, in terms of successful state regulation, transparency and community access. It was believed for decades that the expansion of resource extraction would lead to sustainable development and prosperity by creating a series of multiplier effects by which oil capital would diffuse throughout the economy, starting with commodity-producing regions.[35] Formulated as a linkage theory, this thinking was turned into a powerful bargaining tool in the hands of oil corporations whose activities were, in theory, regulated by the government. In practice, however, the state served the industry interests more often than not, leading to, as Ross put it, an 'undiagnosed policy failure' whereas 'governments appear to have the capacity to foster linkages, yet have commonly failed to do so' (Ross 1999: 305). What seemed to be a sign of diversified development and infrastructural investment was an illusion that disappeared as extractive operations downsized, leaving local businesses '"linked" to nothing', which is likely to be the future of the Tengiz area (Frickel and Freudenburg 1996).

The increased public pressure in the 1990s resulted in tougher control over extracting industries in Western states, especially in the sphere of environmental protection. This development, which coincided with the rise of oil prices, pushed MNCs to move most of their operations to developing countries and emerging nations, including Kazakhstan amongst others.[36] Desperately seeking capital investment, these countries have framed their markets with investor-friendly policies in order to obtain lucrative multi-billion contracts. These contracts, however, designed for the Third World, legally guarantee the autonomy of oil companies and their economic activities from the government, minimizing incentives for public involvement.[37] This was also the time when the problems associated with resource curse gained prominence across many oil states. The research on resource politics, however, has remained inimical to global connections of the phenomenon, limiting its scope to individual nation-states that have failed to democratize and prosper despite (or because of) booming oil economies on their soil.

The government of Kazakhstan has made an effort to use its oil wealth to establish a viable basis for long-term economic growth through the diversification of economy and by putting on reserve a large fraction of the increased oil revenue.[38] It has also installed a fiscal regime designed to attract reinvestment, promote the integration of upstream businesses in the downstream and petrochemicals, and capture linkages with non-oil sectors of the national economy. On a corporate front, strong accomplishments have been reported in this regard: TCO has increased its domestic workforce by 17 per cent since 1993 and entered multiple agreements with domestic companies, the total worth of which is almost $1 billion.[39] Likewise, PFD boasts the ratio of domestic and foreign employees as 20:1, respectively, a self-declared achievement. This selective reporting has silenced less impressive facts, however; for example, that the dollar value of the domestic labour within the total PFD workforce is only 25 per cent despite significant numerical representation; and TCO, the largest oil project in Kazakhstan, has been rated as one of the most non-transparent enterprises nationwide, which does not even have a website, where it could otherwise specify the names of all contractors, the procedures that selected them, the value of domestic contracts in relation to those with foreign firms and the intermediary chains between them and the sponsor company.[40] In this chapter, I have tried to expose this crude reality behind corporate reports and develop an understanding of social and economic effects that oil production has generated around Tengiz.[41]

Notes

1 *The IMF country report No. 04/362*, November 2004; *The IMF country report No. 05/240*, July 2005; 'Kazakhstan Country Analysis Brief' *Energy Information Administration*: Official Energy Statistics from the US Government, 2005. See Chapter 2 for more detail data on oil production.

2 In 2004, Kazakhstan derived about 30% of total government revenue from the oil sector, compared to only 6% in 1999. *The IMF country report No. 05/240*, July 2005, p. 12. This transformation has been based on the dynamic growth of existing upstream enterprises and the 'world-class' discovery of Kashagan in 2000, the largest hydrocarbon reserve in the Caspian Sea containing over 30 billion barrels of 'sweet' oil. Kashagan is now one of the three largest known hydrocarbon fields in Kazakhstan along with Tengiz and Karachaganak, the world's largest gas condensate field.

3 This consistent malfunction, especially among large oil-exporters, has been known as a 'resource curse'. The analytical puzzle it involves has shaped recent debates on resource-abandoned states, their politics and economics (see Chapter 2).

4 The SGP would increase oil recovery and the sour gas technology would reinject by-products of oil extraction into the ground. *TengizChevroil (TCO) Sour Gas Injection and Second Generation Project, Tengiz Oil Field, Kazakhstan*, available online at http://hydrocarbon-technology.com.

5 The situation with local communities is a theme in its own right and will be discussed in a separate paper. There a growing body of scholarship discussing resource development from the perspective of local stakeholders that have provided a clearer view of the impact of mining projects on resource areas, e.g. Bunker (1985), Sawyer (2004) and Jorgensen (2003).

6 'Overadaptation' is a concept denoting a high degree of infrastructural adjustment of resource-dependent regions to a given form of extractive industry (Frickel and Freudenburg 1996: 447).

7 The present study is part of a larger project on local and national impacts of the petroleum industry. Two institutions supported the fieldwork and writing stages for this study, including the Social Sciences & Humanities Research Council of Canada and the Max Planck Institute for Social Anthropology.

8 'Proletarskya "Mayevka" na Tengize izbrala novogo proflidera', *Gorodskoy park*, Atyrau, 14 May 1998.

9 Here I refer primarily to Ferguson (2006). Also, Ethan B. Kapstein 'Multinational Risks', *The Wall Street Journal*, 10 May 2006 (the author of Kapstein 2006).

10 L. Monastyrskya, 'Ostat'sya nadolgo namereny nashi amerikanskiye partnery', *Prikaspiyskaya Kommuna*, 20 June 1992.

11 It is a fairly common assumption that nomads subsist on pristine nature. To the contrary, as a form of ecological adaptation, pastoral nomadism transforms the environment to serve its needs. For a succinct discussion, see Humphrey and Sneath (1999).

12 At the time that the Soviet state embarked on Tengiz in the early-1980s, the economy could no longer contain labour excesses, so Moscow orchestrated a large-scale labour relocation from downsizing enterprises in the European part of the USSR to the newly established industrial site.

13 The area hosts a total of four camps. The Tengiz colony centres on three of them, excluding the one belonging to the companies developing Kara Arna, a minor field near Tengiz.

14 This cost includes maintenance of the infrastructure, access to shared facilities, room and board as well as transportation costs between home and the work place.

15 Except those who work in various offices in the new headquarters that TCO built in Atyrau.

16 This statement reflects basic assumptions of a staple theory, stipulating that resource boom promotes broad-based economic development based on reinvestment of

the capital generated outside the region (for a succinct presentation of this theory see Watkins (1963)). It has been later developed in a linkage theory, which will be discussed later in this chapter.

17 Workers' comments, from the minutes of trade union meetings with the TCO administration (1997–98), cited in Kizatova (1998).

18 The administration refused to sign the original document, walking out of the negotiations. A major point of disagreement was a status of the collective bargaining agreement in relation to the oil contract with the government. The union voted out the statements placing union documents in a subordinate position to the contract, which rendered the collective bargaining agreement pointless (Kizatova 1996).

19 'To stop an abusive behavior of Americans on our own land', the comment goes, 'we'll use the most extreme measures!'. Workers' comments, from the minutes of trade union meetings with the TCO administration (1997–98), cited in Kizatova (1998: 99).

20 The transport department was treated as an essential part of the enterprise, sharing all the risks and hardships involved in the oil production. In 1989, for example, at the time of a fatal blow out at Tengiz, they performed heroic work, rescuing people and equipment (sources: Kulsary Museum and interviews). So the plan to eliminate the department generated unease among many workers.

21 At the time, workforce reduction in the course of reorganization (as opposed to transfer to another company) was prohibited by law in Kazakhstan. It has been determined that TCO violated the Partnership Chart since the Board of TCO Partners did not authorize the reorganization. Original correspondence cited in Kizatova (1998: 99).

22 Both situations generated massive publicity internationally. See Hersh (2001) and the Hydrocarbons Technology website at http://hydrocarbon-technology.com under 'TengizChevroil' for a sober discussion of politics and controversy over the financing of SGP/SGI in 2002.

23 Santiago (2006) and Turner (1980). That said, we need to keep in mind that in both cases the effort of oil workers was downplayed and misused by the state in the aftermath of revolutions.

24 Exxon/Mobil website, under 'Projects in Kazakhstan'. The original information is cited as following: TCO territory 'includes a production area of 380 thousand gross acres encompassing the Tengiz field, an associated processing plant complex, and the adjacent Korolev field. TCO also holds a prospective exploration license that covers over 600 thousand gross acres surrounding the production license'. This site is the only mention of specific pertaining to TCO territory otherwise unavailable to the public.

25 TCO hired PFD in 2002 to provide engineering, procurement and construction management services.

26 Here I draw on the notion of 'good' and 'bad' jobs within the US context (Austin 2005: 167–8).

27 The minimal wage in Kazakhstan is 12,000 tenge/month (approximately $90) based on 40 hours of work per week.

28 In Kazakhstan, every enterprise and organization is legally obliged to transfer 10% of each wage into their employees' individual pension accounts. At the time of hiring, wages are commonly quoted to employees after pension deductions and taxes. Concerning safety measures: based on conservative estimates, every year at Tengiz about four or five workers die. Causes of death have remained undetermined; local residents and workers attribute the deaths to toxic pollution at the plant complex. Based on the circumstances of death described by the witnesses, it is possible that they were caused by heart failure. Many labourers work for months without rest for 12–13 hours a day in the open field, even when the temperature is as high as 46°C.

29 Local authorities also placed two policemen at the checkpoints in Shanrak and TCO villages. By 2006, however, the TCO administration squeezed them out using the

same tactics as in the case of the union leaders – first they denied them access to the canteen, then the right to enter the camp grounds outside the checkpoint.

30 Interview with a worker in July 2006. This information is supported by the state reports published in August. 'Komissiya eshe raz konstatirovala chto nashi rabochiye bespravny', *Ak Zhaik*, 31 August 2006: 35/766.

31 Office workers referred to one case, however, when several women from PFD reported sexual assaults. The office, they said, met with the company administration, which fired the offender. The audit resulted with the closure of three companies, including the canteen service Zambo whose employees joined the strike in May. These individual cases, however, brought little improvement to the situation with female workers in general.

32 The existing Federation of Trade Unions, a nationwide bureaucratic structure that could lend some support to workers, could be found nowhere near Tengiz since the late-1990s and, especially, after the demise the labor movement at TCO.

33 See Karl (1997a, 1997b), Ross (2001), Sachs and Warner (2001) and a review article by Ross (1999).

34 Corporate invisibility perhaps lends its authority to the conventional wisdom that unlike other industrial and agricultural resources mineral reserves are controlled by the state regardless of exploitation matters, which put the state in the spotlight of analysis. Watts (2004: 53) provides a critical reflection on the absence of oil multinationals in the resource-politics scholarship.

35 The causal relationship between industry's linkages and economic development was established in Hirschman (1958). Hirschman's theory was subject to criticism and revisions, see, for example, Yotopoulos and Nugent (1973).

36 Based on industry sources, cited in Coelho (2005).

37 Most often those are PSAs that were introduced for the first time in the late 1950s, but became the most widespread type of contracts in the 1990s. For a discussion of the earlier contracts in relation to PSA see Sawyer (2004). PSAs have been designed to secure oil companies from unstable and unpredictable conditions in Third World countries. However, they have also served to help multinationals to multiply their profits at the expense of the state (Muttitt 2005; www.carnweb.org).

38 In 2005, the IMF reported an 'impressive' growth trend in the Kazakhstan's non-oil sector: 8% per year since 1998 with strong chances to be sustained over the coming years. *IMF staff country report No. 05/240*, July 2005 pp. 3–5.

39 Kazinform, 4 September 2006, available at www.inform.kz and Ak Zhaik, #35/766, 31 August 2006.

40 The *National Business*, Almaty, September 2005/9(23): 14–15.

41 This volume was already in press when another outbreak of violence took place at Tengiz in October 2006. Centring on the same company (SK) and revolving around the same issue of labour abuse, it indicates that the state failed to take control over the situation around Tengiz. See Saulesh Yessenova, 'Worker Riot at the Tengiz Oilfield: Who is to blame?', *Central Asia Caucasus Analyst* 9/4, 21 February 2007, at http://www.cacianalyst.org/view_article.php?articleid=4725.

11

CONCLUSIONS

Boris Najman, Richard Pomfret and Gaël Raballand

The energy exporting countries of the Caspian Basin were among those countries which suffered the most severe fall in output during the transition from central planning. At the same time they tended to rank well below average in the degree to which they pursued economic reform, as measured, for example by the EBRD transition indicators. Since the late 1990s, however, they have enjoyed some of the highest output growth rates in the world – this is especially true of Azerbaijan, Kazakhstan and (albeit discounting the official data) Turkmenistan, and to a lesser extent Russia and Uzbekistan. This book addresses the question of whether the oil boom-driven growth is sustainable and can provide a platform for long-term economic development, or whether the Caspian Basin countries will be blighted by the resource curse.

Although the Caspian Basin economies have clearly benefited from an oil boom (Chapter 2), the concept of a 'resource curse' is neither easy to define nor to grapple with analytically (Chapter 3). The emphasis in trade theory on real exchange rate effects, the so-called Dutch disease, is not the main source of a 'curse' outcome, and indeed there is no evidence of Dutch disease effects in Kazakhstan (Chapter 4). This leads to the paradox set out by the Lead Counsellor at the European Bank for Reconstruction and Development (EBRD):

> Partly through effective macroeconomic management and the creation of stabilization funds, governments in the energy rich countries have thus far seemed to inoculate themselves against the 'Dutch disease' – the reduction in competitiveness of manufactured and other tradable goods that comes with increases in the real exchange rate, which in turn undermines growth. So, have the energy exporters in Eurasia ... finally cured themselves of the 'resource curse'?
>
> (Rousso 2006: 3).

The desirable intertemporal macroeconomic management and use of the stabilization fund in Kazakhstan is analysed in Chapter 5, while the Azerbaijan stabilization fund is analysed in Chapter 8. One problem of fiscal management is creating an appropriate balance between central control and decentralized decision-making – a balance which is far from being achieved in the highly centralized states of Central Asia (Chapter 6).[1]

An alternative approach to analysing the impact of the oil boom is to utilize the high quality household survey data available in Kazakhstan and Azerbaijan to assess the transmission mechanisms from the oil boom to household expenditure. It is well-known that the energy sector provides little direct job creation. In Kazakhstan there is also little in the way of official transfer of resources, and the main transmission seems to be through informal earnings and overwhelmingly to the benefit of households in the two main cities, the financial capital Almaty and the political capital Astana (Chapter 7). In Azerbaijan, there is less geographical split because the oilfields are close to the only major city, Baku, and there is more evidence of official transfers to the disadvantaged, for example, to support internally displaced persons (Chapter 8).

Even more disaggregated approaches to the issue utilize research on the behaviour of the foreign investors in the energy sector and detailed fieldwork on a major oilfield. These lead to diverging perspectives, with more optimistic prognoses based on the potential for good behaviour by the investors (Chapter 10) and less optimistic prognoses emerging from fieldwork at the Tengiz oilfield (Chapter 11). To the extent that local jobs are created outside direct oil production in the Tengiz area, they are mostly in small enterprises.

To what extent are the Caspian Basin countries a valuable case study or are they *sui generis*? As with any countries they have their own history, geography and culture, but their experience may be of more general interest for assessing the resource curse because they were new states with sudden increases in their known petroleum reserves. Corruption levels are high and institutions far from good, but institutional change may be easier in countries which are still in the process of nation-building. Moreover, the existence of independent states with varying responses to the oil boom provides material for comparative analysis; in this book we have focused on the two main existing producers, Azerbaijan and Kazakhstan, but they could be joined by Turkmenistan and, less likely, Uzbekistan, as important oil producers.

What are the policy choices facing the Caspian Basin energy producers? This book has focused on what to do with oil revenue, but a prior decision for any mineral producer is whether to produce or not. The rate of depletion, or how much oil to leave in the ground, is a choice variable.[2] Even though oil dominates the economies of Azerbaijan and Kazakhstan, they are marginal to world supplies, i.e. they are price-takers in the world oil market. If oil prices are going to be higher in the future, then it may be desirable not to pump as much oil as possible in the short-run. The problem with the depletion rate as a policy variable is that it is notoriously difficult to predict the direction of world oil prices; in 1998 when prices fell below $10 a barrel, predictions inside and outside the industry were of prices falling even further in the early 2000s.[3] If oil prices were to fall back to such low levels, then Caspian oil, with its high transport costs to the major markets, could become uncompetitive; in that scenario there is a case for exploiting the oil as fast as possible.

A more direct policy implication of the research reported in this book concerns the use to be made of the revenue from oil. Very little of that revenue flows to domestic workers or to suppliers to the oil industry. The main distribution mechanisms are through the government budget. Thus, the government decides the extent to which the oil revenue is used for investment or for saving. The oil fund is a mechanism for channelling the revenue to investment. Public spending, boosted by revenue from oil, can also promote investment in physical and human capital. On the other hand, using the revenue for social programs or dissipating it via corruption directs the revenue to current consumption; the ultimate multiplier effects will depend upon institutional conditions, and much of the redistribution in Kazakhstan and Azerbaijan is through informal earnings.

What then does the future hold? One aspect which all the contributors to this book agree to be important but which is hardly tackled here is the political environment. All of the regimes are highly centralized and the character of the individual presidents matters. This was perhaps clearest in Turkmenistan, where President Niyazov (or, as he preferred to be known, Turkmenbashi the Great) created an extreme personality cult and brooked no alternative centres of opinion or decision-making. Turkmenbashi died in December 2006 as the manuscript was being finalized for publication and the future prospects for Turkmenistan will depend critically on the post-Niyazov regime. All of the Caspian Basin countries have ranked very poorly in terms of governance and the prevalence of corruption,[4] but it is possible that some of the leaders may start to look to their legacy now that they and their families and cronies are rich.[5] Apart from domestic developments a further political uncertainty is the prospect of regional conflict, either a hotting up of the cold war between Azerbaijan and Armenia or regional conflict in Central Asia between the two would-be hegemons, Kazakhstan and Uzbekistan, or between one of them and one of the smaller countries, most likely over water (Spechler and Spechler 2006).

A key issue is the extent to which the energy-rich countries can put in place appropriate growth-friendly institutions before an energy downturn arrives. All commodity price history points to busts following booms, and indeed the former Soviet Union experienced such a pattern in dramatic form. The 1970s oil boom gave new life to the moribund Brezhnev regime, leading to international assertiveness in Afghanistan and some domestic innovation with the succession of Gorbachev, but the drop in world oil prices in 1986 undermined the ability of Gorbachev to maintain support for economic reform, contributing to the disorderly collapse of the centrally planned economy after 1987 and the dissolution of the Soviet Union in 1991. Whether an oil-price downturn will have such dramatic impact on the Soviet successor states is unlikely, but it could contribute to either increased repression or regime collapse and leave the region exposed to external intervention as various great powers compete for influence.

Notes

1 The Central Asian countries and Azerbaijan are often characterized as having super-presidential regimes, with power heavily concentrated in the office of the President (Collins 2006). The 'tulip revolution' in the Kyrgyz Republic in March 2005 was the first serious check on presidential power and the 2006 Constitution provided for a significantly increased role for the Parliament. Whether that role is realized in practice and whether it influences regimes elsewhere in the region are among the key political questions facing the Caspian Basin countries.

2 Apart from the price argument, another reason why it may be desirable not to pump as much oil as possible in the short-run is the possibility that the quality of governance will improve. This is quite likely in Central Asia if we think in decades rather than years, but it is unlikely that the incumbent governments would accept this reason for delaying exploitation of their countries' oil reserves.

3 In 1999 major oil companies like Shell and BP Amoco were operating on the assumption that the world oil price for the next five years would average $10. The *Economist* ('Cheap Oil', 6 March 1999) thought this was over-optimistic and that, due to new technologies and the availability of substitutes for oil, a more realistic projection was of prices between $5 and $10 per barrel.

4 In the 2006 edition of the corruption perception index of Transparency International, Azerbaijan ranked one hundred and thirtieth and Kazakhstan one hundred and eleventh.

5 None of them seems willing to risk the uncertainty of democracy. Although both incumbent presidents would probably have won a fair election, the 2005 presidential elections in both Azerbaijan and Kazakhstan were characterized by widespread irregularities. In neither country does the Parliament operate as an independent check on presidential authority. However, both regimes have shifted significantly towards the USA and the West, which they would like to act as a counterweight to the regional influence of Russia and, in Kazakhstan's case, China. President Aliyev is one of the few leaders to have good working relations with both presidents, Putin and Bush, and President Nazarbayev, long one of Russia's closest allies in the CIS and the Eurasian Economic Community, made a high-profile official visit to Washington in September 2006 during which President Bush lauded Kazakhstan as a 'free nation'.

REFERENCES

Abdiev, K.S. (2003) *Regiony Kazakhstana*, Almaty: Kazakhstan Republic Statistical Agency.

Ahmad, E. and Singh, R. (2003) 'The Political Economy of Oil Revenue-Sharing in a Developing Country: Illustrations from Nigeria', IMF Working Paper 03/16, Washington, DC: IMF.

Aliyev, K. (2006) *Whither Azerbaijan's Oil Profits?*, RFE/RL Report posted 20 September, www.eurasianet.org.

Anderson, K. and Pomfret, R. (2002a) 'Relative Living Standards in New Market Economies: Evidence from Central Asian Household Surveys', *Journal of Comparative Economics*, 30(4): 683–708.

—— (2002b) 'Spatial Inequality and Development in Central Asia', School of Economics Working Paper, University of Adelaide; reprinted in R. Kanbur, A.J. Venables and G. Wan (eds) (2006) *Spatial Disparities in Human Development: Perspectives from Asia*, Tokyo: United Nations University Press: 233–69.

—— (2003) *Consequences of Creating a Market Economy: Evidence from Household Surveys in Central Asia*, Cheltenham: Edward Elgar.

Aroca, P. (2001) 'Impact and Development in Local Economies Based On Mining: The Case of Chilean II Region', *Resources Policy*, 27(2): 119–34.

Austin, D.E. (2005) 'Women's Work and Lives in Offshore Oil', in N. Dannhaeuser and C. Werner (eds) *Markets and Market Liberalization: Ethnographic Reflections, Research in Economic Anthropology*, vol. 24, Houston, TX: Texas A&M University: 163–206.

Auty, R.M. (1999) *Why is the Diversification of Manufacturing Not Occurring in Azerbaijan?* Washington, DC: ECSPE, World Bank.

—— (2001) *Resource Abundance and Economic Development*, Oxford: Oxford University Press.

—— (2007a) 'Patterns of Rent-extraction and Deployment in Developing Countries: Implications for Governance, Economic Policy and Performance', in G. Mavrotas and A. Shorrocks (eds) *Advancing Development: Core Themes in Global Economics*, London: Palgrave Macmillan.

—— (2007b) 'From Mining Enclave to Economic Catalyst: Large Mineral Projects in Developing Countries', *Brown Journal of World Affairs*, 13(1) 135–45.

Auty, R.M. and Mikesell, R.F. (1998) *Sustaining Development in Mineral Economies*, Oxford: Oxford University Press.

Bagirov, S., Akhmedov, I. and Tsalik, S. (2003) 'State Oil Fund of the Azerbaijan Republic', in S. Tsalik (ed.) *Caspian Oil Revenues: Who Will Benefit?*, New York, NY: SOROS Foundation: 89–125.

Barnett, S. and Ossowski, R. (2003) 'Operational Aspects of Fiscal Policy in Oil-Producing Countries', in J.M. Davis, R. Ossowski and A. Fedelino, *Fiscal Policy and Implementation in Oil-Producing Countries*, Washington, DC: International Monetary Fund.

Baschieri, A., Falkingham, J., Hornby, D. and Hutton, C. (2005) *Creating a Poverty Map for Azerbaijan*, World Bank Policy Research Working Paper No. 3793, Washington, DC: World Bank.

Beegle, K. (2003) 'Profile of Living Standards in Kazakhstan', ms., Washington DC: World Bank.

Benigno, G. and Thoenissen, C. (2003) 'Equilibrium Exchange Rates and Capital and Supply Side Performance', *Economic Journal*, 113(486): 103–24.

Bergman, M. (2003) *Interregional Inequality and Robin Hood Politics*, Stockholm School of Economics/Economic Research Institute (SSE/EFI) Working Paper Series in Economics and Finance No. 523, Stockholm: SSE/EFI.

Bevan, D., Collier, P. and Gunning, J. (1999) *The Political Economy of Poverty, Equity and Growth: Nigeria and Indonesia*, Oxford: Oxford University Press.

Blanchard, O. and Shleifer, A. (2000) *Federalism With and Without Political Centralisation. China Versus Russia*, National Bureau of Economic Research Working Paper No. 7616, Cambridge, MA: NBER.

BP (2002) *Executive Summary: Environmental and Social Impacts of the AGC Full Field Development*, London: BP.

—— (2003) *Regional Review: Economic, Social and Environmental Overview of the Southern Caspian Oil and Gas Projects*, Baku: BP.

—— (2004) *BP Azerbaijan: Sustainability Report 2003*, London: BP.

Breton, A. (1996) *Competitive Governments: An Economic Theory of Politics and Public Finance*, Cambridge: Cambridge University Press.

Brown, J.C. (1992) *Oil and Revolution in Mexico*, Berkeley, CA: University of California Press.

Bunker, S.G. (1985) *Underdeveloping the Amazon: Extraction, Unequal Exchange, and the Failure of the Modern State*, Urbana and Chicago, IL: University of Illinois Press.

Center for Economic Research (2004) *The Major Directions of Reforming the Government at the Local Level* (in Russian), Center for Economic Research Report 2004/05, Tashkent: CERR.

Chapman, K., MacKinnon, D. and Cumbers, A. (2004) 'Adjustment or Renewal in Regional Clusters: A Study of Diversification Among SMEs in the Aberdeen Oil Complex', *Transactions of the Institute of British Geographers*, 29(3): 389–96.

Clements, K.W. and Frankel, J.A. (1980) 'Exchange Rates, Money and Relative Prices: The Dollar–Pound in the 1920s', *Journal of International Economics*, 10(2): 249–62.

Coelho, K. (2005) 'The Footprint of the Offshore Oil industry on Community Institutions', in N. Dannhaeuser and C. Werner (eds) *Markets and Market Liberalization: Ethnographic Reflections, Research in Economic Anthropology*, vol. 24, Houston, TX: Texas A&M University.

Cohen, M. (2006) 'The Effect of Oil Revenues on Transition Economics: The Case of Azerbaijan', *Geopolitics of Energy*, 28(6).

Collier, P. and Hoefler, A. (2000) *Greed and Governance in Civil War*, Policy Research Working Paper 2355, Washington, DC: World Bank.

Collins, K. (2006): *The Logic of Clan Politics: Regime Transformation in Central Asia*, New York, NY: Cambridge University Press.

Cooke, K. (2005) 'Poor Azerbaijan Prepares to Get Rich', *BBC News online*, 3 May 2005.

Corden W.M. (1984) 'Booming Sector and Dutch Disease Economics: A Survey', *Oxford Economic Papers*, 36(3): 359–80.

Coudouel, A. and Marnie, S. (1999) 'From Universal to Targeted Social Assistance: An Assessment of the Uzbek Experience', *MOCT-MOST: Economic Policy in Transitional Economics*, 8(4): 443–58.

Crespo-Cuaresma, J., Fidrmuc, J. and MacDonald, R. (2005a) 'The monetary approach to exchange rates in the CEECs', *Economics of Transition*, 13(2): 395–416.

Crespo-Cuaresma, J., Fidrmuc, J. and Silgoner, M.-A. (2005b) 'On the Road: The Path of Bulgaria, Croatia and Romania to the EU and the euro', *Europe-Asia Studies*, 57(6): 843–58.

Crowson, P. (1998) 'Economic rent and the mining industry', *Raw Materials Report* 13(2): 22–5.

Cukrowski, J. (2004) 'Russian Oil: The Role of the Sector in Russia's Economy', *Post-Communist Economies*, 16(3): 285–96.

Cummings, S.N. (2000) *Kazakhstan*, London: Royal Institute of International Affairs.

Dabla-Norris, E., Martinez-Vasquez, J. and Norregaard, J. (2000) *Making Decentralization Work: The Case of Russia, Ukraine, and Kazakhstan*, Georgia State University International Studies Program Working paper 00-9, Atlanta, GA: Georgia State University.

Davoodi, H.R. (2002) 'Assessing Fiscal Vulnerability, Fiscal Sustainability and Fiscal Stance in a Natural Resource Rich-Country', in *Republic of Kazakhstan – Selected Issues and Statistical Appendix*, IMF Country Report No. 02/64: 7–31, Washington, DC: IMF.

—— (2005) *Long-Term Prospects for the Real Value of the Tenge*, IMF Country Report No 05/240, 29–38, Washington, DC: IMF.

Davoodi, H. and Zou, H. (1998) 'Fiscal Decentralization and Economic Growth: A Cross-Country Study', *Journal of Urban Economics*, 43(2): 244–57.

de Mello, L. and Barenstein, M. (2001) *Fiscal Decentralization and Governance: A Cross-Country Analysis*, IMF Working Paper/01/71, Washington, DC: IMF.

Desai, R.M., Freinkman, L. and Goldberg, I. (2005) 'Fiscal Federalism in rentier regions: Evidence from Russia', *Journal of Comparative Economics*, 33(4): 814–34.

Di Boscio, N. (2004) 'Taking the Lead: Mining and the Challenges of Economic Development', paper presented at the International Mining Seminar, CEPMLP, University of Dundee.

Dienes, L. (2002) 'Reflections on a Geographic Dichotomy: Archipelago Russia', *Eurasian Geography and Economics*, 43(6): 443–58.

Djalili, M.-R. and Kellner, T. (2003) 'Géo-Economie des Hydrocarbures de la Caspienne', *Risques et Management International*, 2: 61–94.

Ebel, R. (2001) 'The American Policy in Central Asia, Unchanged but Flexible', presentation to a conference organized by Défense Nationale Review.

Ebel, R.D. and Yilmaz, S. (2002) *On the Measurement and Impact of Fiscal Decentralization*, Washington, DC: World Bank.

Égert, B., Drine, I., Lommatzsch, K. and Rault, C. (2003) 'The Balassa–Samuelson Effect in Central and Eastern Europe: Myth or Reality?', *Journal of Comparative Economics*, 31(3): 552–72.

Égert, B., Halpern, L. and MacDonald, R. (2006) 'Equilibrium Exchange Rates in Transition Economies: Taking Stock of the Issues', *Journal of Economic Surveys*, 20(2): 257–324.

Eggert, R.G. (2002) *Mining and Economic Sustainability: National Economies and Local Communities*, MMSD Paper 19, London: International Institute for Environment and Development (IIED).

Enikopolov, R. and Zhuravskaya, E. (2003) *Decentralization and Political Institutions*, Centre for Economic Policy Research Discussion Paper No. 3857, London: CEPR.

Epstein, P. and Winter, M. (2004) *Assessment of Intergovernmental Relations and Local Governance in the Republic of Uzbekistan*, Washington, DC: The Urban Institute.

Ernst & Young (2005) *Kazakhstan Oil and Gas Tax Guide*, Almaty: Ernst & Young.

Esanov, A., Raiser, M. and Buiter, W. (2006) 'Nature's Blessing or Nature's Curse? The Political Economy of Transition in Resource-based Economies', in R.M. Auty (ed.) *Energy Wealth and Governance in the Caucasus and Central Asia*, London: Routledge, 39–76.

European Bank for Reconstruction and Development (EBRD) (2001) *Transition Report 2001: Energy in Transition*, London: EBRD.

—— (2006) *Transition Report 2006: Energy in Transition*, London: EBRD.

Faruqee, H. (1995) 'Long-Run Determinants of the Real Exchange Rate: A Stock-Flow Perspective', *IMF Staff Papers*, 42(1): 80–107.

Ferguson, J. (2006) *Global Shadows: Africa in the Neoliberal World Order*, Durham, NC: Duke University Press.

Fisman, R. and Gatti, R. (2002) 'Decentralization and Corruption: Evidence across Countries', *Journal of Public Economics*, 83(3): 325–46.

Forsyth, P.J. and Kay, J. (1980) 'The Economic Implications of North Sea Oil Revenues', *Fiscal Studies*, 1(3): 1–28.

Frankel, J.A. and Romer, D. (1999) 'Does Trade Cause Growth?' *American Economic Review*, 89(3): 379–99.

Frickel, S. and Freudenburg, W.R. (1996) 'Mining the Past: Historical Context and the Changing Implications of Natural Resource Extraction', *Social Problems*, 43(4): 444–66.

Garcia-Mila, T. and McGuire, T. (1996) *Do Interregional Transfers Improve the Economic Performance of Poor Regions? The Case of Spain*, Department of Economics and Business, Universitat Pompeu Fabra, Economics Working Papers No. 2007, Barcelona: Universitat Pompeu Fabra.

Gelb, A. et al. (1988) *Oil Windfalls: Blessing or Curse?* New York, NY: Oxford University Press.

Gelb, B. (2006) *Caspian Oil and Gas: Production and Prospects*, CRS Report for Congress, available at www.ncseonline.org/NLE/CRSreports/06Oct/RS21190.pdf.

Goldman Sachs (2005) *Introducing the Goldman Sachs Energy Environmental and Social Index*, London: Goldman Sachs.

Grafe, C., Raiser, M. and Sakatsume, T. (2005) *Beyond Borders: Reconsidering regional trade in Central Asia*, European Bank for Reconstruction and Development Working Paper No. 95, London: EBRD.

Granovsky, E.I. (2003) *Problems of Sustainable Development of the Atyrau City and the Atyrau Region*, Almaty: Kazakh State Research Institute for Science and Technical Information.

Groen, J. (2000) 'The Monetary Exchange Rate Model as a Long-run Phenomenon', *Journal of International Economics*, 52(2): 299–319.

Gustafson, T. (1989) *Crisis Amid Plenty*, Princeton, NJ: Princeton University Press.

Gylfason, T. (2001) 'Natural Resources, Education and Economic Development', *European Economic Review*, 45(4–6): 847–59.

REFERENCES

—— (2002) 'Natural Resources and Economic Growth: What is the Connection'? ms, University of Iceland.

Gylfason, T., Herbertsson, T.T. and Zoega, G. (1999) 'A Mixed Blessing: Natural Resources and Economic Growth', *Macroeconomic Dynamics*, 3(2): 204–25.

Hallwood, C.P. (1988) 'Host Regions and the Globalization of the Offshore Oil Supply Industry: The Case of Aberdeen', *International Regional Science Review*, 11(2): 155–66.

Hausmann, R. and Rigobon, R. (2003) 'An Alternative Explanation of the Resource Curse: Theory and Policy Implications', in J. Davis, R. Ossowski and A. Fedelino (eds) *Fiscal Policy Formulation and Implementation in Oil-Producing Countries*, Washington, DC: IMF.

Hayek, F.A. (1945) 'The Use of Knowledge in Society', *American Economic Review*, 35(4): 519–30.

Herbertsson, T.T., Skuladottir, M.G. and Zoega, G. (1999) *Three Symptoms and a Cure: A Contribution to the Economics of the Dutch Disease*, Working Paper No. W99:10, Institute of Economic Studies, University of Iceland.

Hersh, S. M. (2001) 'The Price of Oil: What Was Mobil up to in Kazakhstan and Russia?', *New Yorker*, 9 July: 48–65

Hirschman, A. (1958) *The Strategy of Economic Development*, New Haven, CT: Yale University Press.

Hoyos, C. (2006) 'Caspian Oil Field to Produce 25% More', *Financial Times*, 26 November.

Human Rights Watch (2003) 'From House to House: Abuses by Mahalla Committees', *Human Rights Watch Tashkent*, 15(7), (D).

Humphrey, C. and Sneath, D. (1999) *The End of Nomadism?*, Durham, NC: Duke University Press.

Humphreys, D. (2000) 'A Business Perspective on Community Relations in Mining', *Resources Policy*, 26(3): 127–31.

Huther, J. and Shah, A. (1996) *A Simple Measure of Good Governance and Its Application to the Debate on the Appropriate Level of Fiscal Decentralization*, Washington, DC: World Bank.

Ikein, A. and Briggs-Anigboh, C. (1998) *Oil and Fiscal Federalism in Nigeria*, Aldershot: Ashgate.

Institut Ekonomičeskich Issledovanij pri Ministertve Ekonomiki i Bjudžetnogo Planirovanija (2003) 'Analiz gosudarstvennych funkcij, ich optimizacija, povyšenie effektivnosti i kačestva ich predostavlenija', unpublished ms, Almaty.

Institute for Economic Research under the Ministry of Economics and Budget Planning (2005) 'Fiscal decentralization in Kazakhstan' (in Russian), unpublished ms, Almaty.

International Finance Corporation (2000) *Investing in People: Sustaining Communities through Improved Business Practices: A Community Development Resource Guide for Companies*, Washington, DC: International Finance Corporation.

International Monetary Fund (IMF) (2002) *Cross-Border Issues in Energy Trade in the CIS Countries*, IMF Policy Discussion Paper 02/13, Washington, DC: IMF.

—— (2003a) *Republic of Kazakhstan: 2003 Article IV Consultation – Staff Report*, IMF Country Report No. 03/210, Washington, DC: IMF.

—— (2003b) *Republic of Kazakhstan: Selected Issues and Statistical Appendix*, IMF Country Report No. 03/211, Washington, DC: IMF.

—— (2004) *Republic of Kazakhstan: Selected Issues*, IMF Country Report No. 04/362, Washington, DC: IMF.

—— (2006) *World Economic Outlook: October 2006*, Washington, DC: IMF.

Isham, J., Woolcock, M., Pritchett, L. and Busby, G. (2003) *The Varieties of Resource Experience: How Natural Resource Export Structures Affect the Political Economy of Economic Growth*, Middlebury College Economics Discussion Paper No. 03-08, Middlebury, VT.

Ivashenko, O. (2004) 'Geographic Profile of Living Standards in Kazakhstan: Where Are the Poor?', unpublished ms.

Jorgensen, D. (2003) 'Hinterland History: Mining and its Cultural Consequences in Telefolmin', paper presented at the workshop Mining Frontiers: Social Conflicts, Property Relations and Cultural Change in Emerging Boom Regions, Max Planck Institute for Social Anthropology, 18 June.

Jovanovic, B. (2001) 'Russian Roller Coaster: Expenditure Inequality and Instability in Russia, 1994–98', *Review of Income and Wealth*, 47(2): 251–71.

Kagirov, S. (1992) 'Povesti o Zhguchih Delah' (Problemy Tengiza), *Prikaspiyskaya Kommuna*, 12 August.

Kalyuzhnova, Y. (1998) *The Kazakhstani Economy: Independence and Transition*, Basingstoke: Macmillan.

Kalyuzhnova, Y. (2006) 'Overcoming the Curse of Hydrocarbon: Goals and Governance in the Oil Funds of Kazakhstan and Azerbaijan', *Comparative Economic Studies*, 48(4): 583–613.

Kalyuzhnova, Y. and Kaser, M. (2005) 'Prudential Management of Hydrocarbon Revenues in Resource-Rich Economies', paper for Economic Commission for Europe Spring Seminar, Geneva.

Kapstein, E.B. (2006) *Economic Justice in an Unfair World*, Princeton, NJ: Princeton University Press.

Karl, T.L. (1997a) *The Paradox of Plenty*, Berkeley, CA: University of California Press.

—— (1997b) 'The Perils of the Petro-State: Reflections on the Paradox of Plenty', *Journal of International Affairs*, 53(1): 31–48.

Kashani, H.A. (2005) 'Regulation and efficiency: an empirical analysis of the United Kingdom continental shelf petroleum industry', *Energy Policy*, 33(7): 915–25.

Kawagoe, T. (1998) *Interregional Resource Transfer and Economic Growth in Indonesia*, World Bank Policy Research Working Paper No. 1882, Washington, DC: World Bank.

Kemp, A. (2005) 'The Management of Petroleum Wealth: UK Experience', paper presented at Reading University, Centre for Eurasian Studies, 10 June.

Kizatova, T. (1996) 'Glasnost po-amerikanski', *Ak Zhaik*, 23 February.

—— (1998) 'Legko li stat' shevroidom?', *Russian Petroleum Investor*, 3: 98–101.

Klein, B., Crawford, R.G. and Alchian, A.A. (1978) 'Vertical Integration, Appropriable Rents, and the Competitive Contracting Process', *Journal of Law and Economics*, 21(2): 297–326.

Knell, M. and Stix, H. (2003) *How Robust are Money Demand Estimations? A Meta-Analytical Approach*, Österreichische Nationalbank Working Paper No. 81, Vienna: Österreichische Nationalbank.

Korhonen, I. (2004) *Does Democracy Cure a Resource Curse?*, Bank of Finland Institute for Economies in Transition Discussion Paper 18/2004, Helsinki: Bank of Finland.

Kornai, J. (1986) 'The Soft Budget Constraint', *Kyklos*, 39(3): 3–30.

Kronenberg, T. (2004) 'The Curse of Natural Resources in the Transition Economies', *Economics of Transition*, 12(3): 399–426.

Kutan, A.M. and Wyzan, M.L. (2005) 'Explaining the Real Exchange Rate in Kazakhstan, 1996–2003: Is Kazakhstan Vulnerable to the Dutch Disease?', *Economic Systems*, 29(2): 242–55.

REFERENCES

Lane, F.C. (1958) 'Economic Consequences of Organized Violence', *Journal of Economic History*, 18(4): 401–17.

Leschenko, N. and Troschke, M. (2006) *Fiscal Decentralization in Centralized States: The Case of Central Asia*, Osteuropa-Institut München Working Paper No. 261, Munich: Osteuropa-Institut München.

Lin, J.Y. and Liu, Z. (2000) 'Fiscal Decentralization and Economic Growth in China', *Economic Development and Cultural Change*, 49(1): 1–22.

Lohmus, P. (2005) 'Fiscal Management of Kazakhstan's Oil Wealth', in *Republic of Kazakhstan – Selected Issues, IMF Country Report No. 05/240*, Washington, DC: IMF: 12–19.

Luong, P.J. (2000) 'Kazakhstan: The Long-Term Costs of Short-Term Gains', in R. Ebel and R. Menon (eds) *Energy and Conflict in Central Asia and the Caucasus*, Lanham, MD: Rowman and Littlefield.

—— (2003) 'Economic Decentralization in Kazakhstan: Causes and Consequences', in P.J. Luong (ed.) *The Transformation of Central Asia: States and Societies from Soviet Rule to Independence*, Ithaca, NY: Cornell University Press.

MacDonald, R. (1998a) 'What Determines Real Exchange Rates? The Long and Short of It', *Journal of International Financial Markets, Institutions and Money*, 8(2): 117–53.

—— (1998b) *What Do We Really Know About Real Exchange Rates?*, Österreichische Nationalbank Working Paper No. 28, Vienna: Österreichische Nationalbank.

MacDonald, R. and Ricci, L. (2002) *Purchasing Power Parity and New Trade Theory*, IMF Working Paper No. 32, Washington, DC: IMF.

McKay, J. (1984) 'Baku Oil and Transcaucasian Pipelines, 1883–1891: A Study in Tsarist Economic Policy', *Slavic Review*, 43(4): 604–23.

McLure, C., Martinez-Vazquez, J. and Wallace, S. (1999) *Fiscal Transition in Kazakhstan*, Manila: Asian Development Bank.

Maeso-Fernandez, F., Osbat, C. and Schnatz, B. (2005) 'Pitfalls in Estimating Equilibrium Exchange Rates for Transition Economies', *Economic Systems*, 29(2): 130–43.

Mahmutova, M. (2003) 'Division of Expenditure Tasks Between Levels of Budget System in Kazakhstan', Kazakhstan Institute of Management project research materials, unpublished ms, Almaty.

Manzano, O. and Rigobon, R. (2001) *Resource Curse or Debt Overhang?*, National Bureau of Economic Research Working Paper No. W8390, Cambridge, MA (rev.ver. published in D. Lederman and W.F. Maloney (eds) (2003) *Natural Resources and Development: Are They a Curse? Are They Destiny?*, Stanford, CA: Stanford University Press).

Mathieu, P. (2004) 'An Analysis of Kazakhstan's Petroleum Potential', in *Republic of Kazakhstan – Selected Issues and Statistical Appendix, IMF Country Report No 04/362: 17–31*, Washington, DC: IMF.

Matsuyama, K. (1992) 'Agricultural Productivity, Comparative Advantage and Economic Growth', *Journal of Economic Theory*, 58(2): 317–34.

Meese, R. and Rogoff, K. (1983) 'Empirical Exchange Rate Models of the Seventies: Do They Fit out of Sample?', *Journal of International Economics*, 14(1): 3–24.

Mining, Minerals, and Sustainable Development Project (2002) *Breaking New Ground: Mining, Minerals and Sustainable Development*, London: Earthscan.

Monastyrskya, L. (1992) 'Ostat'sya nadolgo namereny nashi amerikanskiye partnery', *Prikaspiyskaya Kommuna*, 20 June.

Mulkey, D. and Hodges, A.W. (2004) 'Using IMPLAN to Assess Local Economic Impacts', mimeo, Department of Food and Resource Economics, Gainesville, FL: University of Florida.

Musgrave, R.M. (1959) *The Theory of Public Finance*, New York, NY: McGraw Hill.

Muttitt, G. (2005) *Crude Designs: The Rip-Off of Iraq's Oil Wealth*, PLATFORM with Global Policy Forum, Institute for Policy Studies (New Internationalism Project), New Economic Foundation, Oil Change International and War on Want, November.

Myradova, C. *et al.* (2006) 'Administrativnaj Reforma na Mestach', *Ekonomičeskie Obosrenija*, 64(1).

Neary, J.P. and Van Wijnbergen, S. (eds) (1986) *Natural Resources and the Macroeconomy*, Cambridge, MA: MIT Press.

Nietalieva, I., Wesseler, J. and Heijman, W. (2005) 'Health Costs Caused by Oil Extraction Air Emissions and the Benefits from Abatement: The Case of Kazakhstan', *Energy Policy*, 33(9): 1169–77.

Nikolaev, E. (1992) 'Oil and One More Time, Oil', *Prikaspiyskaya kommuna*, 25 June.

North, D. (1990) *Institutions, Institutional Change and Economic Performance*, Cambridge: Cambridge University Press.

Nuriev, S. (2003) 'Voprosy fiskal`noj decentralizacii v Respublike Uzbekistan', *Bozor, Pul, Va Kredit*, 11.

Nuritdinov, H. (2005) 'Fiscal Decentralization in Uzbekistan' (in Russian), unpublished ms, Institute for the Deepening of Market Reforms under the State Property Committee, Tashkent.

Oats, W. (1972) *Fiscal Federalism*, New York, NY: Harcourt Brace Jovanovich.

OECD (2004) *Economic Outlook 2004: Fiscal Relations Across Levels of Government*, Paris: OECD.

Olcott, M.B. (2002) *Kazakhstan: Unfulfilled Promise*, Washington, DC: Carnegie Endowment for Peace.

Papyrakis, E. and Gerlagh, R. (2004) 'The Resource Curse Hypothesis and its Transmission Channels', *Journal of Comparative Economics*, 32(1): 181–93.

Peck, A. (2003) *Economic Development in Kazakhstan: The Role of Large Enterprises and Foreign Investment*, Abingdon: RoutledgeCurzon.

Persson, T. and Tabellini, G. (2000) *Political Economics: Explaining Economic Policy*, Cambridge, MA: MIT Press.

Pesaran, M.H., Shin, Y. and Smith, R.J. (2001) 'Bounds Testing Approaches to the Analysis of Level Relationships', *Journal of Applied Econometrics*, 16(3): 289–326.

Pomfret, R. (1995) *The Economies of Central Asia*, Princeton, NJ: Princeton University Press.

—— (2002) *Constructing a Market Economy: Diverse Paths from Central Planning in Asia and Europe*, Cheltenham: Edward Elgar.

—— (2005) 'Kazakhstan's Economy since Independence: Does the Oil Boom Offer a Second Chance for Sustainable Development?', *Europe-Asia Studies*, 57(6): 859–76.

—— (2006) *The Central Asian Economics since Independence*, Princeton, NJ: Princeton University Press.

Prebisch, R. (1950) *The Economic Development of Latin America and its Principal Problems*, New York, NY: United Nations.

—— (1964) 'Toward a New Trade Policy for Development', in *Proceedings of the United Nations Conference on Trade and Development*, New York, NY: United Nations.

President of the Republic of Kazakhstan (2005) 'On the Medium-Range Conceptual Framework for the Formation and Use of Assets of the National Fund of the Republic of Kazakhstan', Decree No. 1641, 1 September.

Public Policy Research Center (2004) 'Razvitie mestnogo samoupravlenija. strategičeskie voprosy', *Policy Studies*, 2

—— (2005) 'Budget Process in the Caspian Countries: Experience of Kazakhstan and Azerbaidjan', *Policy Studies*, 7(2).

Qian, Y. and Roland, G. (1998) 'Federalism and the Soft Budget Constraint', *American Economic Review*, 88(5): 1143–62

Qian, Y. and Weingast, B. (1997) 'Federalism as a Commitment to Preserving Market Incentives', *Journal of Economic Perspectives*, 11(4): 83–92.

Raballand, G. (2005) *L'Asie Centrale ou la Fatalité de l'Enclavement?*, Paris: L'Harmattan.

Raballand, G. and Esen, F. (2006) 'Economics and Politics of Cross-Border Oil Pipelines – the Case of the Caspian Basin', *Asia-Europe Journal*, 5(1): 133–46.

Radvanyi, J. (1985) 'Régions et Pouvoirs en URSS', unpublished thesis.

Rama, M. and Scott, K. (1999) 'Labor Earnings in One-Company Towns: Theory and evidence from Kazakhstan', *World Bank Economic Review*, 13(1): 185–209.

Rapach, D.E and Wohar, M.F. (2004) 'Testing the Monetary Model of the Exchange Rate Determination: A Closer Look at Panels', *Journal of International Money and Finance*, 23(6): 867–95.

Reno, W. (1995) *Corruption and State Politics in Sierra Leone*, New York, NY: Cambridge University Press.

RGP Institute for Economic Research (2005) 'Fiscal Decentralization in Kazakhstan', unpublished ms, Almaty.

Riker, W. (1964) *Federalism: Origins, Operation, Significance*, Boston, MA: Little, Brown and Co.

Robinson, J. and Torvik, R. (2005) 'White Elephants', *Journal of Public Economics*, 89(2–3): 197–210.

Ross, M. (1999) 'The Political Economy of the Resource Curse', *World Politics*, 51/ January: 297–322.

—— (2001) 'Does Oil Hinder Democracy?', *World Politics*, 53(3): 325–61.

Rossello, J. (2003) 'Regional Redistribution and Growth', *Investigaciones Economicas*, XXVII(2): 369–92.

Rousso, A. (2006): 'Escaping the Resource Trap: Market Reform and Political Governance in the Resource Rich Countries of Eurasia', *China and Eurasia Forum Quarterly*, 4(3), 3–14.

Saavalainen, T. and ten Berge, J. (2006) *Quasi-Fiscal Deficits and Energy Conditionality in Selected CIS Countries*, IMF Working Paper No. 06/43, Washington, DC: IMF.

Sachs, J. and Warner, A. (1995) *Natural Resource Abundance and Economic Growth*, National Bureau of Economic Research Working Paper No. 5398, Cambridge, MA: NBER.

—— (2001) 'The Curse of Natural Resources', *European Economic Review*, 45(4–6): 827–38.

Sala-i-Martin, X. and Subramanian, A. (2003) *Addressing the Natural Resource Curse: An Illustration from Nigeria*, National Bureau of Economic Research Working Paper 9804, Cambridge, MA: NBER.

Santiago, M.I. (2006) *The Ecology of Oil: Environment, Labor, and the Mexican Revolution, 1900–1938*, Cambridge: Cambridge University Press.

Sawyer, S. (2004) *Crude Chronicles: Indigenous Politics, Multinational Oil, and Neoliberalism in Ecuador*, Durham, NC: Duke University Press.

Schynbekov, D. (2005) 'Finansovye osnovy mestnogo chozjajstva: vzaimootnošenija s respublikankskim bujdžetom Finansy Kazachstana', 1: 72–8.

Seabright, P. (1995) 'Accountability and Decentralisation in Government: An Incomplete Contracts Model', *European Economic Review*, 40(1): 61–86.

Shleifer, A. and Vishny, R. (1993) 'Corruption', *Quarterly Journal of Economics*, 108(3): 599–617.

Shokmanov, Yu. (ed.) (2004) *Financy Respubliki Kazakhstana 1990–2003*, Almaty: Kazakhstan Republic Statistical Agency.

Singer, H. (1950) 'The Distribution of Trade between Investing and Borrowing Countries', *American Economic Review*, 40(2): 473–85.

Slinko, I. (2002) *The Impact of Fiscal Decentralization on the Budget Revenue Inequality among Municipialities and Growth of Russian Regions*, Economics Education and Research Consortium – Russia and CIS Working Paper, Moscow: EERC.

Smailes, A. (2001) 'Toxic town', *Central Europe Review*, 3(3), available at www.ce-review.org/01/3/smailes3.html.

Smailov, A.A. (ed.) (2001) *Regional'nyî Statističeskiî Ezhegodnik Kazakhstana*, Almaty: Kazakhstan Republic Statistical Agency.

Spechler, D.R. and Spechler, M.C. (2006): 'Trade, Energy, and Security in the Central Asian Arena', in A. Tellis and M. Wills (eds) *Trade, Interdependence, and Security: Strategic Asia 2006–07*, Seattle, WA and Washington, DC: National Bureau of Asian Research: 204–38.

State Program on Poverty Reduction and Economic Development (2003) 'Azerbaijan Progresses Towards the Achievement of the Millennium Development Goals', *Annual Report (Baku)*, Baku: State Program on Poverty Reduction and Economic Development..

Stevens, P. (2003) 'Resource Impact – Curse or Blessing? A Literature Survey', *Journal of Energy Literature*, 9(1): 3–42.

Stock, J. and Watson, M.W. (1993) 'A Simple Estimator of Cointegrating Vectors in Higher Order Integrated Systems', *Econometrica*, 61(4): 783–820.

Sutyagin, V. (2000) 'S Vashington Post' problemy u nas shozhi, hotya i ne sovsem', *Prikaspiyskaya Kommuna*, 22 July.

Tabata, S. (1998) 'Transfers from Federal to Regional Budgets in Russia: A Statistical Analysis', *Post-Soviet Geography and Economics*, 39(8): 447–60.

Tanzi, V. (1995) 'Fiscal Federalism and Decentralization: A Review of Some Efficiency and Macroeconomic Aspects', paper prepared at the World Bank's Annual Bank Conference on Development Economics, Washington, DC, May.

Tiebout, C. (1956) 'A Pure Theory of Local Expenditures', *Journal of Political Economy*, 64(5): 416–24.

Timofeev, A. (2002) *Fiscal Decentralization and Soft Budget Constraints*, Economics Education and Research Consortium – Russia and CIS, Working Paper No. 01/12, Moscow: EERC.

Transparency Kazakhstan (2004) *Problems and Outlook of the National Foundation of the Republic of Kazakhstan*, Almaty: Civic Foundation.

Troschke, M. and Ufer, H. (2007) *Fiskalische Dezentralisierung und regionale Disparitäten in Kasachstan*, Working Paper Nr. 262, Munich: Ost-Europa Institut.

Tsalik, S. (2003) *Caspian Oil Windfalls: Who Will Benefit?*, Caspian Revenue Watch, Central Eurasia Project, New York, NY: Open Society Institute.

Turkmenmillichasabat (Turkmen Ministry of Information and State Statistics) (2005) 'Decentralization of State Governance and Local Self-government Development in Turkmenistan' (in Russian), unpublished ms, Aschgabad.

Turner, L. and Hurd, R.W. (2001) 'Building Social Movement Unionism: The Trans-formation of the American Labor Movement', in L. Turner, H.C. Katz, and R.W. Hurd (eds) *Rekindling the Movement: Labor's Quest for Relevance in the 21st Century*, Ithaca, NY: Cornell University Press: 9–26.

Turner, T. (1980) 'Iranian Oil Workers and 1978–79 Revolution', in P. Nore and T. Turner (eds) *Oil and Class Struggle*, London: Zed Books.

Unayama, T. (2003) 'Product Variety and Real Exchange Rates: The Balassa–Samuelson Model Reconsidered', *Journal of Economics*, 79(1): 41–60.

United Nations Development Programme (UNDP) (2004) *Poverty in Kazakhstan: Causes and cures*, Report UNDPKAZ 08, Almaty: UNDP.

United States Department of Energy Information Administration (2005) *Kazakhstan: Major Oil and Natural Gas Projects*, available at www.eia.doe.gov/emeu/cabs/kazaproj.html.

—— (2006) *Azerbaijan: Production-Sharing Agreements*, available at www.eia.doe.gov/emeu/cabs/Azerbaijan/azerproj.html.

Verme, P. (2001) *Transition, Recession and Labour Supply*, Aldershot: Ashgate.

Wakeman-Linn, J., Aturupane, C., Danniger, S., Gvenetadze, K., Hobdari, N. and Le Borgne, E. (2004) *Managing Oil Wealth: The Case of Azerbaijan*, Washington, DC: IMF.

Warner, M. (2005) *Meeting the Social Performance Standards of the International Project Finance Institutions*, London: Overseas Development Institute.

Watkins, M. (1963) 'A Staple Theory of Economic Growth', *Canadian Journal of Economics and Political Science*, 29(2): 141–58.

Watts, M. (2004) 'Resource Curse? Governmentality, Oil and Power in the Niger Delta, Nigeria', *Geopolitics*, 9(1): 50–80.

Weingast, B.R. (1995) 'The Economic Role of Political Institutions. Market-Preserving Federalism and Economic Growth', *Journal of Law, Economics and Organization*, 11(1): 1–31.

Wheeler, B. (2003) *Economic Impact of Present and Future Mining Operations at Waihi*, available at www.marthamine.co.nz/econ_employ.html.

Woller, G.M. and Philipps, K. (1998) 'Fiscal Decentralization and Economic Growth: An Empirical Investigation', *Journal of Development Studies*, 34(4): 139–48.

Wood, A. (1999) 'Natural Resources, Human Resources and Export Composition: a Cross-Country Perspective', in J. Mayer, B. Chamber and A. Farooq (eds) *Development Policies in Natural Resource Economies*, Cheltenham: Edward Elgar.

Wooster, J. (2000) 'The Intergovernmental Fiscal Reform in Kazakhstan: Progress to Date and Recommendations for the Future', *Kazakhstan Economic Trends*, 36–53.

World Bank (2000) 'Kazakhstan Public Expenditure Review', *World Bank Report 20489-KZ, Vol. II*, Washington, DC: World Bank.

—— (2003) *Final Report of the Extractive Industries Review*, Washington, DC: World Bank.

—— (2005) *Staying Competitive: The Challenge of Managing Kazakhstan's Oil Boom*, Washington, DC: World Bank.

—— (2006) *Indicators of Governance 2005*, Washington, DC: World Bank.

Yotopoulos, P.A. and Nugent, J.B. (1973) 'A Balanced-Growth Version of the Linkage Hypothesis: A Test', *Quarterly Journal of Economics*, 77(2): 157–66.

Zhang, T. and Zou, H. (1998) 'Fiscal Decentralization, Public Spending, and Economic Growth in China', *Journal of Public Economics*, 67(2): 221–40.

Zhuravskaya, E. (2000) *Incentives to Provide Local Public Goods. Fiscal Federalism, Russian Style*, Economics Education and Research Consortium – Russia and CIS, Working Paper No. 99/15, Moscow: EERC.

INDEX

Abdiev, K.S. 113
Afghanistan 4n5
Ahmad, E. and Singh, R. 119
Anderson, K. and Pomfret, R. 115, 128, 129, 130
Artemyev, A. 18
augmented Dickey-Fuller (ADF) test 52
Austin, D.E. 197
Auty, R.M. 33, 165, 170, 171, 173; and Mikesell, R.F. 161, 173
Azerbaijan, and conflict with Armenia 134; data on 132–3, 143–5; dependency on government in 133; economic activity/geography of 137–43, 148–9, 156n10–n12; evidence on reallocation of oil revenue in 146–51; expectations in 18–19, 20; foreign contracts in 133, 134–5; identification strategy/ estimation method in 143–5; oil-propelled growth in 134–6, 155n5; oil/gas exports 9; regulatory framework in 136–7; revenue redistribution in 132–51; and state benefits 144–5, 149, 156n14–n16; structural changes in 142–5; and targeting to oil-poor 146–51; uneven benefits in 132
Azerbaijan household budget survey (AHBS) 143
Azerbaijan Oil Fund 20, 28n18
Azeri, Chirag and Gunashi (ACG) fields 134

Bagirov, S. *et al.* 166
Baku–Tbilisi–Ceyhan (BTC) pipeline 2, 16, 135–6, 155n6
Baku–Tbilisi–Erzerum (BTE) pipeline 135–6, 155n6
Balassa–Samuelson model 46, 47–8, 49, 58

Barnett, S. and Ossowski, R. 72
Beegle, K. 128
Benigno, G. and Thoenissen, C. 49
Bergman, M. 133
Blair, T. 25
Blanchard, O. and Shleifer, A. 74
Breton, A. 74
Bunker, S.G. 196

Caspian Basin, and appropriate growth-friendly institutions 201; and benefits of oil boom 199; effect of transition from central planning on 199; future possibilities 201; as major oil producing region 9; and policy choices/ implications 200–1, 202n3; potential of 9, 26n1; as valuable case study 200
Caspian oil, analysis of 3–4; background to 3; capital-intensive nature of 3; and disjunction of discontents 3, 4n6; and Dutch disease effects 3; handicaps 1; impact/sustainability of boom 2–3; importance of 1; improved pipeline 1–2; major discoveries 1; stagnation of 1; strategic importance of 2
Caspian Pipeline Consortium (CPC) 2, 4n4
Caspian Revenue Watch 176, 194
Chapman, K. *et al.* 162
Chinese National Petroleum Company 2
Clements, K.W. and Frankel, J.A. 63
Coelho, K. 198
Cohen, M. 16, 18, 19
Collier, P. and Hoefler, A. 37
Commonwealth of Independent States (CIS) 45, 166
Corden, W.M. 3, 40
corporate policy, and environmental damage 168, 170; and establishment of stakeholder committees 170–1;

and extension of PSA conditions
171–2; and foreign investment 160;
and lobbying capacity of local groups
172–3; and policies to improve impacts
of extraction 168–73; and reining of
social activity 170; and sustainable
linked economic activity 161–2, 166–8
Coudouel, A. and Marnie, S. 86
Crespo-Cuaresma, J. *et al.* 63
Cukrowski, J. 27

Dabla-Norris, E. *et al.* 119
Davoodi, H.R. 45, 72
de Mello, L. and Barenstein, M. 75
Desai, R.M. *et al.* 75
Di Boscio, N. 160
Dienes, L. 3, 128, 152
Dutch disease 3, 33, 40n7, 160, 173,
199; and balance of payments 34;
Balassa-Samuelson effect 46; and
current account surplus 34; data
description 51; and de-industrialization
35–6; econometric methods 52–3; and
economic growth 35–6; estimation
results 55–8; evidence for 45; and
exhaustibility 36; and fiscal policy
33, 40n6; and governance 37; and
imports 34–5; initial undervaluation
53–5; and linkages 36; and loss
of competitiveness 33–4; nominal
exchange rate 46–9; and offshore
saving 35; and real exchange rate 33–7,
40–1n9–n18; real exchange rate 49–51;
terminology 34; and trade balance 34;
and volatility 36

early reform zones (ERZs) 159, 170
Ebel, R.D. 9, 11; and Yilmaz, S. 75
Economist Intelligence Unit 132
Égert, B. *et al.* 49, 63
Eggert, R.G. 160, 161
Elliott-Rothenberg-Stock (ERS) test 52
Enikopolov, R. and Zhuravskaya, E. 75
enterprise profit tax (ENPT) 79, 92
Epstein, P. and Winter, M. 107
Ernst & Young 128
Eurest Raytheon Support Services (ERSS)
187
European Bank for Reconstruction and
Development (EBRD) 199
Evans, R. 28
Extractive Industries Transparency
Initiative (EITI) 25–6, 166

Faruqee, H. 50
Ferguson, J. 196
fiscal decentralization, and administrative
reform 79–84; and analysis of
expenditure assignment 84–92;
analysis of revenue assignment/sharing
92–8; background 73; and balance with
central control 199–200; and collapse
of USSR 78; comparative perspective
89–90, 98; current status 79–84;
different rates of 83; and direct/indirect
subsidies 79; expenditure side 77;
international comparison of indicators
76; and local autonomy 78–9, 80, 84,
90, 92, 106n4, 107n11; and provision/
implementation of laws 80–1, 83,
84; revenue side 77–8; and Russian
doll model 78; starting points 78–9;
theoretical considerations 74–6
fiscal policy 37; domestic/foreign saving
37–8; importance of 38; optimal 66;
volatility issue 38, 41n20
fiscal sustainability, and future oil
production 68; and maintaining
constant level 67; and management
of oil wealth 64–6; and NFRK 70–2;
non-oil deficit path 66–70, 67n8; and
resource revenue 64–72; and rules
67; and savings 67–8; and spending
decisions 66
Fisman, R. and Gatti, R. 75
Forsyth, P.J. and Kay, J. 132
Frickel, S. and Freudenburg, W.R. 195,
196

Garcia-Mila, T. and McGuire, T. 133
gas industry 14, 22, 27n8, 28n21
governance 22–3, 25, 37; and best practice
environmental standards 168, 170; and
consequences of enthusiasm/windfall
revenue on society 194; constraints on
166–8; corruption in 201; and
democracy 202n5; and high share of
rent 160; and inadequate financial
markets 166, 168; and long-term
economic growth 195; and negative
impacts of mismanaged revenue 161;
Northeast Scotland case study 162–4;
problems encountered 164–5; public
pressure on 195; relationship with oil
industry 194–5; and rent seeking 168;
and self-appointed lobby groups 161;
and size of local fiscal linkage 160; and
social capital deficiency 165–6; and

Printed in Great Britain
by Amazon.co.uk, Ltd.,
Marston Gate.